MY IRISH TABLE

MY IRISH TABLE

RECIPES FROM THE HOMELAND AND RESTAURANT EVE

Cathal Armstrong & David Hagedorn

PHOTOGRAPHY BY SCOTT SUCHMAN

TEN SPEED PRESS

Berkeley

CONTENTS

~

To Mam, Da, and Meshelle,
who put me on the right road years ago
and keep me there now.

ACKNOWLEDGMENTS

FROM CATHAL: My sincerest gratitude to my children, Eve and Eamonn, for allowing Meshelle and me to use their names on our restaurants and for putting up with their parents' crazy schedules; to my mother-in-law, Carmen Salang, who took care of the kids whenever we needed her to while we worked on this book; to Alice Hanson for all the prep and time she put in; to Jeremy Hoffman and Ryan Wheeler for keeping me organized; to David Hagedorn for driving me to the edge of insanity; to Master Jason Yoo for keeping me fit and stress-free throughout this process; to our business partners Todd Thrasher and Maria Chicas; to my brothers and sisters, who lent us their stories; to Joy Tutela, our agent; and to Scott Suchman for the terrific photographs.

FROM DAVID: Very special thanks to my husband, Michael Widomski, who never complained about eating Roast Leg of Pork and Dublin Coddle three days in a row (but drew the line at Steak and Kidney Pie); to Meshelle and Cathal Armstrong for bringing up this crazy idea in the first place; to Sally Swift, a supportive pal with great advice; to Carol Spier, the dearest friend I still haven't met in person and fellow hater of the serial comma; and to my sister, Claire, and my posse, Nycci Nellis, Amber Pfau, and Amanda McClements, who let me prattle on endlessly about this project.

INTRODUCTION

I WAS BORN IN DUBLIN IN 1969, the third eldest of six children. My birthday, August 16, is likely familiar to the rest of the world as the day that Elvis Presley died, but in my food-centric Irish family, it was known as the night we'd be feasting on prawn cocktail, rack of lamb, and corn on the cob for dinner—my menu of choice.

On any given day in my Mam and Da's kitchen, until I moved to the United States at twenty years of age, the conversation centered around food. Although my mother, Angela, was acclaimed for her superlative baking skills, it was my father, Gerry, who did most of the cooking for our household.

Da was an avid gardener who took pride in cooking with the sixty-plus kinds of fruits and vegetables he grew on our Dublin property on Watson Road. It was extremely rare for the times that a family living in Dublin would have such a garden—and that a man would cook.

At home, dinnertime was sacrosanct. While other families hurriedly scarfed down fish fingers in front of the telly, we Armstrongs loitered over three- and four-course meals. That's probably why I never got As in school—I didn't have time to study because we were too busy eating dinner all night.

Hoping to instill in us kids an appreciation of the land, Da insisted that we tend the garden. One of my most enduring memories is of having to get up at six in the morning and spread mounds of horse manure (shite being the correct Irish term) that had been delivered and dumped in the front yard at four a.m. This was also a source of mockery from the other kids in the neighborhood.

Da was a successful tour operator who sold package holidays to the Continent, mainly Spain, so he had the means and opportunity to expose me to diverse cuisines—and he did. Throughout my childhood, it was not unusual for Da to pack up the family at a moment's notice and take us to Tunisia, Greece, or Spain for a week or two, where we would feast on rabbit paella, Valencia chicken, couscous, or moussaka.

At the tender age of seven, my parents started shipping me off to France to spend my summers as an exchange student, learning the language and absorbing French culture, especially that which revolved around food. The family with whom I lived, the Baudins, took me on regular excursions around the countryside and to the sea, where I became familiar with the gustatory wonders of France: Normandy apples, Brittany butter, foie gras, croissants and baguettes, chocolate, wine (eventually), and the freshest mussels and oysters.

~

Mine was a wonderful and rich life, but when I was fourteen, everything turned upside down. The laws governing Ireland's travel industry were altered and Da's business disintegrated. We weren't exactly destitute, but our family fell on hard times. More than just a hobby now, gardening became the family's primary food source. It remained a central source of our diet even after Da opened a new business, this time one focusing on business travel. Things began to look up for him.

I went to Coláiste Eoin, a high school where everything was taught in the Irish language. After graduating in the late eighties, the midst of the tech revolution, I went on to study computer programming. While I was in school, I got a part-time job washing dishes at a Dublin pizza joint called Da Vincenzo. It didn't take me long to realize that being in a restaurant environment was more fun than computers. The heat, the chaos, the camaraderie, hanging out until the wee hours of the morning, rolling pizza dough, going to the clubs on Leeson Street and drinking cheap wine until the sun came up—it was all just so intoxicating. I woke up in class one day and decided it was time for me to quit school. I was now a full-time dishwasher at Da Vincenzo; it was there that the thought of cooking professionally took root.

Because I had a strong work ethic, I always offered to pitch in where I could. I started learning basic knife skills and was soon doing a lot of the prep work (chopping vegetables, grating cheese, picking herbs, peeling garlic) and performing some of the everyday cooking tasks, like making red sauce or stocks.

One of the chefs took ill one day and the owners asked me to cover him for a couple of weeks, which turned into several months. They threw me on the line and talked me through it as best they could, but I was more or less thrown to the wolves. I caught on pretty quickly and clearly had an affinity for cooking; after a few months I started referring to myself as a "chef."

After his original objections, Da warmed up to the idea of me being in the restaurant business. Even though I had only been at it for a short while, he got it into his head that it was time for me to open a restaurant of my own and got the money up for it with some friends of his.

We opened The Baytree in 1989 in Monkstown, a suburb of Dublin, and needless to say it was a disaster. I clearly didn't really know anything about cooking, the history, the technique, the science, etc., and knew even less about running a kitchen and an entire restaurant. (Food cost? Labor cost? Health permit? Those were foreign notions to me.)

I had the audacity to serve what I thought was classic French food. I thought it would be provocative to keep the front door of the restaurant closed and have guests ring a doorbell to gain admittance— not exactly a welcoming business strategy. I was always in the red and the deeper in the hole I got, the less I wanted to be there. On the day Dublin's most revered food critic came calling, I had earlier decided not to open and was at the pub instead. "The Baytree was mysteriously closed," the critic noted in the paper the next day.

Ten months after opening, we closed. I had learned some good lessons—don't drink all the booze; don't spend all the cash; don't hire your friends—but Da didn't consider that education worth the cost. He set forth a new plan for me: go to the States for a few months, make some money, come home to get back to computers, and forget about the restaurant business for good.

That's not how things turned out.

~

When I arrived in the United States from Ireland in 1990 at the age of twenty, I was broke and had no idea what to do with my life. I got a job as a short-order cook at Murphy's, an Irish pub in Washington, D.C., and found myself going down a nowhere road: drinking, skipping out on apartments, and frittering away my meager earnings.

At the bar there one night, I met Greggory Hill, the chef of New Heights, a neighboring restaurant that was well regarded. I'm not exactly sure how it happened, but a few whiskeys later I had a second job there as a nighttime line cook. Gregg hooked me up with a third job, working at Cities, a trendy (and now long defunct) Washington eatery.

During my stint as a pizza maker at Cities, I met my future wife, Meshelle, the restaurant's twenty-one-year-old manager. I knew immediately that she was the one who would set my life on the right track—and that my father's plan was no longer an option. I resolved that I would not leave Meshelle, nor would I return to Ireland as I had since left it: defeated.

The problem was, my visa had long expired and I was an unwanted guest of the United States. Fortuitously, or perhaps by pure Irish luck, I entered and won an immigration lottery. Part of that process required me to return to Ireland, register at the U.S. embassy, and swear an allegiance to pay taxes for the time I had been working in the States illegally. There was a possibility that I would be declined at the embassy and never see Meshelle again. It was very dramatic and emotional, but things worked out; in 1991 I obtained my green card, granting me the legal status to live and work in the United States. Somewhere along the way, Da resigned himself to the fact that he couldn't control how my life would turn out.

Upon my return to Washington, D.C., I went back to work at New Heights and threw myself into a self-imposed apprenticeship. I showed up at noon every day even though I was scheduled to be there at three. During this time, I learned a lot of rudimentary cooking techniques from Gregg and his sous-chef: butchering, sauce-making, and charcuterie-making, among others.

At this point, things were going well. I was establishing my career as a serious cook, and I became engaged to Meshelle. When Gregg took a position at another restaurant (called Gabriel), I followed him. There I met a young chef named Neil Annis, who recognized my ability and told me that to advance my career, I should go to work for Jeffrey Buben, a chef for whom he had worked in the past. I applied for a job at chef Buben's much-acclaimed Vidalia Restaurant in March of 1993. The interview consisted of one question: "Do you want to work or do you want to talk?"

"I'll work," I said. And so the next phase of my career began.

~

Vidalia was a whole new world, and a much more challenging kitchen than any other I had ever worked in. At a rapid pace, an education was forced upon me. To say that Buben was a taskmaster and a tough person to work for would be a gross understatement. Tensions ran high in the kitchen and by attrition and default, I wound up as the sous-chef after only a few months. I was severely underqualified.

On the first New Year's Eve I worked at Vidalia, I was somehow on the meat station, cooking filet mignon by pan-roasting it, a method with which I was completely unfamiliar. (I explain the technique on page 118.) We did about 300 covers for dinner that night, and after the sixtieth or so steak was sent back for being overcooked, chef Buben gave up screaming at me. I thought the infamous vein up the center of his forehead would explode. He no doubt knew he had put me in a position I wasn't ready for, but still I felt pretty worthless. It was a good thing we were closed the next day and I had time to lick my wounds before returning to the lion's den.

In subsequent years, as Buben and I worked hand and hand together (mine was held to the stove), my knowledge of classic French cooking and the discipline it took to produce it became honed and I rose quickly through the culinary ranks. I recognized that I was good at cooking; the better I got at it, the more confident I became and the more fun it was. It was the same kind of high I got from playing hurling—the adrenaline of the dinner rush, the intensity, the satisfaction of working as a finely tuned team, the thrill of cooking great food. The business seemed to be in my blood, so it was only natural that I would revisit the idea of opening a restaurant of my own.

In 1997, Meshelle and I married and began to pursue the restaurant dream together. Our first child, Eve, was born in 1999. By then I had been promoted. I was now the chef de cuisine of Buben's newly opened and much-hyped restaurant, Bistro Bis, a stone's throw from Capitol Hill. There I cooked for various notables, from Ted Kennedy to Muhammad Ali.

One Monday, Jeff called me and told me that Julia Child was coming to lunch on Thursday. I prepared a special menu and ordered the freshest special ingredients to be delivered, but she showed up unannounced a day early and I had to scramble.

I don't remember what I made, but it must have passed muster. I learned later that they had had arrangements somewhere else for Thursday that Julia insisted on canceling so that she could return to Bis a second day in a row, with none other than famed chef Jacques Pépin in tow. That was one of the highest points of my career. I remember I made sorrel soup, but other than that, the day was a blur.

During my years at Bis, I learned how to manage staff, control food and labor costs, and run a large, busy operation. It was a sense of proprietorship that would come in handy in the not-too-distant future; by the early 2000s, Meshelle and I were developing plans to open our own place.

~

By this time, Ireland was in the midst of a cultural resurgence and a culinary revolution. The significance of this is great, because the concept of Irish cuisine is a twentieth-century development.

Ireland had been under English rule for hundreds of years. The fertile countryside's output (cash crops, meat) went to landowners, leaving the mostly rural population to subsist on potatoes, the only crop they could grow for themselves. From 1845 to 1848, the Great Potato Famine occurred when a blight wiped out the potato crop, causing mass starvation. An estimated one million people died; millions of others emigrated throughout the remainder of the nineteenth century and into the twentieth century.

In 1949, Ireland withdrew from the British Commonwealth and strived to develop an economy driven by its primary resource: agricultural products. Due to continuing high unemployment and low GDP, college-educated people in Ireland continued to emigrate because there weren't any jobs for them.

Finally, in the early 1990s, the government drastically changed regulations and made it possible for foreign investors to do business in Ireland tax-free; money and people poured in. In 1995, the population in Ireland grew for the first time since 1845. During this time (1995–2007), known as the Celtic Tiger period, the Irish economy, including the hospitality industry, exploded. A new breed of Irish chefs emerged that was dedicated to a modern cuisine based on ingredients indigenous to Ireland.

Among the pioneers of this movement were chef Derry Clarke of L'Ecrivain Restaurant and chef Ross Lewis of Chapter One Restaurant, both in Dublin, and Darina Allen, the doyenne of modern Irish cooking and owner of Ballymaloe House in Shanagarry in County Cork.

The resources Irish chefs have at their disposal are abundant. Agriculturally, Ireland is very wealthy. It's on the same latitude as Newfoundland, but very different in this way: the Gulf Stream comes across the Atlantic from Florida and keeps the climate moderate, making it conducive to growing produce year-round. Grass-fed beef and lamb are superlative. Irish butter ranks among the finest butters of the world, as do artisanal cheeses such as Cashel Blue and Dalhallow. As an island country, Ireland is also rich in fish and seafood, such as plaice, mussels, oysters, and Dublin Bay prawns, some of the most delectable shellfish you'd ever want to eat.

~

In 2004, Meshelle and I opened Restaurant Eve, a fine-dining establishment we named after our daughter. (Our son, Eamonn, was born in 2002. We named our fish and chip joint, Eamonn's, A Dublin Chipper, after him.) We divided the ninety-seat restaurant, situated in a charming converted townhouse in Old Town Alexandria, Virginia, into two distinct dining rooms: the casual but upscale Bistro and the slightly more formal Tasting Room, where we offer five-, seven-, and nine-course tasting menus. The restaurant met with instant acclaim.

Just as the Irish chefs based their menus on their local ingredients, so did I, buying produce, meat, eggs, cheese, fish, and seafood from the finest farmers of the Delmarva region. I did, however, work cherished Irish ingredients and dishes into the mix, with the likes of Kerrygold butter, brown bread, and colcannon popping up on my modern American menus.

In 2006, Food & Wine magazine named me one of the ten best new chefs in the United States. Before getting on the plane to accept the award in Aspen, Colorado, an employee of mine handed me a copy of Michael Pollan's The Omnivore's Dilemma, which proved revelatory.

Until then, I had been a supporter of sourcing products locally, but only because they were the freshest ingredients I could lay my hands on. Thanks to Pollan, I realized I needed to make a deeper commitment: to make a real effort to educate and lead by example. Da had pointed the way long before; I just hadn't connected the dots.

Now I did. I planted my own garden at the restaurant to honor my family's traditions. There we grow a multitude of fruits and vegetables, including peaches, heirloom apples, herbs, tomatoes, and peas. I committed to going green, changing all the chemicals in our establishments to environmentally friendly ones. I began to participate in myriad fundraising activities that support the proliferation of farmers' markets. (I serve on the Board of Directors of FRESHFARM Markets, which manages and promotes several producer-only markets in the metropolitan Washington, D.C., area.)

In 2010, I created an organization called Chefs as Parents, whose mission is to effect change in school lunch programs and educate children and parents about the value of healthful, local, nutritious foods. For that, the White House hailed me as a "champion of change" who does "extraordinary things to out-innovate, out-educate and out-build the rest of the world."

~

On an October night in 2011, I stood at the front door of Restaurant Eve congratulating President and Mrs. Obama on their wedding anniversary as they made their way to The Bistro for dinner. Afterward, I chatted with them about their recent trip to Ireland. As a kid washing dishes in a Dublin pizzeria, I could not have fathomed conversing with the president of the United States any more than I could have envisioned an empire that included Restaurant Eve, the Majestic Café, two branches of Eamonn's, A Dublin Chipper and PX cocktail lounges, and Society Fair, our gourmet emporium and wine bar.

My success as an internationally recognized four-star chef, an owner of multiple restaurants, and a leader in the sustainable food movement has its roots firmly in my Irish upbringing. Without the shepherd's pie, black pudding and onions, and Mam's apple pie of my youth, the Kerrygold Butter–Poached Lobster with Parsnips, Pork Belly with Braised Cabbage and Poached Apples, and Pan-Roasted Rockfish with Mushroom Reduction and Mock Risotto of Restaurant Eve could never have been.

This book is a collection of traditional Irish dishes close to my heart, family recipes (with a few spins here and there), and refined, Irish-inspired dishes from Restaurant Eve.

It is a culinary coming of age story of an Irishman, a chef, and, most importantly, a son.

A NOTE ABOUT SALT

"With all thine offerings thou shalt offer salt." Leviticus 2:13

At my restaurants, we use Italian sea salt for cooking everything because it is unrefined and has a nice, mineral quality. The salt used in the recipes in this book, unless otherwise indicated, is kosher salt.

CHAPTER ONE

First Things First: Irish Breakfast Like at Home

Breakfast is always hearty in Ireland, but it's more expansive on Sunday than any other day of the week. It would not be unusual to serve eggs, an array of pork products, fried potatoes, tomatoes, brown bread, and toast all at one meal.

Whenever we land at Dublin airport, always in the morning, we call Mam and she says, "Right, right. I'll put the breakfast on." We know that the instant we walk in the door the undisputedly porcine and faintly sweet smell of sizzling, fat-rich sausage links, disks of white and black pudding, and slices of cured bacon will greet us, luring us immediately into the kitchen.

Pork is one of the most commonly consumed meats in Ireland because it has always been much less expensive than beef, which, except for stew or scrap meat, was reserved for special occasions. Pork is beloved. A butcher in Dublin once told my dad that the bin men wouldn't pick up the trash unless he gave them a pound of bacon and a pound of sausages, which they would then eat raw behind the butcher shop. That is a little bit beyond my own comfort zone, but it is an indicator of how important pork was, and still is, to the country's people.

Our daughter, Eve, likes Irish sausage and American bacon; our son, Eamonn, likes American sausage and Irish bacon. I'd like to say there is some entertaining way that we resolve this issue, but the truth is we are just indulgent parents and usually wind up making both kinds of sausage and bacon. The more pork, the merrier.

And not to be underestimated are the, shall we say, medicinal benefits of a hearty Irish breakfast or a plate of rashers and chips; they are ideal hangover cures. A rasher sandwich is one of the greatest meals ever—when you get home from the pub feeling a little tipsy, you can't beat it.

Irish Breakfast

A traditional Irish breakfast typically includes finely textured breakfast sausage, white pudding (a coarse, poached pork sausage with herbs, bread crumbs, and spices), black pudding (a rich, poached sausage made with pork blood, fat, and spices), back and/or streaky rashers, fried potatoes, tomatoes, buttered toast, and sunny-side up eggs. In our house, add to that plenty of brown bread, orange marmalade, and raspberry jam.

In addition to laying out how to put such a feast together, I've included recipes to make Restaurant Eve's Pork Loin Bacon, breakfast sausage, white pudding, and black pudding from scratch. These all must be prepared ahead of time and can be refrigerated or frozen. If you'd prefer to make your life a little easier by buying some or all of these items, they are available at www.foodireland.com.

Timing is everything when making Irish breakfast because so many components have to come together at the same time. The best way to get the job done is to do it in steps, starting with the things that take the longest and can most withstand being held in a warm oven. Choose your preferred Breakfast Tomatoes recipe (page 12) and make them first because they hold well. Be sure to have cold, cooked potatoes on hand. (Irish people generally do, but Americans may have to plan ahead.) Fry the eggs at the very last minute.

{ SERVES 4 }

Breakfast Tomatoes (page 12)

1 tablespoon canola oil

4 thick (2-ounce) Breakfast Sausages (page 17)

8 ounces White Pudding (page 20), casing removed, cut crosswise into 1-inch slices

8 ounces Black Pudding (page 22), casing removed, cut crosswise into 1-inch slices

4 (1/4-inch) slices Restaurant Eve's Pork Loin Bacon (page 14) and/or back or streaky rashers

4 boiled or peeled baked potatoes, cold, halved lengthwise, and sliced into 1/2-inch slices

Kosher salt

1 tablespoon unsalted butter

8 large eggs

Brown Bread (page 192), sliced

4 slices toast, buttered

Orange Marmalade (page 24)

Raspberry Jam (page 26)

Begin with the tomatoes: Preheat the oven to 200°F. Prepare your chosen breakfast tomatoes recipe and transfer them to a small serving plate or bowl; place in the oven to keep warm.

Cook the meats: In a large nonstick slope-sided sauté pan or well-seasoned cast-iron skillet over medium heat, heat the oil until it shimmers. Pan-fry the sausage links, turning them often until they are hot in the center, 10 to 15 minutes for the links. Add the white and black pudding slices after the sausage has cooked for about 5 minutes, and cook, turning often with tongs, for 5 to 7 minutes,

or until they are lightly browned and warm on the inside. Transfer everything to a large ovenproof platter and place in the warm oven. Using the same pan, sauté the bacon slices for 1 minute on each side until lightly browned and then transfer them to the platter in the oven.

Cook the potatoes: In the same pan with the meat drippings and over medium heat, fry the potatoes, spreading them evenly on the bottom of the pan. Season with salt and fry for several minutes on both sides until well browned. Transfer the potatoes to the platter with the breakfast meats.

{continued}

Finally, make the eggs: In a nonstick pan over medium heat, heat the butter until it bubbles. Crack the eggs into the pan and cook them sunny-side up, 2 to 3 minutes, depending on your desired degree of doneness. Separate the eggs with the flat end of a spatula and transfer them to a platter. Serve immediately with the breakfast tomatoes, brown bread, toast, orange marmalade, and raspberry jam.

Breakfast Tomatoes Three Ways

Broiling is the easiest and most popular method of preparing tomatoes for breakfast in Ireland. Sautéing them in olive oil, which I call Tomatoes in a Pan, is another option. This is how my father always prepared them. Whenever I'd try to chef them up with garlic and onions, he'd turn his nose up and grumble, "No! That doesn't go in there!"

In our Virginia house, Meshelle's Tomato Thing wins the day. Being American, Meshelle didn't grow up eating tomatoes with breakfast and was dismayed when she first came across a barely cooked, flavorless one on her breakfast plate, probably in some pub in Ireland. She'd always leave them on her plate.

But one morning I spruced them up with onions, garlic, and bay leaves and made a believer out of her to the point where she'd request "that tomato thing you made that time, honey." So that's how her preferred breakfast tomatoes came to be called Meshelle's Tomato Thing.

❧ EACH RECIPE SERVES 4 ❧

Broiled Tomatoes

2 small tomatoes, halved crosswise
Kosher salt and freshly ground black pepper

Position the oven rack about 4 inches from the heating element and preheat the broiler. Season the tomatoes with salt and pepper and set them cut-side up in a small gratin dish. Broil until soft and hot, but not necessarily browned, 2 to 3 minutes.

Tomatoes in a Pan

1/4 cup olive oil
2 tomatoes, cored and coarsely chopped
Kosher salt and freshly ground black pepper

In a slope-sided sauté pan over medium-high heat, heat the oil until it shimmers. Sauté the tomatoes until soft, stirring occasionally, about 10 minutes. Season to taste with salt and pepper.

Meshelle's Tomato Thing

1/4 cup olive oil
1/2 yellow onion, chopped
4 large cloves garlic, thinly sliced crosswise
2 tomatoes, cored and coarsely chopped
4 fresh bay leaves
1/2 teaspoon kosher salt
1/2 teaspoon ground black pepper

In a slope-sided sauté pan over medium-high heat, heat the oil until it shimmers. Stir in the onion and garlic and lower the heat to medium. Let the vegetables cook, stirring occasionally, until the onions are translucent and soft, but not brown, about 5 minutes. Add the tomatoes, bay leaves, salt, and pepper and cook for 10 more minutes, until most of the water has evaporated. Discard the bay leaves. Serve hot or at room temperature.

Restaurant Eve's Pork Loin Bacon

The bacon we make at Restaurant Eve is cured pork loin. I think people would be more into curing if they realized how simple the process is, involving little more than making a wet marinade with water, spices, salt, and, if the recipe calls for it, sugar, then letting meat sit in it for several days in the refrigerator. (See the sidebar On Irish Bacon, opposite.)

Since the curing process for this recipe takes 3 days, it's advisable to make a big batch, dividing what you don't use into reasonable portions and freezing them for later use. Cured pork loin will last for 4 days in the refrigerator, wrapped tightly in plastic wrap. Freeze for up to 3 months, wrapped tightly in plastic wrap and then with aluminum foil.

Use cured pork loin as you would bacon; in addition to our Irish Breakfast, it is delicious in dishes such as the Irish BLT (page 138) we serve at Restaurant Eve.

{ MAKES 2½ POUNDS, ABOUT 25 (¼-INCH) SLICES }

1 quart water

1 cup kosher salt

½ cup sugar

1 quart water frozen into ice cubes (2 pounds)

1 small head garlic, unpeeled, halved crosswise

1 yellow onion, quartered

2 tablespoons pink curing salt, such as sel rose or Insta Cure #1 (see Resources, page 263)

½ teaspoon black peppercorns

½ teaspoon yellow mustard seed

½ small bunch fresh sage

1 (2½-pound) boneless pork loin, preferably Kurobuta or Berkshire, top layer of fat intact

Make the brine: In a large pot over high heat, bring the water to a boil. Add the kosher salt and sugar, stirring until they are dissolved. Remove from the heat and stir in the ice to completely cool the brine. Add the garlic, onion, curing salt, peppercorns, mustard seed, and sage.

Cure the pork: Place the pork loin in a 2½-gallon zip-top bag placed in a large bowl. Pour the brine into the bag. Seal the bag, removing as much air as possible so that the pork is completely submerged. Refrigerate the pork in its brine for 3 days. After

3 days, rinse the pork completely in cold water. Discard the brine. Blot the loin dry on all sides with paper towels. Depending on how soon you plan to use the bacon, refrigerate or freeze it. (See recipe note.)

To cook the bacon: Heat a little canola oil in a slope-sided sauté pan over medium-high heat until it shimmers; use 1 teaspoon of oil for 4 slices of bacon. Sauté the bacon slices for 1 minute on each side until lightly browned.

In Ireland, there are four types of bacon: smoked and unsmoked versions of streaky rashers and back rashers. Streaky and/or back rashers are found in every household in Ireland and are eaten pretty much every day. The streaky rasher comes from the pig's fat-riddled belly, like American bacon. The back rasher is the loin with usually about $\frac{1}{2}$ or 2 inches of the belly attached to it. My Da hated smoked bacon. The recipe for unsmoked back rashers I make in my restaurants (Restaurant Eve's Pork Loin Bacon) is on page 14, opposite.

To make your own unsmoked streaky bacon, refer to the Boiling Bacon recipe on page 122. Once the bacon comes out of the brine and is rinsed and dried, set it on a wire rack uncovered in the refrigerator for 5 days, flipping it over every day. After that, it is ready to be sliced and cooked.

If you have sufficient skill and knowledge to smoke meat safely, you could make smoked streaky bacon by smoking it rather than drying it in the refrigerator.

Sausage making need not be an intimidating process. If you are organized and have the right tools for the job, it really doesn't take that much time, even if it does require an initial investment to purchase the equipment. Plus, making sausage is fun to do with kids—they love it and it teaches them that, sometimes, good things in life take time.

All of your sausage making needs can be found at www.sausagemaker.com.

You will need:
- Curing salt, usually a mix of table salt, pink dye, sodium nitrite, and sometimes sodium nitrate; this inhibits bacterial growth and helps the meat retain a rosy hue.
- Casings, either natural or synthetic (usually collagen) ones. Before they are stuffed, natural (hog) casings need to be soaked in cold water and to have cold water run through them. This ensures cleanliness and will show you whether there are any tears in them.
- A meat grinder, either hand-crank or electric, with fine and coarse grinder plates. (The meat grinder attachment of a stand mixer works well, too.)
- A table-mounted, hand-crank sausage stuffer, which is preferable to a stand mixer outfitted with a stuffing attachment. This dedicated machine keeps you from having to perform a balancing act while trying to push the meat into the grinder, guide the stuffing into the sausage, and keep the sausage dangling from the stuffer until it is long enough to reach the table. Make sure the machine is clamped firmly to the worktable so it doesn't slide all over the place.

- An extra pair of hands comes in handy when making sausage, allowing one person to feed the stuffer while the other works air pockets out of the casing as the meat passes through the extruder.
- A sausage pricker, whose fine prongs pierce natural casings enough to release air but not so much as to provide an exit for precious cooking juices.
- A remote digital thermometer. This thermometer consists of a probe attached to heatproof wire that plugs into a countertop register. The probe digitally reads the internal temperature and sounds an alarm when the desired temperature is reached so it allows you to monitor the internal temperature of the item you are baking throughout the cooking process.

Some preparation tips:
- Make sure the meat and water used are very cold at all times. This helps the fat stay suspended in the meat's protein as long as possible during the cooking process so that it goes into the meat instead of being leached out. This makes the difference between succulent and dry sausage.
- You want to get rid of air pockets; juices will collect and expand in the sausages during cooking and cause the casings to burst. The result will be a dry sausage. Gently knead the coil as it comes off the extruder to rid it of air pockets.
- Leave some slack in the beginning and end of the sausage casing—that way you will have plenty of room to massage the air pockets out of the finished rope.
- If you are making links, alternate the direction in which you twist them: one clockwise, the next counterclockwise, etc. If you don't, they can unravel.

Breakfast Sausage

The process of sausage making is not as difficult as it is time-consuming, and there's really no reason why home cooks should feel intimidated about making sausage from scratch. When you do, you know exactly what is going into your food—a real plus, especially if you don't really know much about the butcher or market where you're buying these products already made.

It pays to make extra sausages and keep them on hand for cocktail parties, for special occasions, or when guests drop in unexpectedly for breakfast. No birthday celebration in our house is complete without them, made into half-size links. Store the links in freezer-proof zip-top bags for up to 3 months.

For this recipe, you'll need some sausage-making equipment; see On Sausage Making (opposite). You'll find some useful tips there, too.

{ MAKES 16 (2-OUNCE) LINKS }

1 tablespoon fresh sage leaves, packed

1 teaspoon canola oil, plus more for frying

1/2 cup finely minced yellow onion

2 pounds boneless pork shoulder, preferably Kurobuta or Berkshire, cut into 2-inch chunks

1 cup panko bread crumbs

1 tablespoon fine sea salt

1 teaspoon freshly ground white pepper

2 teaspoons chopped fresh thyme leaves

1/2 cup ice water

Two 32- to 35-millimeter-wide (1 1/4- to 1 1/3-inch-wide) hog casings, each about 4 feet long

2 cups torn pieces of French bread

Blanch and chop the sage leaves: Bring a small pan of water to a boil; prepare a small bowl of ice water. Submerge the sage leaves in the boiling water for 10 seconds. Drain them and immediately submerge in the ice water. Drain again and squeeze dry on a kitchen towel. Chop them and measure 2 teaspoons; reserve any remaining for another use.

Sweat the onion: In a small slope-sided sauté pan over medium heat, heat the 1 teaspoon of oil until it shimmers. Add the onion and let sweat, stirring frequently with a wooden spoon, until translucent, about 2 minutes. Set aside.

Mix the sausage filling: Outfit a meat grinder with a 1/4-inch grinder plate and grind the pork. Grind the pork again, mixing in the onion. Transfer

the pork to a food processor. Add the panko, salt, pepper, thyme, and sage; pour in the ice water and process for 1 minute, until the ingredients are incorporated but the mixture retains some texture. Transfer the mixture to a bowl; cover and refrigerate while you prepare the casings.

Clean the casings: Soak the hog casings for 10 minutes in cold water. To clean each one, thread one end onto the faucet, and run cold water through it for several seconds.

Attach a casing and fill the stuffer: Untwisting it as you go along, thread a casing onto the extruder tube of a sausage stuffer. Remove the pork mixture from the refrigerator and fill the bowl of the sausage stuffer with it. Place the French bread on top of it. (This is going to push all of the stuffing

{continued}

out of the machine so you don't waste any of it.) Start passing the meat through the stuffer until it comes to the end of the extruder. (This gets rid of air trapped in the machine.) Pull about 2 inches of casing off the end of the tube and knot it.

Fill the casing: Crank the stuffer and fill the casing, using slow, steady movement. That way, as you go, you can gently work out with your fingers any air pockets within the casing. (An extra pair of hands really comes in handy for this part of the process.) As the filled casing comes off the extruder, it will naturally form into a coil. If at any time during the process you come across a tear in the casing, cut it off, knot the end, and start another coil. You may need to use the second casing.

Tie off the filled casing: The moment you see bread coming through the extruder, stop filling the casing. Leaving a few inches of slack, cut the casing and knot it. (To start cleaning the machine, finish running the bread through it and discard it.)

Shape the links: Twist the filled coil(s) into links at 4-inch intervals, alternating the direction in which you twist: one clockwise, the next counter-clockwise, etc. Using a sausage pricker, prick the sausages at approximate 1-inch intervals. Place the links on a cookie rack set over a baking sheet and allow them to dry in the refrigerator uncovered for 24 to 48 hours, turning them over halfway through.

Cook the sausage: Heat a little canola oil in a slope-sided sauté pan over medium-high heat until it shimmers. (Use 1 teaspoon of oil for 4 sausages.) Pan-fry the sausages, turning often, until they are golden brown and cooked through but still juicy, about 10 to 15 minutes.

White Pudding

White pudding is a poached coarse pork sausage made with herbs, bread crumbs, and spices; for serving, it is sliced, removed from the casing, and pan-fried. It's something every Irish household has on hand and every butcher shop makes and sells. Pork shoulder has the right amount of fat in it for making sausage: about two-thirds lean to one-third fat. The poached sausages, wrapped in plastic wrap and then aluminum foil, can be refrigerated for 3 days or frozen for up to 3 months.

For this recipe, you'll need some sausage-making equipment; see On Sausage Making (page 16). You'll find some useful tips there, too.

{ MAKES 2 1/2 POUNDS, ABOUT 20 (1-INCH, 2-OUNCE) SLICES }

2 1/2 pounds boneless pork shoulder, preferably Kurobuta or Berkshire, cut into 2-inch chunks

1 cup ice water

2 1/2 cups panko bread crumbs

3 large eggs, lightly beaten

2 teaspoons chopped fresh basil

2 teaspoons chopped fresh thyme

2 teaspoons chopped fresh marjoram or oregano

4 cloves garlic, chopped

2 teaspoons kosher salt

2 teaspoons freshly ground white pepper

Three 60-millimeter-wide (2 3/8-inch) collagen sausage casings, each 2 feet long

2 cups torn pieces of French bread

Canola oil for pan-frying

Mix the sausage filling: In a meat grinder fitted with a 1/4-inch grinder plate, grind the pork in two batches, refrigerating the half that isn't being used at the time. Transfer half of the ground pork to a food processor. With the machine running on a medium speed, add the ice water; process to mix. Transfer to a large bowl, add the other batch of pork along with the panko, eggs, herbs, garlic, salt, and pepper and mix well. (The best tools to use here are your hands.) Cover and refrigerate the mixture while preparing the casings.

Attach a casing and fill the stuffer: Soak all 3 casings in cold tap water for a few minutes to make them supple. Thread 1 casing onto the sausage stuffer. Remove the pork mixture from the refrigerator and fill the bowl of the sausage stuffer with it. Place the French bread on top of it. (This is going to push all of the stuffing out of the machine

so you don't waste any of it.) Start passing the meat through the stuffer until it comes to the end of the extruder. (This gets rid of air trapped in the machine.) Pull about 2 inches of casing off the end of the tube and tie it off with kitchen twine.

Fill the first casing: Crank the stuffer and fill the casing, using slow, steady movement. That way, as you go, you can gently work out with your fingers any air pockets within the casing. (An extra pair of hands really comes in handy for this part of the process.) When the casing is almost full, pull the end off the extruder and tie it off.

Fill the remaining casings: Repeat the process with the other 2 casings. The moment you see bread coming through the extruder, stop filling the last casing and tie off its end. (To start cleaning the machine, finish running the bread through it and discard it.)

Ready the pan for poaching: Use a pan deep, wide, and long enough to cook the 3 sausages in a water bath without their touching the bottom. (A 6-inch-deep hotel pan, see Resources, page 263, is what professionals use and is a useful thing for a home cook to have. You can also use a deep flameproof roasting pan.) Position the pan over two front-to-back burners on the stove and place a thick kitchen towel in the bottom of it. To determine how much poaching water you will need, put the sausages in the pan and add enough cold water to cover them by 2 inches. Remove them from the pan.

Poach the pudding: Heat the water over medium-high heat until it is warm. Put the sausages in the pan and cover them with a thick towel and a rack or heatproof plate to make sure they remain submerged while poaching. Increase the water's heat to 160°F and maintain that temperature throughout the cooking process, using ice cubes to do so if necessary. Cook the sausages until they reach an internal temperature of 165°F (about 80 minutes). Using a remote digital thermometer takes the guesswork out of this process.

Cool and wrap: Remove the pan from the heat and let the sausages rest in their cooking water for 1 hour. When they are cool enough to handle, transfer them to a tray. Discard the cooking liquid. Cover and refrigerate the sausages for 4 hours, or overnight. To store, wrap each sausage in plastic wrap and aluminum foil and refrigerate or freeze them.

Cook the pudding: Slit the casing with a knife, peel it away, and discard it. Cut the log into 1-inch-thick slices. In a nonstick slope-sided sauté pan over medium heat, heat a little canola oil until it shimmers (1 teaspoon of oil for 4 slices). Pan-fry the pudding slices, turning often, until they are lightly browned and warm in the center, about 5 to 7 minutes.

Black Pudding

Black pudding, a rich, poached sausage made with pork blood, fat, and spices, is one of those things you either love or hate. It is definitely an acquired taste, like a pint of good stout. I love eating it, but I'm not crazy about making it. If you have a problem with the sight of blood, this isn't the dish for you. Note that black pudding doesn't have any meat in it. Traditionally, it was a way for farmers to use up every bit of an animal, including the blood. The sausage gets thickened with cereal and/or grain, which absorbs moisture as the pudding cooks. To serve it, you remove the casing, slice it into rounds, and pan-fry it.

You're pretty much on your own finding pig's blood, unless you happen to know a pig farmer, as we do. We get ours from one of our local Virginia farmers. I've seen it in Asian markets from time to time.

To store black pudding, cut it into whatever size batches you prefer. Wrap them in plastic wrap and aluminum foil and refrigerate for up to 3 days or freeze for up to 3 months.

For this recipe, you'll need some sausage-making equipment; see On Sausage Making (page 16). You'll find some useful tips there, too.

∫ MAKES 3 POUNDS, ABOUT 48 (1-INCH, 1-OUNCE) SLICES ∫

1 quart fresh pig's blood (see recipe note)

$4^1/_2$ cups panko bread crumbs

8 ounces pork fat, ground (ask your butcher for this)

1 quart whole milk

1 cup cooked pearl barley

1 cup uncooked rolled oats (not instant)

$^1/_4$ teaspoon four-spice blend (see sidebar, page 23)

1 tablespoon kosher salt

Two 32- to 35-millimeter-wide ($1^1/_4$- to $1^1/_3$-inch-wide) hog casings, each about 4 feet long

2 cups torn pieces of French bread

Canola oil for pan-frying

Mix the sausage filling: In a large bowl, stir the blood, panko, pork fat, milk, barley, oats, spices, and salt to combine well. Cover and refrigerate.

Clean the casings: Soak the hog casings for 10 minutes in cold water. To clean each one, thread one end onto the faucet and run cold water through it for several seconds.

Attach the casing and fill the stuffer: Untwisting it as you go along, thread a casing onto the extruder tube of a sausage stuffer. Remove the filling from the refrigerator and fill the bowl of the sausage stuffer with it. Place the French bread on top of it. (This is going to push all of the stuffing out of the machine so you don't waste any of it.) Start passing the filling through the stuffer until it comes to the end of the extruder. (This gets rid of air trapped in the machine.) Pull about 2 inches of casing off the end of the tube and knot it.

Fill the casing: Crank the stuffer and fill the casing, using slow, steady movement. That way, as you go, you can gently work out with your fingers any air pockets within the casing. (An extra pair of hands really comes in handy for this part of the process.) As the filled casing comes off the extruder, it will naturally form into a coil. If at any time during the process you come across a tear in the casing, cut it off, knot the end, and start another coil. You may need to use all the casings.

Tie off the filled casing: The moment you see bread coming through the extruder, stop filling the casing. Leaving a few inches of slack, cut the casing and knot it. (To start cleaning the machine, finish running the bread through it and discard it.)

Poach the pudding: Using a sausage pricker, prick the coil at approximate 1-inch intervals. Place a thick kitchen towel in the bottom of a wide, heavy casserole. Put the pudding coil on the towel and add enough cold water to cover it by 2 inches. Place another towel and a wire mesh rack over the coil to make sure it remains submerged. Cook the pudding over low heat until it reaches an internal temperature of 165°F (about 80 minutes). Using a remote digital thermometer takes the guesswork out of this process.

Drain the pot and run cold water over the pudding. When it is cool enough to handle, transfer it to a tray. Cover and refrigerate for 4 hours, or overnight.

Cook the pudding: Remove and discard the casing and cut the pudding diagonally into 1-inch slices. In a nonstick slope-sided sauté pan over medium heat, heat a little canola oil until it shimmers (1 teaspoon of oil for 4 slices). Pan-fry the pudding slices, turning often, until they are warm in the center, about 5 to 7 minutes.

ABOUT FOUR-SPICE BLEND

Four-spice blend is also known as quatre épices, a blend of spices often used to flavor pâtés in French cooking. Although cooks have been known to come up with their own combinations of spices, the one you see most often is ground cloves, ground ginger, ground nutmeg, and ground white pepper. Proportions vary, but I use equal parts. Combine 1 tablespoon of each and store in an airtight container to have on hand. Makes about 1/4 cup.

Orange Marmalade

This is my Ma's recipe. In Ireland, she uses something called Sure-Set sugar, which has pectin in it. That product doesn't exist in the States that I've found. You can cut the rind into the size strips you wish depending on what kind of texture you prefer for your marmalade. I like to cut the rinds into 1/4-inch slices; others prefer 1/2-inch squares or just a coarse chop. All the grocery stores in Ireland sell thick-cut and thin-cut marmalade.

Preserving the marmalade requires a precise method that calls for special equipment; see Canning Instructions, page 25. Preserved marmalade needs to set for at least 2 weeks after it's made—plan ahead.

{ MAKES ABOUT 7 (1/2-PINT) JARS }

1 1/2 pounds (about 4 medium) oranges, preferably Seville, stems removed

3 1/2 cups water

6 cups sugar

Juice of 1 lemon

1 (1 3/4-ounce) box Sure-Jell pectin

Boil the oranges: Place the whole oranges in a deep, heavy-bottomed saucepan, preferably just wide enough to contain them in a single layer. You want the pot to be deep because boiling sugar takes up a lot of volume and you don't want gooey syrup spilling all over your stove. Cover the oranges with 3 cups of the water and boil over high heat for 10 minutes, until the oranges are tender. Transfer the oranges to a cutting board. Set the pot of cooking liquid aside.

Cook the pulp: When the oranges are cool enough to handle, cut them in half crosswise. Use a dessert spoon to scoop all the pulp from the rind and into a medium saucepan. Add the remaining 1/2 cup of water. Over medium-high heat, boil the pulp for 30 minutes, until it is mushy. Press the mixture with the side of a wooden spoon to facilitate breaking down the pulp as it cooks.

Strain the pulp: Set a large strainer over the pot of reserved cooking liquid. Transfer the pulp to the strainer and press down on the fruit with your wooden spoon to extract all of its juice. (What you're doing here is extracting all the natural pectin in the fruit, which will help set the marmalade.) Discard the pulp.

Cook the marmalade: Cut the rinds into 1 by ½-inch strips (there should be about 1½ cups). (See recipe note.) Add the rinds to the pot with the cooking liquid. Stir in 5½ cups of the sugar and the lemon juice. Boil the liquid hard over high heat for 10 minutes, stirring occasionally and skimming and discarding any white foam that rises to the top.

Add the pectin: While the marmalade is still boiling, combine the pectin and the remaining ½ cup of sugar in a bowl. Ladle 1 cup or so of hot cooking liquid into the pectin mixture, whisking until smooth. Whisk that mixture back into the hot marmalade. Return the marmalade to a boil and boil for another 2 minutes, stirring occasionally. (The consistency, already quite syrupy, won't change discernably.)

Can the marmalade: Can and store the marmalade per the instructions below. As the marmalade cools, invert and reinvert the jars every so often to distribute the peel evenly throughout. Store them in a cool place for at least 2 weeks to allow the marmalade to deepen in flavor and finish setting.

CANNING INSTRUCTIONS

You will need:
- A 16-quart canner or large pot
- Canning jars
- Lids (must be new to ensure a seal)
- Rings (screwtops)
- A lid lifter (not vital, but useful; it's a magnetized wand that picks lids and rings out of the canner)
- A wide-mouth funnel (makes ladling much easier)
- Jar tongs (so you don't burn yourself)
- To sterilize your jars, fill a large pot, preferably a canner, with water and bring to a boil. Submerge the jars in the water, add the lids and rings, and simmer (do not boil) for 10 minutes. Keep the jars hot until ready to use. (You can transfer the lids and rings, using a lid lifter if you have one, to a wire rack set over a baking sheet.)
- While the recipe you're making is hot, ladle it through a funnel into the sterilized jars (leave ¼ inch of headspace for jam and marmalade and ½ inch for piccalilli). Wipe the rims with a clean cloth. Place the lids on the jars and screw the rings on until just tightened. Don't force them.
- Bring the canner water to a boil and put the jars in it upright and 2 inches apart. (A tool called a jar holder comes in handy for this.) The jars should be covered with at least 2 inches of water. Boil the jars for 7 minutes (jam and marmalade) or 15 minutes (piccalilli).
- Using jar tongs, transfer the jars to a wire rack set over a baking sheet and allow them to cool for 24 hours. The lids should "ping" to indicate that the seals are complete, but they may not. To test, press the top of the lid with your fingertip. If it moves up and down, the seal isn't complete; that means you have to process that jar's ingredients again as above. Store jars in a cool, dark place for up to a year.

Raspberry Jam

We always had raspberries growing in the garden. As kids, we would run around and play and then eat the berries for energy, competing with the birds for them. Late in the summer when the crop was harvested, Mam would make raspberry jam for the year. The smell of raspberry jam cooking takes me right back to that place.

When making most berry jams, you must have equal weights of fruit and sugar or the jam won't set properly, because the ratio of natural pectin to sugar will be off. That is why I give the weights for these ingredients in this recipe and strongly suggest that cooks employ them: use the cup equivalencies at your own risk. Never use frozen fruit. It is important not to overcook the fruit. If you do, you lose the very berry-ness of it and have wasted your time and resources. The texture of this jam will be loose because I rely on the natural pectin only instead of adding powdered pectin. The jam's color will be bright, unlike the gelatinous, overly sweet, jarred stuff you usually find on grocery store shelves.

Preserving the jam requires special equipment; see Canning Instructions, page 25.

*❧ **MAKES 5 (¹/₂-PINT) JARS** ❧*

1 pound, 11 ounces fresh raspberries (about 4 pints)
1 pound, 11 ounces sugar (about 3³/₄ cups)
Juice of 1 lemon

In a large saucepan over high heat, bring the raspberries, sugar, and lemon juice to a boil and boil for exactly 2 minutes, stirring often to release the berries' juices. Can and store the jam per the instructions on page 25.

~⁎⟩ A Perfect Breakfast ⟨⁎~

In the early 1990s, Meshelle and I took a trip to Darina Allen's world-famous Ballymaloe House in Shanagarry. On the way, we stayed at a bed and breakfast near the village of Schull, in County Cork. The breakfast there turned out to be one of the most memorable of our lives.

The lady of the house made Danish pastries, hot scones, and homemade jam from scratch, served Durrus Farmhouse Cheese from a nearby creamery, milk from her own cows, and of course a full Irish breakfast. The table teemed with the famous Clonakilty black pudding, white pudding, rashers, sausages, tomatoes—the lot. We stuffed ourselves to the gills and marveled at our good fortune.

After breakfast, as we were heading out to Ballymaloe, I handed the lady my credit card for the very steep IR£25 bill ($30) comprising our overnight stay there and the meal, which on its own must have cost her at least $30 to produce. She didn't, however, accept credit cards, so I volunteered to go into town just a couple of minutes away and get cash from the ATM.

"Don't be ridiculous," she said. "Just send me a check when you get home."

Meshelle was just flabbergasted at the fulsomeness of our Irish hospitality. I wish I could remember the name of the place. We might have been dreaming.

CHAPTER TWO

Rugby Matches, Croke Park, and Hurling Practice

All of the dishes in this chapter are intended to be snack foods—casual, lazy, Sunday-afternoon-watching-the-game food.

More than anyone else I've ever met, my mother is a mad sports fanatic. There was always some sporting event on the TV when I was at home—golf, cricket, rugby, tennis, horse racing—it didn't really matter. If there was a particularly important sporting event, the television was allowed to be on during dinner.

Just about every week, we'd pack a picnic and make a pilgrimage to Croke Park, a stadium in central Dublin that serves as the headquarters for the Gaelic Athletic Association, to watch matches. (It's one of the largest stadiums in Europe, seating more than 80,000 people.) We supported the "Dubs," of course, and pretty much any hurling match that was being played. When I was in secondary school at Coláiste Eoin, I fell in love with this ancient Celtic sport, first mentioned in 1829 BCE and cited often in Irish folklore. I played it almost every day.

Guinness World Records refers to hurling, an amateur-only sport, as the fastest field sport in the world. It is one of the fiercest, most exciting sports to play and watch. It involves two teams of fifteen players using long-handled paddles (hurleys) to try and score goals (brutally, I might add) by hitting a ball (sliotar) into each other's nets or over the goalposts set directly in front of them. A game takes place over two 35-minute halves, with a 15-minute break in between. Believe me, after working that vast field, 140 yards by 90 yards, it feels more like 70 hours than 70 minutes, but the thrill is like nothing else.

When I was around thirty and living in the States, I went home for a visit. On one particular day, everyone was out except my father. Da had such a big, domineering personality that I just felt odd being alone in the house with him during that phase of my life and this day ended with just him and me watching a big match on TV. Da got out a bottle of sherry and he made a tapas bar for us to eat while we watched the match: salami, cheese, Chicken Liver Pâté (page 30), tinned sardines in tomato sauce (my recipe for fresh ones is on page 45), and Spanish Omelet with Alioli (page 48). Over those snacks and a day of watching sports together, we connected in a way we never had before, as adults, parents, and men. It was a real rite of passage for me.

Chicken Liver Pâté

My mother used to make this for us from scratch, but you can find a good version of it at every deli in Ireland. When preparing the pâté, take the time to trim the livers well. Also, use good Cognac or brandy; the recipe doesn't call for much of it, so now is not the time to skimp. Paying attention to details always makes a difference in the end.

The recipe yields a big batch and can be halved easily, but I like to freeze it in ½-cup portions (sealed with a thin layer of clarified butter) to have on hand for parties or unexpected guests. Whenever I need some, I just bring it to room temperature, scrape off the butter (saving it to use for sautéing vegetables), and serve it with melba toast or sliced French bread. (See How to Clarify Butter, page 253.)

Prepare the pâté at least 12 hours in advance to give it time to set it and allow its flavors to mellow.

⟨ MAKES ABOUT 4 CUPS ⟩

1 large yellow onion, coarsely chopped

2 cloves garlic, coarsely chopped

2 large fresh bay leaves

1¼ cups unsalted butter, at room temperature

2 pounds chicken livers, trimmed of all veins and sinews

1 teaspoon kosher salt

½ teaspoon freshly ground black pepper

1 tablespoon good-quality Cognac or other brandy

Cook the livers: Place the onion, garlic, bay leaves, and ¾ cup of the butter in a large slope-sided sauté pan over medium heat. Sauté for 25 minutes, stirring occasionally, until the onion is translucent but not at all brown. Add the livers, salt, and pepper. Raise the heat to medium-high and cook until the livers are firm but still pink in the center, about 3 minutes. Stir in the Cognac. Discard the bay leaves.

Finish the pâté: Transfer the liver mixture to a food processor along with the remaining ½ cup of butter and purée until smooth, scraping the sides of the bowl down a few times. Taste the pâté and add more salt or pepper if you wish. Spoon the pâté into whatever size food storage containers you prefer. Refrigerate for at least 12 hours to set the butter. It will keep refrigerated for a day beyond that, or you can freeze it for up to 3 months, but serve at room temperature.

Egg and Onion Salad

The first time I made this at Restaurant Eve for a party, my chef de cuisine looked at me like I was nuts for putting all the onions I did into it. We actually had a wager on it, which I clearly won. (Feel free to chop the onions smaller and decrease the amount you put in the salad if you wish, but I like it plenty oniony. In fact, I'd be happy to call the dish Onion and Egg Salad.) The salad is great as a dip with chips, makes a terrific open-faced sandwich on toasted ciabatta, and is tasty on a bed of greens as a lunch. You'll see I don't use pepper in this dish; if I were using store-bought eggs, I might use a touch of it because they need all the help they can get, as you really have no idea how fresh those eggs are. It's not unusual for eggs in grocery stores to be on the shelf for many months and over time their flavor diminishes.

By the way, don't stick your hand in the egg water. (See Witches and Warts, below.)

❋⟩ SERVES 6 ⟨❋

6 large eggs
¹/₂ cup mayonnaise, preferably homemade (page 247)
1 large yellow onion, diced
¹/₄ cup chopped fresh chives
¹/₂ teaspoon kosher salt

Hard-boil the eggs: Place the eggs in a saucepan and cover them with cold water. Bring the water to a rolling boil and keep it boiling over high heat for 10 minutes. Run cold water over the eggs to arrest the cooking process; peel them immediately.

Mix the salad: Cut the eggs into eighths (in quarters lengthwise and then in half crosswise). Place them in a bowl. Add the mayonnaise, onion, chives, and salt and mix well with a wooden spoon. Cover and refrigerate for at least an hour to allow the flavors to meld. Serve chilled or at room temperature, which I prefer. The salad can be made up to 2 days ahead and refrigerated, no longer.

~❋⟩ Witches and Warts ⟨❋~

My grandmother always said that if you put your hand into egg water it would give you warts. If you need a cure for warts, come and see me. I have a special trick that I learned from a witch woman in Alicante. It takes two weeks and the first step is that I pass the magic on to you. You put your spit on the wart every morning before you brush your teeth and every night after you brush your teeth. Works every time, but I have to give you the magic first. And that's not cheap.

Potato and Leek Soup

Potato and leek soup served warm with plenty of Brown Bread (page 192) is one of the great staples of Irish pub grub. It is always on Meshelle's must-have list when in Ireland. When we first put it on the menu at Society Fair, I tried to change the traditional method of making it by bumping up the cream, which wound up being totally unnecessary: another case of the old-fashioned way being the best way. However, if you want the dish to be vegetarian, it's fine to substitute vegetable broth for the chicken stock.

{ MAKES 6 CUPS, SERVING 6 TO 8 }

1/4 cup unsalted butter, at room temperature

4 large leeks, white and light green parts only, sliced lengthwise and coarsely chopped, well washed (see How to Clean Leeks, below)

2 russet potatoes, peeled and cut into 1-inch pieces

4 cups chicken stock (page 239)

1 cup heavy cream

Kosher salt

Freshly ground black pepper

Brown Bread (page 192), sliced

Sweat the vegetables: Melt the butter in a heavy casserole over medium heat. Stir in the leeks and potatoes and let them sweat until tender, about 15 minutes.

Cook the soup: Add the stock and cream and bring to a boil over high heat. Lower the heat to medium and simmer the soup for 30 minutes, until the potatoes are completely soft.

Purée the soup: Working in batches, purée the soup in a blender until completely smooth and then pass through a fine-mesh strainer or china cap into a clean pan. Season to taste with salt. Keep the soup warm over very low heat until ready to serve. Ladle into individual bowls and garnish each serving with ground black pepper; serve with brown bread.

To reheat: The soup can be made up to 2 days before serving or frozen for up to 3 months. Reheat the soup in a saucepan over medium heat until hot and then reblend it before serving. The fat in cream soups congeals when chilled and needs to be re-emulsified.

HOW TO CLEAN LEEKS

Leeks are filled with sand. To clean them, you want to chop them coarsely (or however indicated in your recipe) and put them in a very large bowl of cold water. They will float to the top. With your hands, massage the pieces to separate them and allow the sand to sink to the bottom of the bowl. With your hands, scoop the leeks off the surface and into a colander.

Smoked Haddock and Shellfish Soup

Pretty much every fishmonger in Ireland sells smoked haddock, its distinctive dark yellow, smoky-hued flesh on full display in their cases. Plenty of places around the countryside offer smoked haddock soup, but what you usually find is overly smoky and thin, often made with milk and water. I've taken care of that problem with cream and well-made fish stock, and added some shellfish to boot.

You can use any (not endangered, of course) white fish for this soup, such as hake or pollock. You're going to smoke the fish quite easily yourself, so no need to go to a deli for it. (But since you're smoking it on a stove top, you do need a well-ventilated kitchen.) The soup is best made to order—by this I mean, prepare it when you wish to enjoy it, not ahead of time. You will need 2 cups of wood chips, such as hickory, applewood, or mesquite; a flameproof covered casserole; and a wire rack that fits inside it.

} SERVES 4 {

1 pound haddock fillet, pinbones removed

¼ cup unsalted butter, at room temperature

2 leeks, white parts only, sliced lengthwise, diced, and well washed (see How to Clean Leeks, page 32)

1 fennel bulb, diced

1 russet potato, peeled and diced

8 littleneck clams, rinsed clean

8 mussels, debearded (see Mussel Prep, page 93)

2 cups fish stock (page 241)

1 cup heavy cream

¼ cup chopped fresh dill leaves

1 tablespoon chopped fresh thyme leaves

Kosher salt and freshly ground black pepper

Brown Bread (page 192) and butter, for serving

Smoke the fish: Soak the wood chips in cold water for 30 minutes and drain them.

Place the haddock on a wire rack. Spread the wood chips in the bottom of a wide, lidded casserole. Cover the pot and place it over high heat. When you see wisps of smoke escaping from the pot, lift the lid just enough to slide the rack of fish on top of the chips. Close the lid and let the fish smoke for about 4 minutes, until the flesh is white in appearance. Remove the pot from the heat and let the fish sit uncovered until the smoke completely dissipates, about 10 minutes.

Make the soup: Melt the butter in a casserole over medium-high heat. Add the leeks, fennel, and potatoes and let them sweat, stirring occasionally, for 10 minutes, until the leeks are soft but not at all brown. Add the clams and stir until they start to open, about 3 or 4 minutes. Add the mussels, fish stock, and cream and bring the soup to a simmer. Lower the heat to medium and cook until the potatoes are tender and the mussels have opened, about 4 minutes. Flake the haddock into large pieces (use a fork or your fingers) and stir it in the pot with the dill and thyme and cook until just heated through, about 2 minutes. Season to taste with salt and black pepper. Serve immediately, passing brown bread and butter at the table.

~*{ On Pub Food }*~

The pub culture is actually quite well established in Ireland. It started with this notion called the seanchaí (pronounced shan-a-CHEE). The seanchaí was a traveler who would come back from Europe, or wherever he had been traveling, and tell stories. All the villagers would come and sit around the fireplace and find out from the seanchaí what was happening in the world. He was their news source.

That concept gradually developed into what we have today as the Irish pub. When we were kids—young adults—going into pubs, it was very much a social environment. There wasn't any loud music, no bands playing, no one playing the uilleann (pronounced ILL-in) pipes or the electric guitar. You just sat around a table and chatted all night long, telling stories and laughing. And everyone was there. One of the things that charmed Meshelle when she first came to Ireland was that young and old people socialize together so freely and genuinely enjoy each other's company. That natural sense of culture we Irish people have is just so amazing.

There were some pubs that provided food in those years, but not that many. That kind of business has grown over time, especially when smoking in pubs became illegal and owners had to come up with ways to bring the customers they lost back in.

More and more pubs serve food in Ireland now, and the food they do serve is really incredible, like a beautiful natural vegetable soup or a potato and leek soup. And the sandwiches they do—roast beef and roast lamb—are outstanding. It's good, wholesome, inexpensive food made with heart. The Irish pubs you tend to see in America, they're all kind of diddly-idle-doo to me. Irish nachos? That's not my idea of real Irish food. Putting cheddar cheese on a beef patty, calling it a Murphy burger, and claiming that's Irish is like pretending that leprechauns exist.

Oysters with Coriander Mignonette

The coastal waters of Ireland are well populated with oysters, and on occasion my Da would enjoy a dozen or two. There's a huge oyster festival in Galway every year with all sorts of eating and shucking competitions. The most common way to serve them there is with a couple of drops of Tabasco sauce and some lemon juice and a couple of pints of Guinness.

My family used to go to this dive bar in Donegal called Iggy's. At the height of the tourist season, Iggy's served particularly good pub grub and was a great place to get oysters. There, my parents would meet the actor Stephen Rea, a family friend who has a house in Donegal near theirs, and while away the day eating oysters and laughing. My preferred way to serve them is with this coriander dipping sauce.

Note: To crack ice, wrap ice cubes in a clean kitchen towel and beat them against the counter until they break into large pieces.

{ SERVES 6 }

1 teaspoon coriander seeds

1 teaspoon black peppercorns

½ cup apple cider vinegar

½ large shallot, minced

Crushed or cracked ice (see recipe note)

Kosher salt

72 meaty, briny Atlantic Coast oysters, such as Narragansett Bay or Olde Salt

Tabasco sauce, for serving

Lemon wedges, for serving

Make the mignonette: Toast the coriander seeds in a small skillet over medium heat for 3 minutes, stirring occasionally. Transfer them to a spice grinder. Add the peppercorns and grind into medium-coarse grind. Check the mixture to discard any whole seeds or large pieces of spice, which would be unpleasant to the palate. Pour the vinegar into a bowl, then stir in the shallot and spice mix. Cover and refrigerate to allow the flavors to meld, at least an hour.

Present the oysters: Fill 6 deep-welled soup or pasta bowls with crushed or cracked ice and sprinkle a generous amount of kosher salt over each. Shuck the oysters (see How to Shuck Oysters, page 38), and nestle a dozen on each bed of ice. Spoon the mignonette into 6 small ramekins. Serve the oysters with the mignonette, passing Tabasco sauce and lemon wedges at the table.

You will need a tray of cracked or crushed ice, several kitchen towels, and an oyster knife, which is specially designed for opening oysters. A proper oyster knife is like a jailhouse shank. It has a short, sharp-pointed, sturdy blade that is sharp on one edge and blunt on the other.

A well-shucked oyster should look like an oyster, not a beat-up mess. Keep in mind that the oyster's meat is attached to both shells. Your goal when opening the bivalve at the hinge is to work the tip of the oyster knife in, open the oyster, dislodge the meat from the top shell without hacking it up, remove the top shell without losing any of the liquid (liquor) in the bottom shell (cup), and dislodge the oyster from the bottom shell.

First, use a nail or dish brush to scrub the oysters clean under cold running water. To keep an oyster from slipping as you shuck it, place it horizontally (flat side up; cup side down) in the center of a kitchen towel folded into a 12 by 4-inch rectangle. Grasp one end of the towel between your thumb and

index finger and bring it up halfway over the oyster, leaving the hinge side exposed. Use your knuckles to bear down on the oyster enough to give you leverage while with the other hand you work the tip of an oyster knife into the hinge. Lean into the knife just enough to penetrate the hinge, and then gently twist the knife tip from side to side to loosen the shell all the way around.

Now you have to dislodge the oyster from both shells. First, starting at the hinge end, slide the sharp edge of the knife's blade down the wall of the upper shell and slice the flesh free from the muscle attaching it to the shell. Be careful to keep the bottom shell level so as not to lose any of the liquor in the cup. Check for sand and debris around the lip of the oyster and clean it away with a small piece of cheesecloth or paper towel. Using the sharp edge of the oyster knife, sweep under the oyster to dislodge it from the muscle attaching it to the bottom shell. As you work, place each opened, cleaned oyster on the ice.

~⸗{ Tabasco Sauce and Ireland }⸗~

Tabasco sauce is an American condiment, but its creator, John McIlhenny, was Irish. My parents own a house near Annagry in the wild northwest county of Donegal, where he was from. Nearby is the majestic Glenveagh National Park, which was the lavish home of Henry McIlhenny, John's grandson and heir to his fortune. He gifted the entire estate to the Irish people when he died in 1986. He had no children and over the years entertained such notables as Greta Garbo, Clark Gable, Charlie Chaplin, and Marilyn Monroe. I've toured the castle and its beautiful gardens many times, but the one thing that sticks in my mind is that McIlhenny kept twenty-two full sets of china on hand so that his guests would not see the same pattern twice.

Crab and Artichoke Salad with Harissa Mayonnaise

The coastal waters of Ireland are filled with crabs, and we would go fishing for them when we were kids. When my French exchange student friend was staying with us one year, he and I went crabbing off of Dun Laoghaire pier near where you grab the ferry to go to England. He had a fancy reel and all I had was a bit of string with a bone attached to it. At some point, his reel fell into the water, so I climbed down the wall of the pier to try and retrieve it. To keep from plummeting into the sea, I held onto a branch that promptly broke, and I fell into the murky water. This was soon after Jaws had come out in the movie theaters, and I just about ran on the surface of that water to get out of it before a shark could get to me. I was soaking wet for our whole bus ride home, where we returned with neither reel nor crabs.

Crabmeat has a very limited shelf life, only a few days from when it's packaged, so you need to take extra care to keep it cold at all times. This cleaning method seems like a lot of fuss, but it will ensure that your crabmeat will stay fresh as long as possible. True Blue refers to Maryland crabmeat that has been verified as coming from blue crabs. This is the best crabmeat there is in my opinion—sweet, delicate, and rich.

{ SERVES 4 }

1 lemon, halved

4 large artichokes

1/2 cup plus 2 teaspoons extra-virgin olive oil

1 small yellow onion, coarsely chopped

6 cloves garlic, lightly crushed

3 cups chicken stock (page 239)

4 fresh bay leaves

1 tablespoon kosher salt

1 pound True Blue Maryland jumbo lump crabmeat (see Resources, page 263)

1/3 cup chopped fresh chives

1/3 cup Harissa Mayonnaise (page 250)

16 large Bibb lettuce leaves

1 teaspoon freshly squeezed lemon juice

Prep the artichokes one at a time: Fill a medium bowl with cool water and squeeze the juice of half a lemon into it. Reserve the squeezed fruit. Cut off and discard the artichoke's stem, then, using a bread knife, slice all the way through the globe about 1 inch above the bottom and discard the entire top portion. Dip the bottom into the lemon water to keep it from discoloring. Using a sharp paring knife, cut around the base of the artichoke to remove any remaining leaves and tough outer skin until you only see the white flesh of the bottom. Using the tip of the paring knife, cut the cone of fuzzy choke from the center and discard it.

Repeatedly plunge the bottom in the lemon water throughout the process.

Poach the artichokes: In a saucepan over medium heat, heat the 1/2 cup of oil, onion, and garlic until the oil simmers gently. Cook for 10 minutes, or until the onion is tender. Add the chicken stock, bay leaves, and reserved squeezed lemon and bring the liquid back to a simmer. Stir in the salt. Submerge the artichoke bottoms in the liquid and cook for 30 minutes, until a cake tester inserts into them easily. Remove the pan from the heat and let the artichokes cool completely in the cooking liquid.

Set up the cleaning station: Have ready 4 medium mixing bowls. To keep the crabmeat cold as you work on it, fill 2 of the bowls with ice cubes and place an empty bowl over each one. Dump all the crabmeat into one of the empty bowls. Clean crabmeat will go in the other bowl as you work—this setup will keep all of the crabmeat cold at all times. Fill the plastic container the crabmeat came in with ice water.

Clean the crabmeat: Thoroughly wash your hands. Take up a small amount of crab with your finger-tips and feel for bits of cartilage and shell. If you come across any, dip it into the ice water and it will fall right off your fingers. Transfer the clean crabmeat to the bowl reserved for it as you work. Take care to keep the lumps intact as much as possible. Cover and store the cleaned crabmeat in the coldest part of your refrigerator if not using immediately.

Assemble and serve the salad: Set a large mixing bowl over a bowl of ice. Place the cleaned crabmeat in it. Cut each artichoke bottom (no need to blot them dry) into 12 pie-shaped pieces and add them to the crabmeat. Discard the poaching liquid. Add the chives, harissa mayonnaise, and the juice of the remaining lemon half to the bowl; fold the ingredients together lightly with a rubber spatula. In a medium bowl, coat the lettuce leaves with the 1 teaspoon of lemon juice and the remaining 2 tea-spoons of olive oil and line each of 4 soup plates with 4 of the dressed leaves. Mound crab salad onto the center of each plate, dividing equally. You can make the crab mixture a day ahead, but be sure to keep and serve it icy cold.

Gravlax with Dill Sauce and Brown Bread

The first restaurant I worked at was in Dublin. It was called Da Vincenzo and the chef there was named Terry Barman—a weird name for a chef. Terry was only nineteen but very talented, as well as a great guy and a really nice fellow. We became good friends.

Terry had worked in a Norwegian restaurant and would tell me stories about how they'd have gravlax and caviar for breakfast every day. One day he showed me how to make it. It was such a simple dish but so luxurious at the same time. There are iterations of gravlax all over the place, but I think this is the best way to prepare it. It is actually similar to the smoked salmon that Ireland is famous for. You need to start with very fresh salmon, like the North Atlantic salmon we use. I have nothing against West Coast salmon; it is quite delicious, but not fatty enough for gravlax. Do not use farm-raised salmon if possible—it has no flavor whatsoever.

{ SERVES 12 }

1 (4-pound) side of North Atlantic salmon, skin on, pinbones removed

1 cup sugar

2 cups fine sea salt

1 teaspoon good-quality Cognac

1 teaspoon yellow mustard seed

1 large bunch (about 4 ounces) fresh dill, with 12 nice sprigs reserved for garnish

Brown Bread (page 192)

1 cup Dill Sauce (page 247)

12 lemon wedges, for garnish

1/2 cup minced red onion, for garnish

Caviar, for garnish (optional)

Set up the pan: Line a large, rimmed baking sheet with lengths of plastic wrap that extend over the ends and sides by 12 inches (it's helpful to have extra-wide plastic wrap).

Prep the fish: Place the salmon on the baking sheet skin-side down, trimming the small end if necessary to make it fit flush in the pan. Combine the sugar and salt in a bowl and then spoon the mixture over the salmon, covering it completely, like an igloo. Lightly sprinkle the Cognac and mustard seed over the salt mixture. Set aside the sprigs of dill for garnish; break the remainder into 3-inch pieces and spread them evenly over the covered fish.

Cure the fish: Fold the ends of the plastic wrap up over the salt-covered fillet, then fold up the sides. Now wrap the pan with several layers of plastic wrap to ensure that the fillet is completely sealed.

Place a baking pan on top and weight it down with a brick or similar weight. Refrigerate for 24 hours.

Rinse and slice: Remove the plastic wrap from the pan and salmon. Lift the fillet from the pan and rinse it in cool water to remove all the salt and herbs. Pat the fillet dry on paper towels and transfer to a cutting board. To slice it, hold a thin-bladed slicing knife parallel to the board and cut razor-thin slices, working your way down from the top of the fillet. The top slice will be very salty; you may want to discard it.

Assemble and serve: For each serving, overlap several slices on a plate; add slices of brown bread and garnish the gravlax with the dill sauce, lemon wedges, minced red onion, reserved dill sprigs, and, if you like, caviar. Tightly wrapped in plastic, gravlax can be made several days ahead of time and even freezes well for up to 3 months.

Sardines Braised in Spicy Tomato Sauce

The sardines my father ate at home came in a can with a spicy tomato sauce. This is the homemade version of that, using fresh sardines. Like mackerel or bluefish, sardines are an oily fish and are only good if they're very fresh, so I don't recommend making this dish ahead of time.

When buying fresh sardines, you can ask your fishmonger to scale and gut them, or you can do it yourself. Rinse the fish under cold running water. Use your thumbnail to push the scales off, working from the tail to the head; they come off easily. Pat them dry on paper towels. Using the tip of a paring knife, slice open the belly from the tail to the gills. Remove and discard the entrails. Rinse again under cold running water and dry on paper towels.

❊{ SERVES 4 }❊

½ cup extra-virgin olive oil, plus more for drizzling

1 large yellow onion, medium diced

10 cloves garlic, thinly sliced

2 vine-ripened tomatoes, stems and cores removed, coarsely chopped

6 fresh bay leaves

1 teaspoon kosher salt

1 teaspoon red pepper flakes

8 fresh whole sardines (about 1 pound), scaled and gutted (see above)

½ lemon

Crusty bread, for serving

Make the tomato sauce: In a large slope-sided sauté pan over medium-high heat, heat 6 tablespoons of the oil until it shimmers. Stir in the onion and let sweat until it begins to turn translucent, about 3 minutes. Stir in the garlic and cook for 1 to 2 minutes, being careful not to let the garlic brown. Stir in the tomatoes, bay leaves, salt, and red pepper flakes. Lower the heat to medium and simmer the mixture for 10 minutes, until the sauce is thick; keep warm over very low heat.

Prepare the sardines: In another large slope-sided sauté pan over high heat, heat the remaining 2 tablespoons of oil until it shimmers. Lay the sardines in the pan and sauté them for about a minute on each side to lightly brown them. Transfer them to the pan with the tomato sauce and turn the heat under it to medium-high. Simmer the sardines in the sauce for 2 minutes, turning them over once. Drizzle the fish with oil and squeeze the half lemon through a sieve over them; serve immediately, with plenty of crusty bread. The bones of the sardines are edible, but if you prefer, you can use your knife and fork to work the top fillet off and lift out and discard the center spine, exposing the bottom fillet.

Kidneys in Red Wine Sauce

At home, Mam would just stir butter into the pan to thicken the sauce before serving this dish. My alternative, a rich, syrupy reduction of beef or veal stock known as demi-glace, is certainly a luxury item and therefore generally not something you'd find in Irish households, but it sure does take this dish to a much higher level. Kidneys have a very high water content, so to keep them from spattering too much or having them braise instead of sear, you want to make sure that they're dry before you put them into the pan, and that the pan is very hot.

{ SERVES 4 AS A FIRST COURSE }

4 lamb kidneys (4 pieces), cleaned, trimmed, and quartered (see About Kidneys, page 70)

Kosher salt and freshly ground black pepper

1 tablespoon canola oil

1 large shallot, minced

1/2 cup dry red wine

1 cup veal demi-glace (page 244)

1/4 cup cold unsalted butter, cut into pieces

2 teaspoons chopped fresh thyme leaves

Crusty bread, for serving

Cook the kidneys: Dry the kidneys on all sides with paper towels. Lightly season them with salt and pepper. In a large slope-sided sauté pan over medium-high heat, heat the canola oil until it shimmers. Place the kidneys in the pan, being sure not to crowd them. Let them sear for about a minute on each side. Stir in the shallot and cook for another minute.

Make the sauce: Add the wine to the pan and use a straight-edged wooden spatula to scrape up the brown bits from the bottom. Cook without stirring until the alcohol evaporates, about 3 minutes (the wine volume will reduce slightly). Stir in the demi-glace. Turn the heat to high and let the kidneys cook, stirring occasionally, for 3 minutes, until they are tender and the thickened sauce coats the back of a spoon. Stir in the butter and thyme until the butter melts. (See Making Sauces for Meat, page 142.) Add more salt and pepper if you wish. Serve immediately with plenty of crusty bread.

Black Pudding and Onions

In 2005, my parents bought a house in the Gaeltacht (an area where the Irish language is still spoken as a first language) in Donegal. My Da decided to plant trees and build a high tunnel to grow vegetables. A high tunnel is like a greenhouse and keeps the ground warm longer into the cold weather, thus extending the growing season.

The natives thought he was nuts because all that was there was bog land. I'm sure they still gossip about him every day. My brothers Gerald and Edward and my brother-in-law John Murphy were recruited to plant the trees because I was in America, but I got a chance to dig in the tunnel when I was there visiting. One of the rewards for a hard day's work was black pudding and onions. Hearty and earthy, it really hit the spot on a cold Donegal day.

{ SERVES 4 }

1 tablespoon canola oil

16 (1-inch) diagonal slices Black Pudding (page 22), casings removed

1 small yellow onion, chopped

1 cup veal demi-glace (page 244)

2 tablespoons cold unsalted butter

1 tablespoon chopped fresh thyme leaves

Kosher salt and freshly ground black pepper

Crusty bread, for serving

Sauté the black pudding: Place a slope-sided sauté pan over high heat; add the oil and heat until it shimmers. Arrange the pudding slices in the pan and cook for 30 seconds on each side, until nicely seared. Transfer the slices to a plate.

Sauté the onion: Stir the onion into the pan and lower the heat to medium. Let the onion sweat for 2 minutes, until translucent but not browned. Add the demi-glace. Raise the heat to medium-high and bring the liquid to a boil. Whisk in the butter all at once until melted.

Assemble and serve: Return the pudding slices to the pan and cook for 2 minutes, until the sauce is slightly reduced and thickened. Stir in the thyme. Season with salt and pepper to taste. Serve with plenty of crusty bread.

Spanish Omelet with Alioli

This dish, served here with a garlic sauce on the side, is so prevalent in Spain that I refer to it as their pizza. It's not an Irish dish, of course, but by virtue of my family's frequent travels to the Continent it became a part of Da's repertoire and so I'm including it in this book.

When I was six years old, we went to Spain on vacation and my parents let me stay on an extra week with a family they knew after they went home. The husband was in construction and was building a discotheque, so I sat there and drank espresso all day while he worked. There was always one of these omelets in the refrigerator when we got home. That was my first introduction to the Spanish omelet—and coffee. I was probably pretty buzzed on the plane back to Ireland.

The Spanish eat this omelet cold, hot, at room temperature, whatever, so make it up to 2 days ahead of time and keep it on hand.

{ SERVES 8 TO 10 }

2 cups extra-virgin olive oil
1 pound (3 medium) russet potatoes, peeled and cut into 1-inch cubes
14 large eggs, beaten
1 teaspoon kosher salt
1¹/₂ cups Alioli (page 251)

Cook the potatoes: Preheat the oven to 350°F. Place the oil and potatoes in a large, ovenproof nonstick slope-sided sauté pan over medium-high heat. Bring to a simmer and cook, stirring occasionally, for 10 minutes, until the potatoes are soft but not completely cooked through. Turn off the burner. Strain the hot oil into a bowl. Return the potatoes to the pan off the heat. (Let the oil cool and reserve it for another use.)

Cook the omelet: Using a rubber spatula, stir the eggs and salt into the pan with the potatoes. Then turn the heat to medium and cook the eggs, stirring constantly, bringing up the curds from the bottom of the pan and allowing them to cook evenly. Their water will evaporate as protein coagulates and a cohesive mass forms. As that happens, stop stirring, except to run the spatula along the sides of the pan to create a uniform border. Lower the heat and continue to cook the omelet for 5 minutes, until the sides and bottom are set but the top is still wet.

Bake the omelet: Transfer the pan to the oven and bake for 10 minutes, until the omelet is lightly browned on top. Immediately invert it onto a serving platter. Serve it cut into wedges, with alioli on the side.

CHAPTER THREE

What Mam Cooked

My mother, Angela, was one of three sisters born to Paddy and Jane Hughes. They grew up on the north side of Dublin in an area called Whitehall. Paddy, my Granda, died of cancer when I was fairly young, so I used to go over and take care of Granny's garden quite often.

Granny was a wonderful cook. I still remember the taste of her Yorkshire pudding. I must have eaten too much of it, though, because at the end of my stays there she liked to say, "I'd rather keep you for a week than a fortnight."

When my father met my mother at Rathmines College he chased her from the start and would not give up until she agreed to marry him, which she did in 1966. At least that's her version of the story.

They bought a house for IR£6000 (about $14,000) on Thomastown Road in the south side of Dublin and started what turned out to be a big family: five kids of their own and two adopted. Katharine was born first. In 1968, five-year-old Derek was adopted from the nuns at Saint Patrick's Orphanage on the Navan Road, making him the eldest. I was born in 1969, and then my other sister, Clare, two years later. Niall was born a year after Clare and was hit by a car and killed when he was two and I was six. Soon after that, we adopted Gerald, and then very unexpectedly Mam got pregnant with Edward, who was born in 1979.

So you could say my mother had her hands full. She quit her job as a sales agent at KLM to take care of us, and she did most of the cooking during the week while my father built his business as a tour operator.

When I was five, my parents wisely opted for a bigger house, so we left the one with no central heating and moved to a five-bedroom house (with heat!) not far away, on Watson Road.

The kitchen was the activity center of this house. It was a large room, half of it the dining area where we ate most of our meals. It faced into our backyard, with big, bright windows that filled the room with light. Well, what light was available in Dublin. "It gets late very early, doesn't it?" my Da liked to say. We had these dark orange Formica cabinets (it was the seventies after all) and a big wooden table for the family with a banquette along the wall. We all had our assigned seats that never really changed in the thirty years we lived there.

Mam would make snacks for us when we got home from school and then the evening's dinner. When we were sick, she brought us comics to read in bed, called Dr. O'Leary (who did house calls in those days), and made Chicken Noodle Soup (page 53) to nourish our bodies. Mam's cooking is what we now call comfort food, nostalgic offerings such as Irish Stew (page 60), Shepherd's Pie (page 65), Quiche Lorraine (page 57), and her most heralded specialty—apple pie. (That recipe is on page 209.)

What follows are some of Mam's most memorable dishes, from treats awaiting us after school to rib-stickers that got us through cold, wintry Irish nights.

Traditional
Home
Cooked
Fayre
Served
All ~ Day

Chicken Noodle Soup

Chicken noodle soup has great restorative qualities. All of the ingredients in the recipe are known to have medicinal value. Any time we were really sick, my mother or father would make a batch of this soup, which they also served as dinner on cold winter nights even when we were well. My parents always referred to it as Jewish penicillin. When you have those flulike symptoms, not much can make you feel better than chicken noodle soup.

I think the real secret of this soup is that the broth is triple concentrated. You use chicken stock as the base liquid and then intensify it by poaching a whole chicken in it. Then the resulting broth gets reduced, making a more potent soup.

⁕} MAKES 3 QUARTS, SERVING 10 TO 12 {⁕

BROTH

1 (3-pound) whole chicken

1 large yellow onion, coarsely chopped

2 carrots, peeled and cut into 2-inch pieces

3 celery stalks, cut into 2-inch pieces

10 cloves garlic

1 teaspoon black peppercorns

1 large fresh bay leaf

1 large sprig fresh rosemary

1/2 large bunch (1 ounce) fresh thyme sprigs

12 cups chicken stock (page 239)

SOUP

1 tablespoon unsalted butter

1 large leek, well washed and diced (see How to Clean Leeks, page 32)

2 carrots, peeled and diced

1 yellow onion, diced

5 cloves garlic, minced

2 ounces dried spaghetti, broken into 1 1/2-inch pieces

2 tablespoons fresh thyme leaves

Crusty bread, for serving

Make the broth: Place the chicken in an 8-quart stockpot and cover it with the remaining broth ingredients. Bring to a simmer over high heat. Lower the heat to medium and cook for 45 minutes, using a large ladle to skim and discard any foam and fat that rise to the top. Set a colander in a large bowl and transfer the poached chicken to it. Strain the stock through a fine-mesh sieve into a separate container. Clean the pot and return it to the stove.

Make the soup: Over medium heat, melt the butter until it bubbles. Add the leek, carrots, and onion and sweat for 5 minutes, until they are starting to get tender. Stir in the garlic and cook for 1 minute. Add the chicken broth. Raise the heat to high and bring the broth to a boil. Boil until the broth is reduced by a third, about 30 minutes.

Dice the chicken: Meanwhile, when the chicken is cool enough to handle, remove the skin and debone the meat. Remove and discard all cartilage, fat, veins, and tendons from the meat and then dice it. Strain any liquid in the bowl under the colander into the pot of boiling broth. Set the chicken aside.

Finish the soup: Once the broth is reduced, add the spaghetti to it and continue to cook for another 15 minutes so that the starch releases from the pasta to thicken the soup slightly. Add the chicken and thyme and heat through. Adjust the seasoning. Serve in individual bowls with crusty bread on the side. The soup can be refrigerated for up to 3 days and frozen for up to 3 weeks.

Cheese on Toast

I'm including this ridiculously easy recipe because it's something we'd have after school all the time. My mother didn't put tomatoes or chili powder on it. I learned to do it this way at my first real restaurant job, as a dishwasher at a place called Da Vincenzo. Howard, one of the owners there, added the upgrades, which I made permanent.

{ SERVES 4 }

4 slices Pullman Loaf (page 196) or sandwich bread

4 ounces Irish cheddar cheese, thinly sliced

2 Roma tomatoes, cut crosswise into 1/2-inch slices

Salt

4 pinches chili powder

In a preheated toaster oven or broiler, toast the bread on one side until lightly browned. Arrange the bread toasted-side down on a baking sheet. Divide the cheese equally over the bread, covering each slice completely, and then add 2 slices of tomato to each. Season the tomatoes with salt and sprinkle a pinch of chili powder over them. Broil the toast until the cheese is bubbly and the tomatoes are just barely softened.

Potato Pancakes

Whenever we'd have mashed potatoes left over from dinner, Mam would make potato pancakes for an after-school snack the next day. We would have eaten them every day if we were let.

It is a good idea to have a food mill or potato ricer on hand. (See On Making Mashed Potatoes, page 179.)

} SERVES 4 {

2 russet potatoes, peeled and quartered

1½ teaspoons kosher salt

1 large egg, lightly beaten

¼ cup all-purpose flour, plus more for dusting

2 tablespoons canola oil

Sour cream, for serving

Cook and mash the potatoes: Place the quartered potatoes and 1 teaspoon of the salt in a pot and cover them with cold water. Bring the water to a boil, then lower the heat to medium and allow the potatoes to simmer uncovered until cooked through, about 40 minutes. To tell if they are cooked, take a piece out and cut it in half to see if it's soft in the center.

Mix the potato pancakes: Rice the potatoes into a large bowl. Stir in the egg, flour, and remaining ½ teaspoon of salt. Do not overmix. Lightly dust a cutting board with flour and roll the potato mixture into a ¼-inch-thick, roughly 9-inch square, then cut it into 9 smaller squares.

Cook the pancakes: In a large nonstick slope-sided sauté pan over medium-high heat, heat the oil until it shimmers. Cook the pancakes for 2 to 3 minutes on each side until nicely browned. Serve hot with a dollop of sour cream on the side.

Quiche Lorraine

My mother was most famous for her apple pie (page 209), but this quiche was a close second. It's not an Irish dish, obviously, but I'd be remiss (and in trouble) if I didn't include this signature dish of hers.

In the late sixties, before my father got into the travel business, he worked for RTE (Radio Telefís Eireann), the Irish national radio and television channel. One of his colleagues there gave my mother this recipe on the condition that she not allow Da to mess with the recipe, because she knew that he liked to put his own stamp on things and she didn't think her quiche needed stamping.

The hallmark of a great quiche is a silky custard. The key to achieving that is to cook it at a low enough temperature to just set the eggs without letting them soufflé. Also, use the best farm-fresh eggs you can lay your hands on and heavy cream from a reputable dairy. This recipe doesn't call for salt because the bacon we use supplies all that is necessary. If yours doesn't, add 1/2 teaspoon to the cream.

A lightly dressed green salad makes a nice accompaniment for quiche lorraine. You will need a 9-inch deep-dish fluted pie pan.

1 tablespoon canola oil

12 ounces thick-cut streaky (American) bacon, cut into 1-inch pieces (see On Irish Bacon, page 15)

1/4 batch Mam's Quick Puff Pastry Dough (page 204) or 1 (14-ounce) package prepared all-butter puff pastry

8 large eggs, at room temperature, lightly beaten

4 cups heavy cream

Cook the bacon: In a large slope-sided sauté pan over medium-high heat, heat the oil until it shimmers. Cook the bacon, until it is partially rendered and lightly browned, about 10 minutes. Transfer the cooked bacon to a paper towel–lined plate. Discard the fat or save for another use.

Fit the pastry into the pan: On a well-floured surface, roll the dough into a 1/4-inch-thick, 15-inch-diameter circle. Loosely roll the dough onto a rolling pin, then unroll it into a 9-inch deep-dish pie pan or fluted, 2-inch-deep quiche pan with a removable bottom. Press the dough into the bottom and sides of the pan, making sure it comes all the way to the rim. Trim the dough, leaving a 1-inch overhang all around. (It will shrink a bit as it chills.) Cover the pastry with plastic wrap and refrigerate for 30 minutes.

Assemble the quiche: Preheat the oven to 300°F. Trim the pastry even with the sides of the pie pan. Spread the bacon evenly on the bottom of the pie shell. Whisk the eggs and cream together (this custard mixture is known as royale in French cooking) and pour the custard into the shell. To allow for pastry shrinkage, fill the shell no higher than 3/4 inch from the top.

Bake the quiche: Place the filled pan on a foil-lined baking sheet and then in the oven. Bake for 60 to 70 minutes, until the custard is just barely jiggling beneath the surface. Transfer to a wire rack and cool for at least 1 hour before serving. Quiche lorraine can be made the day before and refrigerated, but bring it to room temperature before serving.

Dublin Coddle

This is a classic Dublin peasant dish that Ma made for dinner occasionally and we all hated growing up. It wasn't anything more than breakfast sausage and bacon cooked with milk. So my version is more like a French blanquette, a rich and elegant cream-based stew, with potatoes added, of course. This recipe doesn't call for salt because the bacon we use supplies all that is necessary. If yours doesn't (fry up a little piece of it to see), add $1/2$ teaspoon of it.

{ SERVES 6 }

2 tablespoons unsalted butter

1 yellow onion, diced

8 ($1/4$-inch-thick) slices streaky (American) bacon, cut into 1-inch pieces (see On Irish Bacon, page 15)

1 large russet potato, peeled and cut into $1/2$-inch cubes

8 Breakfast Sausages (page 17), cut into 1-inch pieces

1 cup chicken stock (page 239)

2 cups heavy cream

3 large fresh bay leaves

$1/2$ cup coarsely chopped parsley

2 tablespoons chopped fresh thyme leaves

Crusty bread, for serving

Cracked black pepper, for garnish (optional)

Sweat the onion: In a medium flameproof casserole over medium heat, melt the butter. Add the onion to the pot and let it sweat for about 8 minutes, until soft but not browned at all. (Because this is a white stew, you don't want the onion to take on any color.)

Cook the coddle: Once the onion is translucent, add the bacon and continue to cook over low heat until the bacon is pale pink and a few tablespoons of the fat have rendered, about 10 minutes. Add the potatoes, sausage, stock, cream, and bay leaves.

Raise the heat to medium-high and bring the liquid to a boil. Lower the heat to medium and cook slowly until the potatoes are cooked through, about 30 minutes.

Add the herbs and serve: Remove the coddle from the heat, stir in the parsley and thyme, and serve immediately with lots of crusty bread. If you wish, sprinkle a little bit of cracked black pepper on top. The coddle can be made a day ahead and gently reheated on the stove or in a 300°F oven for 30 minutes.

Irish Stew with Piccalilli

This isn't a dish we would get often at home, which was too bad because we all loved it, especially with picca-lilli, a mustard pickle of cauliflower, onions, and other vegetables. A lot of places in the States serve what they call Irish stew, but it's made with beef. Real Irish stew is not made with beef. At all. Traditionally it is made with lamb neck or shinbones (known as gigot), but I use shoulder chops because they are meatier and you can get a good sear on them, which adds flavor. Irish stew would not really include carrots, by the way, but I add them for sweetness.

{ SERVES 4 }

Kosher salt and freshly ground black pepper

4 (8-ounce) lamb shoulder chops

2 tablespoons canola oil

2 yellow onions, quartered lengthwise

2 carrots, peeled and cut crosswise into 2-inch pieces

3 cloves garlic, thinly sliced

1 large fresh bay leaf

2 russet potatoes, peeled and quartered

3 cups water

3 tablespoons chopped fresh thyme

Piccalilli (page 259)

Brown the chops: Sprinkle salt and pepper liberally over both sides of the lamb chops. In a flameproof casserole over medium-high heat, heat the oil until it shimmers. Brown both sides of the lamb chops well (2 to 3 minutes per side), working in 2 batches so the pot is not crowded. Transfer the browned lamb to a plate and set aside.

Cook the stew: Blot the oil from the pot with a wad of paper towels. Add the onions, carrots, garlic, and bay leaf. Top the vegetables with the chops and any collected juices on their plate. Add the potatoes and water. Bring the liquid to a boil. Lower the heat to medium, cover the pot, and let the chops simmer for 1 1/2 to 2 hours, until the meat is very tender. Adjust the salt and pepper seasoning to taste. Stir in the chopped thyme and serve immediately, with piccalilli on the side. The stew can be made the day before and gently reheated on the stove or in the oven at 300°F for 30 minutes. (See About Stews, page 73.)

President Obama Stew (Chicken Casserole)

There were definitely a few chicken casserole dishes in my mother's repertoire. I was making this variation of one of them on Saturday, October 9, 2011, on what turned out to be an unforgettable evening.

My brother Edward had come over from Ireland that weekend to surprise the kids, Meshelle, and me. So instead of working, I was home that night preparing dinner for all of us. I had just put this stew on the stove and opened a bottle of wine when I got a phone call from the restaurant. I kind of had an attitude about it, asking, "What are you calling me for?"

Then Todd, our business partner and manager, said, "You need to come to work right away—the President is coming." Well, if President and Mrs. Obama are celebrating their nineteenth wedding anniversary at your restaurant, your stew just has to wait.

My brother came with me to Restaurant Eve and ate at the bar while I cooked for the Obamas. And then he met the President and First Lady, even having a conversation with them about Ireland, when they were on their way out. You can bet that that story got a lot of play from my brother when he got back home.

After the First Couple left, Edward and I went back to my house. The late-night snack, of course, was the chicken stew I had left on the stove, now proudly renamed "President Obama Stew."

You can use the back and neck to make a quick stock for this dish by simmering them in water with a bay leaf, some thyme, and mirepoix (chopped onions, carrots, and celery), or freeze them for stock in the future. Serve the dish over steamed rice or Mashed Potatoes (page 181).

⁎⟩ SERVES 6 ⟨⁎

1 (3½-pound) chicken

Kosher salt and freshly ground black pepper

2 tablespoons canola oil

1 large yellow onion, very coarsely chopped

6 carrots, peeled and cut crosswise into ½-inch coins

6 celery stalks, halved lengthwise and cut into 1-inch dice

20 cloves garlic, crushed and coarsely chopped

1 (28-ounce) can whole plum tomatoes (preferably San Marzano), coarsely chopped, and their juices

3 tablespoons all-purpose flour

3 large fresh bay leaves

1 serrano chile, coarsely chopped, with seeds

4 cups chicken stock (page 239)

2 tablespoons chopped fresh thyme leaves

1 tablespoon chopped fresh rosemary leaves (see Notes on Herbs, page 64)

Leaves from 1 large bunch fresh basil (1 cup loosely packed), coarsely chopped

Cut up the chicken: Cut the chicken into 14 pieces, making 6 breast pieces, 2 drumsticks, 2 thighs, and 4 wing joints. Season them well with salt.

Brown the chicken: In a large slope-sided sauté pan over high heat, heat the canola oil until it shimmers. Arrange all of the chicken evenly in the pan skin-side down and cook for 5 minutes, until golden brown. The pieces should release easily from the bottom of the pan; if they don't, let them brown longer until they do. Transfer the pieces to a flameproof casserole, arranging them skin-side up.

Sweat the vegetables: Add the onion, carrots, and celery to the sauté pan, stirring to combine them. Sweat the vegetables for 4 to 5 minutes, until they

{continued}

{President Obama Stew, continued}

are translucent but still a bit firm. As they cook and water releases from them, use a flat-edged wooden spatula to deglaze the pan by scraping up the brown bits from the bottom. Stir in the garlic and then the tomatoes and flour and cook for 2 minutes. Add the bay leaves, serrano chile, chicken stock, thyme, and rosemary.

Cook the stew: Transfer the vegetable mixture to the casserole. Bring to a boil, then decrease the heat to low, cover the pot, and let it simmer slowly for 45 to 60 minutes, until the chicken and vegetables are very tender. Remove the stew from the heat. Taste the sauce and season with salt and pepper if you like. Stir in the basil leaves at the last second before serving. The stew can be made a day before and gently reheated on the stove or in a 300°F oven for 30 to 40 minutes. (See About Stews, page 73.)

NOTES ON HERBS

All herbs have delicate oils in them that provide the majority of their aroma, so it's super important to have a very sharp knife when you're cutting them and not to overwork them. Slice through herbs once and then move your knife over slightly and make another slice, rather than chopping them over and over, making all of their oils wind up on the board.

PINCH THYME OFF with your fingertips and make a small pile of leaves, then cut through them as indicated above.

ROSEMARY is one of the exceptions to the one chop rule. Rosemary has such an intense pine flavor that you don't want to bite into a mass of it. Chop it very finely so that the flavor is evenly distributed throughout the dish.

TO REMOVE THE BITTER RESIN on the surface of rosemary leaves, give them a quick blanch, shock them, and then mince them very, very fine. To blanch rosemary leaves, have ready a bowl of ice water. Bring 2 quarts of water and 1/2 cup of salt to a rolling boil. Place 1/2 cup of picked rosemary leaves in a strainer, dip the strainer basket into the boiling water for 15 seconds, and then plunge it into the ice water. Drain the leaves and squeeze them dry.

Shepherd's Pie

Da calls this dish Shagger's Pie. It was a much-wished-for dish in our house and, like Irish stew (page 60), always came with Piccalilli (page 259) served on the side. Shepherd's pie is an interpretation of a French dish called hachis parmentier. What makes it truly Irish is that there are potatoes in the stew as well as on top of it. Most versions you see are made with beef, and ground beef at that, but that doesn't really make any sense because why would shepherds have beef? Shepherds tend lambs. To impart a touch of elegance, I make the pie with a rich stew of diced lamb shoulder (leg meat works well, too), lamb stock, and aromatic vegetables. No peas, please. They get lost in the mix.

The dish does involve some preparation, but the lamb stock can be made well ahead and frozen for up to 6 months and the stew can be made 2 days in advance. (See About Stews, page 73.) Prepare and add the mashed potatoes just prior to baking. (See On Making Mashed Potatoes, page 179.) It is a good idea to have a food mill or potato ricer on hand.

⟨ SERVES 6 ⟩

STEW

1½ pounds lamb shoulder, trimmed of all fat and sinew, cut into ½-inch cubes

Kosher salt and freshly ground black pepper

2 tablespoons canola oil

1 yellow onion, chopped

4 carrots, peeled and chopped

4 celery stalks, chopped

2 tablespoons all-purpose flour

4 cups lamb stock (page 243) or store-bought beef broth

3 russet potatoes, peeled and cut into ½-inch cubes (2 cups)

2 large fresh bay leaves

2 tablespoons chopped fresh thyme leaves

1 tablespoon chopped fresh rosemary leaves (see Notes on Herbs, opposite)

1 tablespoon chopped fresh oregano leaves

MASHED POTATOES

4 russet potatoes, peeled and quartered

1 tablespoon salt

4 large egg yolks

½ cup unsalted butter

½ cup heavy cream

Piccalilli, for serving (optional, page 259)

Brown the lamb: Pat the lamb cubes dry on all sides with paper towels and season well with salt and pepper. In a large slope-sided sauté pan over medium-high heat, heat the oil until it shimmers. Distribute the meat evenly in the bottom of the pan without crowding it and don't disturb it for several minutes. If you stir the cubes too soon, they will release water and the meat will boil instead of browning. After 3 or 4 minutes, turn the cubes over and brown them on the other side for another 3 or 4 minutes. Using a slotted spoon, transfer the meat to a bowl and return the pan to the heat.

Sweat the vegetables: Add the onion, carrots, and celery, stirring with a flat-edged wooden spatula. As the vegetables cook, water will release and deglaze the pan. Use the spatula to scrape up brown bits from the bottom of the pan. Sweat the vegetables for 4 to 5 minutes. They should be translucent but still a bit firm.

Cook the stew: Stir in the flour and allow it to brown lightly for about 2 minutes. Add the lamb stock, continuing to scrape up any brown bits from the bottom of the pan. Stir in the potatoes,

{continued}

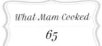

bay leaves, thyme, rosemary, and oregano. Return the meat and its collected juices to the pan. Bring the liquid to a boil. Lower the heat to medium and cover the pot. Simmer for 1¹/₂ hours, until the meat is fork tender. Discard the bay leaves and transfer the stew to an 8-cup baking dish.

Boil the potatoes for mashing: Place the quartered potatoes and salt in a pot and cover them with cold water. Bring the water to a boil, then lower the heat to medium and allow the potatoes to simmer uncovered until cooked through, about 40 minutes. To tell if they are cooked, take a piece out and cut it in half to see if it's soft in the center.

While the potatoes are cooking, preheat the oven to 450°F.

Mash the potatoes: Drain the potatoes, return them to the pot, and stir them over the heat for a couple of minutes. This ensures that they are dry. Rice the potatoes into a mixing bowl. Add the egg yolks, butter, and cream, whisking until the mixture is smooth. Work quickly while the potatoes are hot so they don't become gummy and starchy. Adjust the salt seasoning to taste and allow the potatoes to cool.

⌃ **Top the pie:** Fit a large pastry bag with a large star tip. Spoon the mashed potatoes into the bag. Moving in one direction, pipe large rosettes of potatoes over the lamb mixture, in neat rows or around the perimeter of baking dish. Go over your work and pipe rosettes wherever you see any holes—you want to create a good seal. Alternatively, you can dollop the potatoes over the stew and spread them with a spatula to seal it.

◁ **Bake the pie:** Line a baking sheet with aluminum foil. Set the pie on it and bake for 30 to 35 minutes, until the potatoes are nicely browned and the filling is bubbling. Let the casserole rest for 15 minutes; serve with piccalilli on the side if you'd like.

Steak and Kidney Pie

When my mother makes steak and kidney pie, she puts an upside-down cup in the dish of stew to support the pastry in the center, kind of like a circus tent. It keeps the pastry from sinking into the stew. Then she rolls the pastry scraps into a long snake with the palms of her hands, coils it up, and sticks it in the middle of the crust. It gets brown and crunchy on the outside and doughy on the inside during baking and so was the best part to us kids. We used to fight over who got the snake.

This recipe calls for stew meat, but rib eye also works quite well, as do veal kidneys instead of lamb kidneys. We never used veal kidneys or demi-glace at home, as these were not readily available items. Mam used wine in her stew, which she thickened with a little butter. I use demi-glace instead. It has a slightly syrupy, rich texture and imparts a touch of refinement.

The stew part of the dish can be made 2 days ahead of time. (See About Stews, page 73.) The pastry can be made 3 months in advance and frozen.

} SERVES 8 {

1½ pounds stew beef, such as shoulder or chuck, cut into 1-inch cubes

Kosher salt and freshly ground black pepper

2 tablespoons canola oil

½ pound lamb kidneys, cleaned, trimmed, and cut into 1-inch cubes (see About Kidneys, page 70)

1 yellow onion, cut into ½-inch dice

4 carrots, peeled and cut into ½-inch dice

4 celery stalks, cut into ½-inch dice

2 tablespoons all-purpose flour

½ cup dry red wine

3 cups veal demi-glace (page 244) or store-bought beef stock

2 large fresh bay leaves

1 tablespoon chopped fresh thyme leaves

¼ batch Mam's Quick Puff Pastry Dough (page 204) or 1 (14-ounce) package prepared all-butter puff pastry

1 large egg beaten with 1 tablespoon water, for egg wash (optional)

Brown the meats: Pat the beef cubes dry on all sides with paper towels and season well with salt and pepper. In a large slope-sided sauté pan over medium-high heat, heat the oil until it shimmers. Distribute the beef evenly in the bottom of the pan without crowding it and don't disturb it for several minutes. If you stir the pieces too soon, they will release water and the meat will boil instead of browning. After 3 or 4 minutes, turn the cubes over and brown them on the other side for another 3 or 4 minutes. Add the kidneys and cook for 2 or 3 minutes, until they are lightly browned on both sides. Using a slotted spoon, transfer the meats to a bowl and return the pan to the heat.

Sweat the vegetables: Add the onion, carrots, and celery to the pan, stirring them with a flat-edged wooden spatula. As the vegetables cook, water will release and deglaze the pan. Use the spatula to scrape up any brown bits from the bottom of the pan. Sweat the vegetables for 4 to 5 minutes, until translucent but still a bit firm.

Cook the stew: Stir in the flour and allow it to brown lightly for about 2 minutes. Stir in the red wine and let the alcohol evaporate, about 1 minute. Stir in the demi-glace. Return the meat and its collected juices to the pan. Add the bay leaves. Bring the liquid to a boil, then turn down the heat to low and let the stew simmer uncovered

{continued}

for 2 hours, until the meat is very tender. Remove the pan from the heat. Adjust the salt and pepper seasoning to taste and stir in the chopped thyme. Discard the bay leaves and let the stew cool to room temperature.

Fill the baking dish: Place an ovenproof ramekin or coffee mug upside down in the middle of a 2 1/2-quart (12-inch) round casserole or deep-dish pie pan. (The idea is to create a pedestal to drape the pastry over so it doesn't sink into the meat during baking.) Spoon the stew into the casserole and check to make sure the mug extends about an inch above the meat.

Top the pie with pastry: On a lightly floured surface, roll the pastry into a 1/4-inch-thick, 15-inch-diameter circle. Make a template by cutting a 13-inch-diameter circle from a piece of cardboard and place it in the center of the 15-inch pastry circle. Use a paring knife to cut around it. Lift away the perimeter ring of pastry and, using half of it, roll a 1/2-inch-thick strip of dough long enough to fit around the inside edge of the casserole. Place the strip directly onto the stew and press it into

the side of the pan lightly with your fingertips. Moisten it with water. Now roll the pastry circle lightly onto your rolling pin, then unroll it over the casserole and mug. Trim the edge even with the rim of the casserole. Crimp the edge of the crust with the tines of a fork.

Add the pastry "snake": Use the palms of your hands to roll the remaining dough scraps into a long cylinder about 1 inch in diameter. Roll the cylinder into a pinwheel roughly the size of the mug, or tie it into a loose knot, and place it on the center of the pastry where the mug is protruding. Use a paring knife to cut 1-inch vents into the top of the crust, spaced about 2 inches apart. Refrigerate the pie for 30 minutes so the pastry can rest; after 10 minutes, preheat the oven to 400°F.

Bake the pie: If you want your pastry to have a shiny, finished look, brush it with the egg wash. Bake the pie for 10 minutes, then lower the temperature to 350°F and bake for another 50 minutes, until the pastry is golden brown and you can see the stew bubbling around the edges. Allow the pie to rest for 10 minutes before serving.

ABOUT KIDNEYS

Ask your butcher if you can smell the kidneys before you buy them; if they are fresh they should have no odor at all. If they smell at all ammoniated, do not buy them; they will be bitter. To clean the kidneys, slice them in half lengthwise and use a paring knife to cut away and discard the thick white vein from the center.

Beef Stew

Beef stew is such a hearty, warm, soul-nourishing dish that you can't go wrong with it. That's why it is one of the greatest winter dishes in Ireland. The first time I brought Meshelle to Ireland, my Da made this stew, making it slightly spicy to give it some kick and a little edge. After that, Meshelle was hooked. Even Eve, who doesn't like red meat, loves beef stew. Keep in mind that the spiciness of chiles varies from pepper to pepper, so vary the amount you use to suit your taste. Serve over Mashed Potatoes (page 181).

{ SERVES 6 }

1½ pounds stew beef, such as shoulder or chuck, cut into 1-inch cubes

Kosher salt and freshly ground pepper

2 tablespoons canola oil

1 yellow onion, diced

4 carrots, peeled and diced

4 celery stalks, diced

8 cloves garlic, roughly chopped

2 tablespoons all-purpose flour

3 cups veal demi-glace (page 244) or store-bought beef broth

1 serrano chile, coarsely chopped, with seeds

3 large fresh bay leaves

2 tablespoons chopped fresh thyme leaves

1 tablespoon chopped fresh rosemary leaves (see Notes on Herbs, page 64)

Brown the beef: Pat the beef cubes dry on all sides with paper towels and season well with salt and pepper. In a large slope-sided sauté pan over medium-high heat, heat the oil until it shimmers. Distribute the beef evenly in the bottom of the pan without crowding it and don't disturb it for several minutes. If you stir the pieces too soon, they will release water and the meat will boil instead of browning. After 3 or 4 minutes, turn the cubes over and brown them on the other side for another 3 or 4 minutes. Using a slotted spoon, transfer the meat to a flameproof casserole and return the pan to the heat.

Sweat the vegetables: Add the onion, carrots, and celery, stirring them with a flat-edged wooden spatula. As the vegetables cook, water will release and deglaze the pan. Use the spatula to scrape up brown bits from the bottom of the pan. Sweat the vegetables for 4 to 5 minutes, until translucent but still a bit firm. Stir in the garlic and cook for 1 minute.

Cook the stew: Stir in the flour and allow it to brown lightly for about 2 minutes. Add the demi-glace, scraping up any brown bits from the bottom of the pan. Stir in the serrano chile, bay leaves, thyme, and rosemary. Transfer the vegetables to the casserole and bring it to a boil over medium-high heat. Lower the heat to medium, cover the pot, and braise the meat slowly for 2 hours, until it is very tender. Adjust the salt and pepper seasoning to taste. Serve hot. The stew can be made 2 days ahead and reheated gently on the stove or in the oven at 300°F for 30 to 40 minutes (see About Stews, opposite).

ABOUT STEWS

In general, when you apply heat to food, you're actually applying pressure. In stew making, that pressure makes the meat contract, forcing its flavor into its surrounding liquid. As the meat cools, it relaxes and absorbs that flavor from the surrounding liquid. So you actually achieve an optimal result by preparing stew a day ahead, cooling it completely in its liquid, and gently reheating it the next day. The fact that stews are best made well in advance makes them perfect dishes for parties or family events.

CHAPTER FOUR

Fridays Are for Fish

Food is such an important part of our family dynamic that my parents always have and still to this day shop for provisions in different places: the bakery for bread; the greengrocer for vegetables; one butcher in Foxrock for lamb and a different butcher, Greystones, for beef; the "Protestant" market for chicken; and always to the ladies on Dun Laoghaire pier for fish.

Because we are Catholics, we ate fish on Fridays when I was a child. In an inconspicuous concrete building at the end of the pier, Helen and Geraldine sell only the fish that their husbands catch every day: plaice, haddocks, lobsters, prawns, mussels . . . you name it. It's the best, freshest fish I have ever had anywhere in the world.

The waters around their building are populated with a growing number of enormously fat seals that are an attraction and are the most spoiled animals. Kids come with their mammies and buy fish bones from the ladies to feed them.

When we were kids, our parents usually fed us whiting, which is cheap, while they ate the good fish. Some of the recipes here are interpretations of dishes my parents would have eaten; others are dishes I created for my family using the types of fish the ladies of Dun Laoghaire sell.

~∗{ About Donegal }∗~

For my family, Donegal is a special place. We were drawn there in my childhood by its stark beauty, its feeling of isolation far from the rigors of city living, and its rich, Gaelic roots. Every year when Meshelle, Eve, Eamonn, and I go home to visit, we make a point of spending a few days there. It's about a five-hour drive from Dublin, and the last quarter of the trip is over twisting, winding country roads.

Donegal is in the far northwest corner of Ireland and the terrain is bleak. Ancient forests decayed in this area and created a bogland where nothing much grows. The sky is massive there, as if you're standing on top of the globe. Because of its northerly latitude, in summer it's daylight there until about 10 p.m. and the light in the sky is bizarre and eerie, a mix of various hues of purple, gold, pink, and orange.

Parts of the area have a distinct sense of loneliness. Droichead na nDeor, or the Bridge of Tears, is there. It was at this bridge that emigrants leaving Donegal for the United States or Australia in the 1880s would separate from their loved ones staying behind, never to be seen again.

My father's sister Marie and her husband Don lived in New York and sold everything they had in the States to buy a piece of land and a tiny, two-bedroom house in Donegal in 1973. They went there so Don could write what turned out to be two guides for Americans traveling in Ireland. From time to time over the six years they lived there, Mam, Da and brood would visit them as a family—eight of us, four of them, and, once, my grandparents, too. That's fourteen people in one little country cottage. It was definitely cozy.

Marie and Don moved back to New York, but kept the house. They would stay there in the summertime and my cousin David and I would spend time with them. (An aside here to the family: For the record, Kevin and David broke the window. Steven and I were innocent bystanders.)

Our family had such a love for Donegal that it was only natural my parents would buy a place near my aunt's house, which they did in 2005. Because the area is very rural, it was a challenge to find the kind of food and wine they were accustomed to, but my father made short work of sourcing his needs: Pat Boyle the butcher, Jack the fishmonger, the Green Man in Dunfanaghy, and the farmers' market in Falcarragh to name a few, plus Da's own garden, of course, once he tamed the bog.

Fried Oysters with Horseradish and Green Onion Mayonnaise

A great way to introduce people to oysters is to serve them battered and fried and accompanied with some kind of mayonnaise, such as Horseradish and Green Onion Mayonnaise.

The oysters must be fried just in time to serve. Do not hold them in a warm oven because they will get soggy. Once fried, oysters will retain their heat for several minutes as you fry subsequent batches, but it is not a bad idea to have two skillets going at the same time. You will need a deep-fry/candy thermometer.

∙{ SERVES 6 AS AN APPETIZER }∙

BATTER

3 cups cake flour

3/4 cup cornstarch

2 teaspoons baking soda

1 teaspoon kosher salt

4 cups sparkling water or club soda

OYSTERS

Canola oil, for frying

30 meaty, briny Atlantic Coast oysters, such as Narragansett Bay or Olde Salt (see How to Shuck Oysters, page 38)

All-purpose flour, about 2 cups, for dredging

Horseradish and Green Onion Mayonnaise (page 249)

Make the batter: In a large bowl, use a fork or chopsticks to mix the cake flour, cornstarch, baking soda, and salt; add the club soda and just barely mix. The batter should be lumpy.

Fry the oysters: Line a baking sheet with a double thickness of paper towels. Heat 2 inches of canola oil in a 6-quart heavy casserole over high heat to 350°F. Put the dredging flour in a medium bowl.

Working in batches so as to not overcrowd the pot, dredge each oyster in flour, then in batter, and gently place it in the hot oil. Cook the oysters for a couple of minutes on each side until golden brown. Blot them on paper towels and serve warm with Horseradish and Green Onion Mayonnaise on the side.

Salt-Baked Dublin Bay Prawns with Aioli

This cooking method may be unfamiliar to you, but it is ridiculously easy and really tasty. As the salt layer in the pan bottom gets hot, its radiant heat "bakes" the prawns and their juices mingle with the salt and its infused garlic flavor. The result is juicy, salty deliciousness, here made all the better with an accompaniment of pungent, rich aioli.

*{ **SERVES 4 AS A FIRST COURSE** }*

4 cups rock salt

20 cloves garlic, peeled

12 whole Dublin Bay prawns (about 3 pounds), langoustines, or head-on shrimp (see Dublin Bay Prawns, below)

Aioli (page 251), for serving

Cook the prawns: Spread the salt in the bottom of a 17-inch paella pan or slope-sided sauté pan and dot it with the garlic cloves. Let the salt heat over high heat for 3 minutes. Lay the prawns on top of the salt in an even layer. Cook them for 15 minutes, turning them over halfway through, until they are deep orange. To test for doneness, pull the body and head apart on one. The flesh should be white all the way through.

To serve: Serve the prawns family style by placing the pan right on the table with a crock of aioli on the side. Pull the heads off and suck the juices out of them (delicious!) before discarding them, then peel the bodies and dip the meat in aioli.

DUBLIN BAY PRAWNS

Dublin Bay prawns are one of the great luxury foods of the world and so were always considered a treat when I was growing up because they were so expensive. We would only have them on very special occasions—say, for a christening or when a highly regarded guest came to visit, such as myself on the occasion of my birthday.

Shrimp and prawns are separate species, though the words have come to be used interchangeably. Prawns, however, resemble small lobsters, claws and all, and have sweet, succulent flesh, much more tender than that of lobster or shrimp. They are virtually impossible to source in the United States. Langoustines are the closest approximation to them, but shrimp can also do as a reasonable substitute in many dishes.

~•} About Chippers {•~

Chippers were always the go-to fast food joints for us in Ireland; they were around long before McDonald's was invented and you'll almost always find one close to any pub in Ireland. There's a constant debate about who makes the best fish and chips. In my opinion, and most people agree, Burdock's by Christchurch Cathedral in Dublin does.

When Meshelle was pregnant with Eve in 1998, she was put on bed rest for the ninth month. It was right before Christmas and I was renovating our new house and had just started a new job at Bistro Bis in Washington. My parents came to visit us and when they saw the state of the place, they were like, "No way are you bringing a child into this." So they sent for my brother Edward in Ireland to help me with the construction. But while I was at work and Edward was at home, he and Meshelle were scheming and got the idea in their heads that we should open a chipper. When the right space became available, we did just that, opening Eamonn's on King Street in Old Town Alexandria in 2006.

Definitely one of the best ways to enjoy fish and chips is to make sure you have at least ten pints of Guinness first. One of our neighbors growing up, Jim Corridan (we called him Big Jim Corridan), was this larger-than-life man from County Kerry. I remember we were in the car once coming back from somewhere, and I was at the wheel. I guess I was sixteen or seventeen years old, just learning how to drive. Corridan and my father were sitting in the back seat eating the batter-fried ray they had just gotten from Burdock's. The bones of that fish are purely cartilage, so if you're really crazy or drunk enough, you can eat the whole thing. Corridan ate all of his and the bones my father left. So now there is a note on the Eamonn's menu that reads: "Big Jim Corridan, the only man I ever met brave enough to eat all the bones."

Fish and Chips with Tartar Sauce

Of course, no Irish cookbook is complete without a recipe for fish and chips, the original fast food. There is just something so appealing about that delicate white fish, steaming and moist beneath its golden brown, crispy exterior. (See About Chippers, opposite.) It took six years for me to perfect the recipe for the batter we use at Eamonn's, our Dublin Chipper in Alexandria, Virginia, so I am very proprietary about it. The one I offer here is close, but if you want the authentic version, you can order the mix at www.eamonnsdublinchipper.com.

Because cod is endangered in the Mid-Atlantic, I use pollock that comes from the Gulf of Maine—it's absolutely delectable. But you can use any flaky, white fish you prefer, such as grouper or halibut.

To develop their starch properly, the cut potatoes must be soaked overnight in water, unrefrigerated. (See Making Chips, page 83.) The dry mix for the fish batter will last for months in an airtight container, but the batter, fish, and chips should be made when you are ready to enjoy them. Make sure you have parchment paper on hand to make cones for serving. You will need a countertop deep-fat fryer with a basket or a 6-quart heavy casserole and a mesh spider.

} SERVES 4 {

4 russet potatoes, peeled

Canola oil, for frying

BATTER

3 cups cake flour

3/4 cup cornstarch

2 teaspoons baking soda

1 teaspoon kosher salt

4 cups very cold club soda

Fine sea salt

4 (6-ounce) pieces pollock, no more than 1/2 inch thick, pinbones removed

All-purpose flour, for dusting

Marie Rose Sauce (page 248)

Tartar Sauce (page 248)

Ready the chips: To steady the potatoes on the cutting board, slice 1/2 inch off of each lengthwise to create a flat edge. Flat sides down, cut the potatoes lengthwise into 1/2-inch slices and then cut the slices into 1/2-inch sticks (chefs call these batons). Cut the trimmed edges into batons, too; they will be smaller than the others and therefore especially coveted because they will get extra crispy. Transfer the potatoes to a bowl of water and soak overnight at room temperature.

The next day, prep your workspace: Fill a countertop fryer or 6-quart heavy casserole with canola oil and preheat to 300°F. Line a baking sheet with a double thickness of paper towels and place a wire rack over another baking sheet.

Dry the potatoes: Drain the potato sticks in a colander and dry them thoroughly on a cotton kitchen towel. This will keep them from spattering in the hot oil.

Do the first frying: Fill the fryer basket with potatoes and blanch them at 300°F for 10 minutes, shaking the basket occasionally, until they turn pale brown. (If you are using a casserole, add and remove the potatoes with a mesh spider.) Transfer the blanched chips to the paper towel–lined baking sheet and turn off the fryer (don't empty it). Refrigerate the potatoes for at least 1 1/2 hours.

{continued}

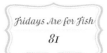

Make the batter: When the potatoes have chilled, preheat the fryer to 350°F and the oven to 180°F. In a large bowl, whisk together the cake flour, cornstarch, baking soda, and salt; add the club soda and whisk until smooth. Do not overmix. Set aside.

Do the second frying: Fry the cold blanched potatoes, shaking the basket occasionally, for 4 minutes, until golden brown. Make sure not to overcrowd the basket so the potatoes fry evenly (fry in batches if you need to). Turn the chips out into a large bowl. Season them immediately with fine salt and then transfer them to the wire rack on the second baking sheet. Place in the oven to keep warm.

Fry the fish: Allow the fryer oil to return to 350°F. Lightly dust the fish fillets with flour and completely immerse them in the batter. Lower the fillets into the oil slowly—do not just drop them in because this can result in splattering oil. Depending on the size of your fryer, you may have to fry in batches; overcrowding reduces the temperature of your oil and produces a soggy product. Fry the fillets until lightly browned on their bottom sides, about 30 seconds. Use tongs to carefully turn the fillets over and continue to fry them for 4 to 5 minutes more, until good and brown. As they come out of the fryer, blot them dry on paper towels. Keep the fried fillets warm on the rack in the oven, next to the chips.

Serve "chipper" style: Make 4 large cones out of parchment paper and fill each with a fish fillet and a handful of chips, offering Marie Rose sauce and tartar sauce on the side.

MAKING CHIPS

Once potatoes are harvested, their sugar begins to convert into starch, so older potatoes are very starchy. For chips, you want potatoes with the right balance of sugar and starch so they get golden brown and very crisp on the outside, but fluffy on the inside. If the potatoes have too much sugar, they'll get soggy in the oil. So it's important that you get potatoes that aren't too fresh, but not ready to sprout buds, either. For our chipper, Eamonn's, we age potatoes for at least a week after delivery, preferably two.

To make perfect chips, remember this formula: soak, blanch, refrigerate, and fry. Also:
- Use russet potatoes.
- Cut peeled potatoes into chips and soak them in water overnight at room temperature. (Refrigerating the potatoes would retard the conversion of sugar into starch in the potatoes.)
- Optimally, you will need a countertop deep-fat fryer with a basket. If not, use a heavy pot filled with canola oil to a depth of 6 inches, allowing for plenty of room above the oil so that it won't boil over during the frying process. Heat the oil over medium-high heat, using a candy thermometer to monitor the temperature of the oil.
- Use clean frying oil; otherwise, your chips may be greasy.
- The key to crispy chips is double frying. The first frying (blanching), at 300°F, cooks the potatoes; the second frying, at 350°F, browns and crisps them.
- Before blanching, pat chips dry to prevent splattering and to keep the oil temperature stable.
- After blanching, refrigerate the chips for at least 1$1/2$ hours. The blanched chips must be cold for the second frying.

Fish and Seafood Pie

When my Da was sick in hospital in 2012, my mother and I took him out one afternoon to have lunch at a great little restaurant called Salt in Monkstown, on the south side of Dublin. His appetite wasn't great, so we ordered lightly. He chose a baked seafood pie that we shared. I wanted to do my own interpretation of that dish because it recalls a fond memory for me.

Use non-oily fish for this pie, such as halibut, hake, haddock, and rockfish. Mild fish are sweet; oily fish such as mackerel and bluefish would just overpower the dish. You can make the filling several hours ahead and refrigerate it in its casserole until you're ready to bake. Prepare and add the mashed potatoes just prior to baking. (See On Making Mashed Potatoes, page 179.) You will need a food mill or potato ricer.

} SERVES 4 TO 6 {

SAUCE

6 tablespoons unsalted butter, cut into pieces, at room temperature

1/2 cup all-purpose flour

2 cups warm whole milk

2 cups warm fish stock (page 241)

1/4 cup chopped fresh dill leaves

1 tablespoon freshly squeezed lemon juice

1 teaspoon salt

FILLING

2 tablespoons unsalted butter, at room temperature

4 leeks, white and light green parts only, sliced lengthwise and diced, well washed (see How to Clean Leeks, page 32)

1 fennel bulb, trimmed and diced

1 1/2 pounds assorted fish fillets (see recipe note), skin and pinbones removed, cut into 1 1/2-inch squares

1/2 pound large shrimp, tails removed, peeled, deveined, and halved crosswise

MASHED POTATOES

4 russet potatoes, peeled and quartered

1 tablespoon kosher salt

4 large egg yolks

1/2 cup unsalted butter, cut into pieces, at room temperature

1/2 cup heavy cream

Make the sauce: Heat the butter in a saucepan over medium heat until it bubbles. Whisk in the flour and cook for 2 to 3 minutes, whisking constantly, until the mixture (chefs call this a roux) is blond in color. Whisking continually, slowly add the milk and then the stock. Bring the sauce to a boil and cook until it thickens, about 3 minutes, whisking continually to keep lumps from forming. Stir in the dill, lemon juice, and salt. Transfer the sauce to a large bowl to cool.

Make the filling: In a large slope-sided sauté pan over medium-high heat, heat the butter until it bubbles. Add the leeks and fennel and let them

sweat for 5 minutes, stirring occasionally, until they are soft and not at all brown. Transfer the vegetables to a bowl to cool. Once they do, stir them into the cooled sauce. Gently fold in the fish and shrimp. Transfer the filling to a 4-quart baking dish.

Cook the potatoes: Place the quartered potatoes and salt in a pot and cover them with cold water. Bring the water to a boil, then lower the heat to medium and allow the potatoes to simmer uncovered until cooked through, about 40 minutes. To tell if they are cooked, take a piece out and cut it in half to see if it's soft in the center. Drain the potatoes, return them to the pot, and stir them over the heat for a couple of minutes. This ensures that they are dry.

Mash the potatoes: Rice the potatoes into a large bowl. Add the egg yolks, butter, and cream, whisking until the potatoes are smooth. Work quickly while the potatoes are hot so they don't become gummy and starchy. Adjust the salt seasoning to taste and allow the potatoes to cool.

Top the pie: Preheat the oven to 450°F. Fit a large pastry bag with a large star tip. Spoon the mashed potatoes into the bag. Moving in one direction, pipe large rosettes of potatoes onto the top of the fish pie in neat rows, or starting around the outside and then working your way into the center in a spiral. Go over your work and pipe rosettes wherever you see any holes—you want to create a good seal. Alternatively, you can dollop the potatoes over the fish filling and spread them with a spatula to seal it.

Bake the pie: Line a baking sheet with foil. Set the pie on it and bake for 30 to 35 minutes, until the potatoes are nicely browned and the filling is bubbling. Remove the casserole from the oven and let it rest for 15 minutes before serving.

Pan-Fried Plaice with Lemon Caper Brown Butter

Plaice is a flat fish, similar to flounder, found off the coast of Ireland. It's a delicate, sweet, white-fleshed fish. For my money, it's a more elegant fish than the esteemed Dover sole.

The recipe calls for Wondra flour, which is an important ingredient to chefs. Wondra is very fine, freeze-dried flour found in the baking aisle of most grocery stores. It comes in a shaker canister with a label that says "for sauces and gravies." Chefs like to use it for dredging sautéed items that call for a delicate coating, such as scaloppini and fish fillets. Wondra forms a thin, crisp coating on the exterior of these foods rather than a stodgy, batter-like layer that often results from using all-purpose flour.

The fish is pan-fried using a basting method similar to pan-roasting. (Frying just uses more oil.) See On Pan-Roasting, page 118.

} SERVES 4 {

BROWN BUTTER

7 tablespoons unsalted butter, cold

1 shallot, minced

2 tablespoons freshly squeezed lemon juice

1 tablespoon Worcestershire sauce

2 tablespoons chicken stock (page 239)

2 tablespoons capers, rinsed and coarsely chopped

3 tablespoons chopped fresh chives

FISH

Kosher salt

2 (2-pound) plaice or flounders, eviscerated, with head, tail, and skin removed (ask your fishmonger to do this; to skin the fish yourself, see photos on page 88)

1/4 cup canola oil

Wondra flour, for dusting

1 tablespoon unsalted butter

1 teaspoon chopped fresh thyme leaves

1 teaspoon chopped garlic

Boiled New Potatoes, for serving (page 178)

Make the sauce: In a small saucepan over medium heat, melt 2 tablespoons of the butter and cook until it stops bubbling and turns pale brown (the color of hazelnuts), about 2 minutes. Stir in the shallots and sauté for 30 seconds. Stir in the lemon juice, Worcestershire sauce, chicken stock, and capers. Stirring constantly, add the remaining 5 tablespoons of butter 1 tablespoon at a time, incorporating each completely into the emulsion before adding the next. Once all the butter has been added, remove the pan from the heat and stir in the chives. Move the pan to a warm part of the stove, but not on a lit burner, while you prepare the fish.

Pan-fry the fish: Sprinkle salt over both sides of each fish. In a large slope-sided sauté pan or well-seasoned cast-iron skillet over medium-high heat, heat the canola oil until it shimmers. Dredge the fish lightly in flour and place them side by side in the pan. Pan-fry the fish for 5 minutes, until nicely browned on the bottom.

Baste the fish: Using a fish spatula, turn the fillets over. Use one hand to tilt the handle of the pan

{continued}

toward you so the oil pools. With the other hand, scoop up some oil in a dessert spoon and baste the fish with it; continue to cook for several minutes more while repeating the basting over and over. To test for doneness, insert a cake tester in the center to the spine bone and press it to your lips. It should feel warm to the touch. (See Testing Meat and Fish for Doneness, below.) When the fish is done, add the butter, thyme, and garlic to the pan and cook for 30 seconds more, basting as before.

Serve the fish: Transfer the fish to a warm platter (discard the cooking oil). Pour the brown butter into a small pitcher or sauceboat. Divide the fish among 4 dinner plates and serve immediately with the brown butter. And boiled potatoes, of course.

TESTING MEAT AND FISH FOR DONENESS

A way of checking meat or fish for the degree of doneness other than using a thermometer is to insert a metal cake tester in the center of what you're cooking and then press it against your lip. For meat, if the tester is cold, the meat is raw; slightly warm it's rare; warm it's medium rare. For fish, insert the tester to the center spine bone or to the center of a boneless piece of fish. It should feel warm when touched to your lip, which indicates that the flesh is cooked all the way through. (Don't use a skewer; it leaves an unsightly hole in your food.)

Being able to rely on inherent knowledge is always preferable than being dependent on machinery. What happens when you can't find the thermometer?

Baked Whole Salmon with Hollandaise Sauce

A whole baked salmon makes a stunning presentation for a banquet or celebration meal, such as a Holy Communion dinner. Serve it with hollandaise sauce, boiled new potatoes, and a simply prepared green vegetable, such as asparagus, peas, or broccoli. When buying salmon, make sure its gills are bright red and its eyes are clear and not sunken into the head. When you sniff the body, it should smell like the sea; its cavity should smell like watermelon.

You can prep the fish for baking several hours ahead of time and refrigerate it, but it should be baked just in time to serve. Make the hollandaise sauce about 40 minutes before the salmon comes out of the oven (25 minutes if its butter has been clarified ahead of time) and set it in a warm place near your cooktop.

{ SERVES 12 TO 14 }

3 tablespoons unsalted butter, at room temperature
1 (10- to 12-pound) eviscerated whole North Atlantic salmon, scaled
2 large bunches fresh thyme, separated into sprigs
1/2 lemon, thinly sliced, seeds removed
Hollandaise Sauce (page 252)

Prepare the foil wrapper: Preheat the oven to 375°F. Lay a sheet of 18-inch-wide aluminum foil slightly longer than your salmon on your work surface. Spread the butter evenly over it.

Prepare the salmon for baking: Towel dry the fish on both sides and lay it in the center of the buttered foil. Spread the thyme and lemon slices inside the cavity. Tightly wrap the foil around the fish, covering it completely. Lay it on a rimmed baking sheet (the sheet will probably be smaller than the fish).

Bake the salmon: Place the salmon, on the baking sheet, in the oven, curling up the tail to make it fit if necessary. (Put foil on the rack underneath the salmon to catch possible drips and keep your oven from becoming a mess.) Bake for 90 minutes, or until the tip of a knife poked through the foil and inserted into the center to the bone is warm.

Unwrap the salmon: Remove the salmon from the oven, place it on a large platter, and let it rest for 10 minutes. Use scissors to slice the foil open (watch out for steam) and then peel the foil away, rolling it up and tucking it under the sides of the fish. Peel away the skin between the gills and the tail, using a dinner knife (you don't want a sharp edge). When you peel back the skin, you will reveal the bloodline. Scrape it away, along with any brown fat beneath it. There should now only be pink flesh visible.

Serve: Slice down the center of the fish to the bone horizontally and then cut portions however thick you want down the sides. They will lift easily off the bones. Once you cut away all the top portions, lift off and discard the fish's spine. Cut portions from the bottom half, scraping away any skin and fat from them. Serve with hollandaise sauce.

~❈{ The Salmon of Knowledge }❈~

Salmon swim from the sea up the River Shannon (the longest river in Europe) to spawn every year. Since ancient times, salmon figure widely in the lore and fare of Ireland. Growing up, a special occasion meal seemed especially good to us when it featured salmon.

There's a great folklore story about salmon. Fionn mac Cumhaill was the leader of the Fianna, an army that protected the high king of Ireland in ancient times. When Fionn was a boy, he was sent to study under the bard Finegas, who lived on the banks of the River Boyne.

Finegas had spent his whole life fishing, hoping to catch the fish Brenden, the Salmon of Knowledge. It was said that the first person to taste the flesh of this fish would have the gift of foresight and the ability to cure a dying man with water from his hands. Soon after Fionn arrived, the fish was caught and set on a spit to cook. The young student was left to supervise while the bard went to the village for supplies, leaving strict instructions not to taste the fish.

As it cooked, a blister rose on the skin of the fish. Fionn popped it with his finger and burned himself. When he put his finger in his mouth to soothe it, all of the knowledge of the fish instantly passed into him.

As soon as Finegas returned from the village he saw the look of Fionn's face and realized that his lifelong quest had been thwarted.

Steamed Mussels with Lemon and Bay Leaf

My love of mussels started at an early age. Beginning when I was seven years old, my Mam sent me to France as an exchange student in the summers so I could learn French. The family I stayed with, the Baudins, lived outside of Paris, but one year we went to Noirmoutier, an island off of France's Atlantic Coast. I have a vivid memory of all of us being outside and eating mussels out of a huge pot.

Eve and Eamonn are huge mussel eaters and very often when we'd go to Ireland, Da would make them this way as a starter. Use small mussels—they are sweeter than large ones—and cook them uncovered. This allows their juices to evaporate and concentrate.

❧ SERVES 6 AS A FIRST COURSE, 4 AS A MAIN COURSE ❧

4 pounds mussels, preferably from American waters, debearded (see Mussel Prep, below)

4 shallots, minced

1/2 cup freshly squeezed lemon juice

4 fresh bay leaves

1/2 cup unsalted butter, cut into pieces, at room temperature

Crusty bread, for serving

Let a large slope-sided sauté pan get smoking hot over high heat. Add the mussels, shallots, lemon juice, bay leaves, and butter and cook uncovered for several minutes until the mussels open and pull away from both sides of the shell. Stir constantly so the mussels cook evenly and the lemon juice and butter emulsify. Serve piping hot with plenty of crusty bread.

MUSSEL PREP

Lightly tap opened mussels against the counter. If they are fresh, they will close back up. If they don't close, discard them. To debeard mussels, rinse them under cool running water and use needle-nose pliers to pull off and discard any black fibers protruding from their shells.

Pan-Roasted Loin of Monkfish
with Fava Bean, Mussel, and Bacon Ragoût

Because of the firm, slightly chewy quality of its flesh and its subtle sweetness, monkfish is often referred to as the poor man's lobster. That is an injustice because it is an absolutely delicious fish in its own right when cooked properly. I like to lightly dust it with Wondra flour and pan-fry it like fried chicken, with a crisp crust and a luscious, pillowy center.

With the fava bean ragoût, it makes a lovely spring dish. Only make the dish when fava beans are in season; frozen fava beans would really sell the dish short.

The method used for cooking the monkfish is known as pan-roasting. (See On Pan-Roasting, page 118.)

{ SERVES 4 }

RAGOÛT

1 cup fresh shelled fava beans (about 1 pound in the shell)

1 tablespoon canola oil

1 cup thickly sliced streaky (American) bacon, diced (see On Irish Bacon, page 15)

1 cup cleaned and quartered cremini mushrooms

2 large shallots, minced

16 medium mussels, debearded (see Mussel Prep, page 35)

1/2 cup chicken stock (page 239)

1/4 cup freshly squeezed lemon juice

2 teaspoons chopped fresh thyme leaves

1/2 cup unsalted butter, cut into pieces, at room temperature

FISH

1/4 cup canola oil

4 (6-ounce) portions monkfish fillet, all bloodline and surrounding membrane removed

Wondra flour, for dredging

1 tablespoon unsalted butter

1 teaspoon chopped fresh thyme leaves

1 clove garlic, minced

Blanch the beans: Place the beans in a small saucepan and cover with cold water. Bring to a boil and boil gently for 3 minutes. Drain and transfer to a bowl of ice water to stop the cooking. If the beans are young and small, you can leave their skins on; if they are older and large, remove the outer skin from each bean by squeezing between your fingers (you may need to pierce the skin with the tip of a paring knife).

Make the ragoût: In a large saucepan over medium-high heat, heat the oil until it shimmers. Cook the bacon, stirring frequently, until it is lightly browned and the fat is partially rendered, about 5 minutes. Add the mushrooms and sauté until tender, about 2 minutes. Stir in the shallots

and cook for 30 seconds. Stir in the beans, mussels, stock, lemon juice, thyme, and butter and cook, stirring occasionally, until the mussels have opened completely, about 3 minutes. Keep warm over very low heat.

Pan-roast the fish: In a large slope-sided sauté pan or well-seasoned cast-iron skillet over medium-high heat, heat the oil until it shimmers. Dredge the fish lightly in flour and place them side by side in the pan. Pan-sear the fish for 5 minutes, until nicely browned on the bottom.

Baste the fish: Using a fish spatula, turn the fillets over. Use one hand to tilt the handle of the pan toward you so the oil pools. With the other hand, scoop up some oil in a dessert spoon and baste the fish with it; continue to cook for several minutes more while repeating the basting over and over. To test for doneness, insert a cake tester into the center to the spine bone and press it to your lips. It should feel warm to the touch. (See Testing Meat and Fish for Doneness, page 89.) When the fish is done, add the butter, thyme, and garlic to the pan and cook for 30 seconds more, basting as before.

Assemble and serve: Remove the pan from the heat and transfer the fillets to a cutting board (discard the cooking oil). Slice them diagonally into ¹/₂-inch slices. Divide the ragoût among 4 soup plates and arrange overlapping slices of monkfish on top. Serve immediately.

Lobster Salad with Citrus Vinaigrette

After we kids were all grown up, my parents sold the house on Watson Road in Dublin and bought a house by the sea in Donegal, an isolated region of northwest Ireland. (See About Donegal, page 76.) To say the land there is not arable would be an understatement, so there was not much of a food culture. Nevertheless, my parents managed to create relationships with purveyors of excellent products. They found a great butcher in Dungloe and for seafood, a guy named Jack. He had a truck that he'd set up on the street in a town called Falcarragh, across from the farmers' market. On a rare, rare occasion, because it was exorbitant, you'd indulge in lobster from him.

With something this special and delicate, you don't want to overembellish it. A few light touches are all you need, like the Citrus Vinaigrette offered here. You can prepare the vinaigrette and cook the lobster a day ahead, then assemble the salad when ready to serve. You will need poultry shears to shuck the lobster.

⟫ SERVES 4 ⟪

4 (1¹/₂-pound) live lobsters

1 fennel bulb, layers pulled apart and cut into very thin strips lengthwise (julienne)

1 red onion, halved lengthwise and cut lengthwise into thin strips (julienne)

8 cups (8 ounces) mixed salad greens (such as radicchio, mizuna, frisée, arugula, Lolla Rossa lettuce, and tatsoi)

¹/₂ cup Citrus Vinaigrette (page 246)

Kosher salt and freshly ground black pepper

Cook the lobsters: Bring a large stockpot of water to a rolling boil over high heat and submerge the lobsters in it. Cook them uncovered for about 12 minutes, until their shells are adobe red all over. To test for doneness, pull the tail off one of the lobsters. The flesh should be white and not at all translucent. Transfer the lobsters to a baking sheet and refrigerate them for about an hour, until completely chilled.

Shell the lobsters: Pull the tails and claws off the lobster bodies; set the bodies aside. Using poultry shears, cut through the middle of each tail's inside shell and remove the tail meat intact. Using a paring knife, make a ¹/₄-inch-deep cut along the back of each piece and remove and discard the black intestinal tract. Place the claws between two kitchen towels and whack them with the back of a sturdy knife. Then use poultry shears to cut through the shells lengthwise, far enough so you can pop out

the claw meat intact (use a cocktail fork or seafood pick to ease the meat out). Grasp the claw meat with one hand and pinch the base with the other to pull out and discard the center cartilage.

Save the shells: You can freeze the shells and bodies to use later for seafood stock or lobster bisque. Discard them if you prefer.

Assemble the salad: Soak the fennel and red onion julienne in a bowl of ice water for 10 minutes to crisp them, then drain and transfer them to a large bowl. Mix in the salad greens and vinaigrette, tossing to coat the leaves well. Season to taste with salt and pepper. Mound the salad on each of 4 pasta plates. Slice each lobster tail into ¹/₂-inch medallions. Arrange the medallions from one tail attractively in the center of each salad, and flank them with a pair of claws, placed at the wide end of the tail to resemble a whole lobster. Serve immediately.

Special Occasions

When I was growing up, my family never really missed an opportunity to celebrate an occasion with food—and a keg or two of Guinness. There would be weeks of planning, notepads strewn about the table, shopping lists, delegations of responsibilities, and the whole thing culminated in hours and hours of fun and revelry.

Although we didn't hesitate to turn Sunday dinners or landmarks like birthdays into big celebrations, many of our special occasions were connected with religious holidays because of our upbringing. One of the greatest holidays probably in the history of all of Ireland was my brother Edward's christening in 1979. He was an unexpected surprise, as my mother was thirty-nine years old at the time. His birth was therefore very exalted.

The festivities surrounding his christening went on for days, and every family member, friend, and acquaintance from far and wide seemed to be in attendance. Mam was there, which may not seem unusual until you know that she wasn't present at my christening—she was still in hospital. In those days, the Church deemed that you had to christen a child

right away in case anything happened to him or her. By the time Edward was born ten years later, they had eased up on that belief.

The big parties always ended with a sing-along. Tony Cowley, my Da's colorful accountant, played the guitar, and Da sang "Waltzing Matilda." The next thing you'd know, it was the next day and there were bodies sleeping everywhere. Breakfast was cooking and yet another meal was on its way.

The recipes in this chapter represent the kinds of foods we'd have at celebratory meals: Sunday dinners at Nana's house, holiday feasts, and the most important event of all—my birthday. You will notice that these meals are mostly centered around roasted meats, because this was the most efficient way to feed a lot of people.

NANA'S SUNDAY DINNERS

❧

NANA, my father's mother, lived in Dublin's inner city. Her name was Martha, but everyone called her Mattie, except for us kids. She lived across the road from her mother, who lived to be ninety-six. We called her Granny Across the Road.

Nana had a tiny three-bedroom house; six kids grew up there. When I was very young, the bathroom was outside, but it was later connected to the house, praise God. The Guinness factory was not far from her house and you could smell it brewing pretty much all the time.

We'd show up there at noon, after Mass, and would still be there into the evening. They'd move the table into the living room from the kitchen and open up the leaf, and we'd cram as many people as we could around it. Always mindful of teaching us kids good manners, Nana would start the meal by saying, "All joints on the table should be carved," meaning that we should not have our elbows on the table.

There was a very animated butcher whose shop was nearby, and he had a great selection of beef. On occasion, we'd have the rare treat of roast beef. Otherwise, it would be a leg of pork or lamb or roast chicken, all served with abundance and a banquet-type atmosphere. I make some of Nana's dishes, like Roast Chicken with Pan Gravy (page 103), as she did; others, like Roast Prime Rib of Beef (page 105), I've added my own embellishments to over the years.

Roast Duck with Sherry Vinegar Gastrique

Even though this isn't a dish Nana made (you wouldn't have seen duck very often in a butcher shop), I'm including this recipe because it's an elegant alternative to roast chicken for a special occasion. The best part of roast duck is the crispy skin, and this dish delivers the goods. It is especially complemented by the gastrique, a sweet-tart sauce, which you can prepare while the duck is roasting. Serve with Lyonnaise Potatoes (page 184) and Creamed Spinach (page 175).

The duck is brined in salt for 24 hours and air-dried in the refrigerator for another 3 hours, so plan your timing accordingly.

◈⟩ SERVES 4 ⟨◈

DUCK

1 (4-pound) Muscovy duck, rinsed in cold water and patted dry with paper towels

1 cup kosher salt

GASTRIQUE

3 tablespoons sugar

1 large shallot, minced

1 celery stalk, finely chopped

1 carrot, peeled and finely chopped

2 cloves garlic, chopped

3 tablespoons sherry vinegar, plus 2 teaspoons for finishing

1 cup chicken stock (page 239)

1 small sprig fresh rosemary

10 sprigs fresh thyme

2 large fresh bay leaves

1 cup veal demi-glace (page 244)

2 tablespoons unsalted butter

1 teaspoon chopped fresh thyme leaves

1/4 teaspoon kosher salt

1/8 teaspoon freshly ground black pepper

Prep the duck: Set a rack over a baking sheet and place the duck on it. Cover its breast with the salt and refrigerate it uncovered for 24 hours. Rinse the duck in cold running water to remove all traces of salt and pat it dry with paper towels. Return it to the rack and air-dry it uncovered in the refrigerator for 3 to 4 hours.

Roast the duck: Preheat the oven to 400°F. Place the duck on a rack set in a roasting pan and roast for 20 minutes. Lower the heat to 300°F and continue to cook for 1 hour and 40 minutes. The skin will be crisp and dark brown and the flesh will be well done. Remove the pan from the oven and transfer the duck to a cutting board to let it rest for 10 minutes.

Begin the gastrique: About 20 minutes before the duck is done, spread the sugar on the bottom of a saucepan and cook it over medium heat undisturbed for a few minutes, until you see a ring of clear syrup around the edge of the pan. Now with a wooden spoon, stir the sugar until it begins to caramelize (take on a golden hue), breaking up any clumps of sugar crystals that may form with the back of the spoon. Continue stirring until the sugar is completely dissolved and the caramel is deep brown. Stir in the shallots, celery, carrots, and garlic. (The caramel will form into clumps.) Increase the heat to medium-high and cook the vegetables for 3 minutes, until they are tender and the caramel is melted.

{continued}

Complete the gastrique: Add the vinegar to the caramelized vegetables and cook for 3 minutes to concentrate the vinegar. Add the stock, rosemary and thyme sprigs, and bay leaves, and continue cooking for 7 minutes, until the liquid reduces by half. Add the demi-glace and cook for another 5 minutes, skimming off and discarding any impurities that rise to the surface. Strain the mixture through a fine-mesh sieve into another saucepan. Bring the liquid to a boil over high heat. Whisk in the butter, thyme leaves, salt, and pepper and cook for 1 minute. Keep warm over low heat until ready to use.

Present the dish: Transfer the duck to a platter and pour the gastrique into a pitcher or gravy boat. Carve the duck at the table, removing the legs first (serve them whole) and then slicing along both sides of the breast. Spoon some gastrique over each portion and serve.

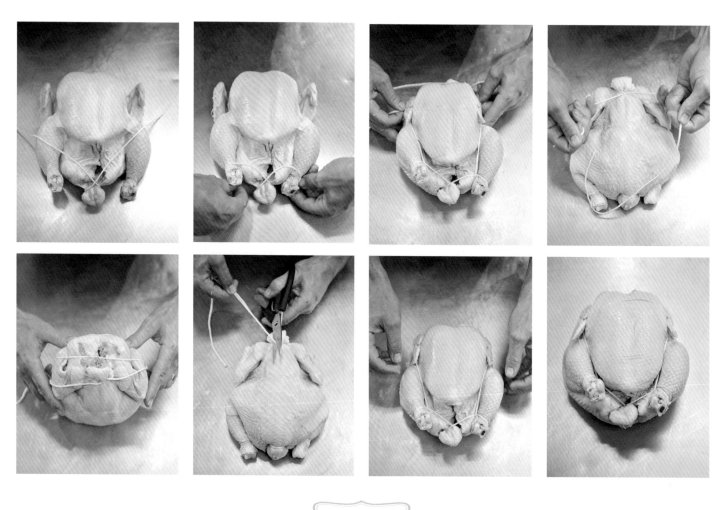

Roast Chicken with Pan Gravy

People ask me all the time what I like to eat, and I think most of the time they expect me to name some fancy dish we make at Restaurant Eve. The truth is, after a long week at work when you're at home with your family, nothing is more appealing than a simple roast chicken. It's easy to prepare and totally comforting. Nana knew that, and so roast chicken made regular appearances on her Sunday dinner table. Now, whenever I make one, stirring the flour into the gravy triggers the memory of my Nana's house and the buzz there'd be on a Sunday afternoon in anticipation of a great dinner. Serve roast chicken with whichever vegetables are in season and any gravy-soaking potatoes you favor.

The best chickens that we've ever used at Restaurant Eve are from Polyface Farms (www.polyfacefarms.com, see Resources, page 263). They are true free-range chickens. The bird has a distinctive flavor, almost like oyster mushrooms. I love the versatility of chicken, using the leftover for chicken salad or sandwiches and soup and using the carcass to make stock.

} SERVES 4 TO 6 {

1 (3 1/2- to 4-pound) whole chicken, neck and giblets removed, if present
1 teaspoon kosher salt
2 tablespoons all-purpose flour
2 cups chicken stock (page 239)
1 clove garlic, crushed

Roast the chicken: Preheat the oven to 450°F. Rinse the chicken in cold water and pat dry with paper towels. Truss it (see photos, opposite) and sprinkle the salt over the top. Place the chicken directly on a flameproof roasting pan and bake it for exactly 1 hour. The chicken should be golden brown and a metal cake tester inserted into the thickest part of the thigh should feel hot to the touch when pressed against your lip (an internal temperature of 165°F if using a meat thermometer). Remove the pan from the oven and transfer the chicken to a platter to rest for 15 minutes.

Make the gravy: Place the roasting pan on a burner over medium heat. Sprinkle the flour over the pan drippings and use a wooden spoon to scrape the browned bits from the bottom of the pan. Add the chicken stock gradually, using a small whisk to stir and scrape bits from the pan. Transfer the gravy to a small saucepan. Stir in the garlic and cook over medium-high heat until the gravy thickens and coats the back of a spoon. Strain it into a gravy boat.

Present the dish: Carve the chicken into individual portions, removing the legs whole and cutting the drumsticks from the thighs, then slicing along both sides of the breast. Spoon gravy over each serving or pass it at the table.

Roast Prime Rib of Beef with Red Wine Sauce and Yorkshire Pudding

My father taught me this method, and once you try it you'll never make roast beef any other way again. The beef will be perfectly cooked, medium rare and rosy pink. This method is for those who prefer their meat that way. There won't be a perceivable difference if your roast is a few ounces more or less than 5 pounds.

Read this recipe all the way through before beginning so you understand the timing of the various steps. Ideally, you'll have a second oven so you can time the pudding to be done at the same time as the beef, which can't be disturbed and requires a different temperature. If you have only one oven, you will make the pudding while the finished roast is resting.

In Irish households, the popover tin for the Yorkshire pudding is used so often that it always stays in the oven, getting more and more seasoned as time goes on. Sometimes Yorkshire pudding doesn't rise well if you make the batter too far ahead of time. I don't recommend making the batter any more than 4 hours or any less than 1 hour before you plan to start cooking.

Instead of traditional gravy, I use scraps trimmed from the beef to make a more formal sauce with red wine reduction and veal stock or demi-glace, as we would at Restaurant Eve. My Nana would serve her beef with Boiled New Potatoes (page 178) and make her gravy from the potato water.

I especially like to serve Horseradish Cream (page 254) with this. In addition to gravy, traditional accompaniments for roast beef include Roasted Potatoes (page 182), "Marrowfat" Peas (page 172), Brussels Sprouts with Bacon (page 165), Glazed Baby Carrots (page 166), Braised Celery with Cashel Blue Cheese (page 170), and Creamed Leeks (page 171). You will need a popover pan with 12 cups.

⟩ SERVES 6 ⟨

PUDDING

3 large eggs

1 cup whole milk

1 cup all-purpose flour

Pinch of fine sea salt

Trimmed fat scraps (from the roast)

ROAST

1 (5-pound) bone-in beef rib roast (2 or 3 ribs)

Medium-grind sea salt

Fresh coarsely ground black pepper

2 tablespoons canola oil

SAUCE

1 tablespoon canola oil

Trimmed meat scraps (from the roast)

1 yellow onion, diced

1 carrot, peeled and diced

1 celery stalk, diced

3 cloves garlic, crushed

1 cup good-quality full-bodied, dry red wine

1 cup veal demi-glace (page 244)

1 small sprig fresh rosemary

1 fresh bay leaf

2 tablespoons cold unsalted butter

1 teaspoon chopped fresh thyme leaves

Kosher salt and freshly ground black pepper

Horseradish Cream, for serving (page 254)

Make the pudding batter: Place the eggs, milk, flour, and salt in a blender or food processor and process on high for 20 seconds. Strain the batter through a fine-mesh sieve into a small bowl. Cover and refrigerate for 1 to 4 hours.

{continued}

Trim the roast: Using a boning knife, trim excess fat from the roast, leaving a ¼-inch layer on top. Cut the trimmed fat into approximately 1-inch pieces and reserve them for rendering later. French the roast by cutting away all of the meat around and between the ends of the ribs to completely denude 2 inches of the bones. Cut the scraps into 1-inch pieces and reserve them to make the sauce later.

Sear the roast: Generously season the roast on all sides with salt and pepper. In a large skillet over medium-high heat, heat the canola oil until it shimmers. Place the roast in the pan and sear it for about 1 minute on the rounded fat-covered side and the two cut ends until it is medium (not dark) brown.

Roast the beef: Place an oven rack in the lower-middle position. Do not preheat the oven. Stand the roast fat side up on a flat rack placed over a rimmed baking sheet and put it on the lower oven rack. Turn the oven to 350°F and bake the roast for exactly 50 minutes. Turn the oven off, and leave the roast inside for 70 minutes exactly. DO NOT open the oven door. When this time has elapsed, remove the roast from the oven. If you do not have a second oven, cover the roast loosely with aluminum foil while you make the Yorkshire pudding.

Make the sauce while the roast is cooking: In a heavy saucepan over medium-high heat, heat the canola oil until it shimmers. Add the trimmed meat scraps (but not the fat scraps), distributing evenly over the pan bottom; let them cook undisturbed for 2 minutes. Turn the scraps over and sear for 2 to 3 minutes more until well browned. Stir in the onion, carrot, celery, and garlic and cook, stirring occasionally, for 3 to 4 minutes, until golden brown. Add the wine and use a flat-edged wooden spatula to scrape any brown bits from the bottom of the pan. Continue to cook until most of the wine has evaporated, 8 to 10 minutes. Stir in the demi-glace, rosemary, and bay leaf. Bring the liquid to a simmer and cook for 12 to 15 minutes, skimming often to remove the impurities and fat that rise to the surface. Strain the sauce through a fine-mesh sieve into another saucepan. Discard the solids and set the sauce aside to finish right before serving the roast.

Render the fat for the pudding: Meanwhile, cook the fat scraps over medium heat in a large slope-sided sauté pan for 30 minutes or so, until all that remains are knobby, spent-looking pieces. Strain the liquefied fat through a fine-mesh sieve into a heatproof bowl and set aside until the roast comes out of the oven. Discard the solids.

Make the Yorkshire pudding: Put the popover pan on the middle rack in the oven; preheat to 450°F.

(If you have a second oven, do this 30 to 40 minutes before the roast is done, depending on how long it takes for your second oven to preheat.) When the temperature is reached, remove the pan from the oven and spoon 1 teaspoon of the rendered beef fat into each cup (reserve any excess fat for another use or another batch of Yorkshire pudding). Ladle the batter (it's fine if it's cold) into the cups, about 3 tablespoons per cup. Return the pan to the oven and bake for 20 minutes, until the puddings are well browned and sound hollow when tapped. They should pop right out of the pan. If they do not, run the tip of a paring knife around them.

Complete the sauce: Ten minutes before the puddings are done, bring the reserved sauce to a simmer over medium-high heat. Whisk in the butter and thyme until the butter is melted. Taste the sauce and season with salt and pepper to taste.

Present the dish: Transfer the sauce to a gravy boat or small pitcher. Spoon the horseradish cream into a small serving bowl. Slice the roast and arrange it on a platter with the Yorkshire puddings arrayed around it. Serve with your chosen side dishes, along with the horseradish cream and the sauce, passed separately.

SAINT PATRICK'S DAY

❧

AT HOME, Saint Patrick's Day is a religious holiday that celebrates Patrick bringing Christianity to Ireland in the fifth century. It is observed with the same kind of reverence that Americans have for Thanksgiving, but more solemn. There's a big parade in Dublin that everybody goes to—just like the Macy's Thanksgiving Day Parade—but every little village has its own parade as well.

On Saint Patrick's Day, we don't drink green beer, we don't dye the rivers green, and we don't get really drunk. It is actually a stay-at-home day on which many pubs are closed.

Saint Patrick's Day usually falls in the middle of Lent when everybody is fasting or abstaining, but on this one day we are given a special dispensation from the Church and are allowed to break the fast and have a celebration. After everybody goes to Mass, the family gathers for an elegant spring meal that typically features Roast Leg of Lamb (opposite), Roast Prime Rib of Beef (page 105), or even Baked Whole Salmon (page 91). One thing you probably won't find on the Irish table is Corned Beef (page 124), which is an American tradition.

Roast Leg of Lamb au Jus with Herb Pesto

When I was very young, we'd go to Nana's house for Saint Patrick's Day. Nana, my father's mother, was a very strong woman, the matriarch of the family. When I was ten years old, she took us to Dublin's Phoenix Park to see Pope John Paul II. We walked all the way from her house to center city, a good hour-and-a-half walk. It seemed to me that all of Ireland was there, and it took all day to get there and back. As we were walking home exhausted that evening, I remember Nana turning to me and saying, "I'm so hungry, I could eat the hind leg off the lamb of God."

Lamb, except for less expensive cuts like shanks, shin bones, or neck meat, was a special occasion meat in my family, reserved for days like Easter and Saint Patrick's Day. One of the most vivid memories I have of growing up is sitting at the oval table in my Nana's living room with her and Granda, the eight of our family, and anyone else lucky enough to have been invited for Sunday dinner's leg of lamb.

Occasionally, I'll be out somewhere and catch a whiff of a leg of lamb roasting, and it takes me back instantly to my place at that table in another time. Too bad if I want to do anything about it, though; Meshelle hates lamb. She never lets me make it at home, but lamb remains one of my preferred meats.

As Nana got older, Saint Patrick's Day dinner shifted to our house. Mam would serve spring lamb with peas because they were the first green vegetables to be seen at that time of year. My version of them is "Marrowfat" Peas (page 172). There were always Roasted Potatoes (page 182), if not also Boiled New Potatoes (page 178) and Mashed Potatoes (page 181). Other nice accompaniments for this dish would be Glazed Baby Carrots (page 166) and Roasted Root Vegetable Purée (page 174).

⁌ SERVES 8 TO 10 ⁑

1 (9-pound) bone-in leg of lamb, H-bone removed by your butcher

2 tablespoons extra-virgin olive oil

2 teaspoons kosher salt

1 cup lamb demi-glace (page 244)

HERB PESTO

1/2 cup extra-virgin olive oil

6 cloves garlic, crushed

1 cup fresh basil leaves

2 tablespoons chopped fresh thyme leaves

2 tablespoons chopped fresh rosemary leaves (see Notes on Herbs, page 64)

1/2 teaspoon kosher salt

Roast the lamb: Preheat the oven to 350°F. Place the leg fat side up in a flameproof roasting pan. Rub it with the oil and season with the salt. Roast for 1 1/2 hours, until a meat thermometer inserted into thickest part of the lamb (but not touching the bone) registers 135°F for medium rare.

Make the pesto: Meanwhile, place the oil and garlic in the bowl of a food processor or blender and pulse briefly. Add the basil and process until a

coarse purée forms. Add the thyme, rosemary, and salt and process briefly, until incorporated.

Add the pesto to the lamb: Transfer the lamb leg to a cutting board and spread 4 tablespoons of herb pesto over it. Cover the leg loosely with aluminum foil and let it rest for 15 minutes.

Make the jus: Meanwhile, skim and discard the fat from the roasting pan. Add the demi-glace to the

{continued}

pan and place over medium-high heat. Use a flat-edged wooden spatula to scrape up all the brown bits from the bottom of the pan.

Present the dish: Pour the jus into a small pitcher or gravy boat. Spoon the remaining pesto into a small serving bowl. Transfer the lamb to a serving platter and carve it at table. At about the middle of the leg, use a carving knife to cut a horizontal wedge the width of the leg and about 2 inches wide, cutting at a 45° angle from both sides until you hit bone. Then cut thin slices from both sides of the wedge. Once you've carved as much meat that way as you can, grasp the bone and stand it on its end with one hand, using your other hand to cut slices off the leg. Spoon some jus over each serving and place a little pesto on the side. Serve with your chosen side dishes.

EASTER

❧

EASTER is a huge holiday for Irish people; the country is, after all, 95 percent Roman Catholic. It is as significant a holiday for us as Christmas, if not even more so. It marks the end of Lent and the beginning of spring. There wasn't any Easter Bunny in my childhood celebrations, but we did get chocolate Easter eggs.

We'd get all dressed up and go to Mass in the morning, then to all my aunts and uncles' houses for a visit and back home by late afternoon for a big family feast. By then we'd be starving. In my early years we would end up at Nana's house, but later on, when she was too old to cook, they'd come to our place, where the preparations for dinner had begun on Good Friday.

It was the first time in forty days and forty nights that we kids were allowed to eat candy, so that was a very big deal. We were on holiday from school and the day after Easter, Easter Monday, was a bank holiday, so everybody, the whole country, really, was in a good mood and the meal extended well into the wee hours, with all the adults asleep on the couch, as usual.

Roast Leg of Pork with Cracklings, Pan Juices, and Applesauce

Leg of pork, which is fresh ham, is something found more commonly on dinner tables in Ireland than in the States because there are so many big families in the Old Country and the cut feeds a lot of people. One of my sister's friends in school had seventeen children in her family. When we had big parties, my Da would say, "We're feeding the 5,000 tonight." Serve it with Braised York Cabbage (page 163), Cauliflower Baked in Cheddar Cheese Sauce (page 167), and some kind of potatoes, naturally. My mother always served homemade applesauce with roast pork, but it's not one of my favorite pairings because I'm not a fan of sweet things with savory dishes. Because of this, I like to balance the sweetness of the applesauce with vinegar. Of course, the better the apples, the better the sauce, so it's worth tracking down Pink Lady apples.

{ SERVES 10 TO 12 }

PORK

1 (12-pound) skin-on hind leg of pork, preferably Kurobuta or Berkshire

4 yellow onions, peeled and quartered

4 large sprigs fresh rosemary

1 head garlic, halved crosswise

1½ cups hard cider, such as Magner's brand

APPLESAUCE

8 apples, such as Bramley, Ida Red, Granny Smith, or Pink Lady, peeled, cored, and coarsely chopped

½ cup apple cider vinegar

¾ cup sugar

Prep the roast: Preheat the oven to 275°F. Cutting crosswise, score the skin of the pork at ½-inch intervals. Do not cut through the flesh. Scatter the onions, rosemary, and garlic in the bottom of a roasting pan large enough to hold the meat. Pour the cider over the vegetables. Set a rack in the pan and place the meat skin-side up on top of it.

Roast the pork: Bake the meat for about 4 hours (allow 20 minutes per pound), until a meat thermometer inserted into the thickest part of the meat (but not touching the bone) registers 165°F. Check the pan often to make sure there is enough liquid in it to keep the vegetables from burning. Whenever there isn't, add a cup or two of water.

While the pork is roasting, make the applesauce: In a saucepan over medium heat, cook the apples, vinegar, and sugar for 15 minutes, stirring occasionally, until the apples are tender.

The applesauce will keep for up to 3 days in the refrigerator.

Make the jus: When the roast is done, transfer it to a cutting board, cover loosely with aluminum foil, and let it rest for 30 minutes. Strain the pan juices into a saucepan and remove the fat from them—there will be a lot of it. Keep the jus warm over low heat until ready to serve.

Present the dish: Pull the crackled skin off the roast, breaking or cutting it into small pieces. Slice the roast in the same direction you scored it and arrange the slices on a serving platter, surrounded by the pieces of crackled skin. Transfer the jus to a gravy boat or small pitcher. Spoon the applesauce into a serving bowl. Serve the meat warm, placing a healthy spoonful of applesauce on each plate. Pass the jus at the table, along with your chosen side dishes.

MY BIRTHDAY DINNER

MY BIRTHDAY is August 16, which since 1977 became known as the day that Elvis Presley died. When people ask me why I wear sideburns now, I attribute it to the fact that we share that day.

For my birthday, from when I was eight years old to about fifteen, my cousins and I, who were of similar age, would go to the movies, followed by a party at the house. Mam would have made all kinds of treats for us to enjoy: Rice Krispie buns, cocktail sausages, chocolate caramel fudge bars. They were the greatest parties.

In our later teen years, the birthday treat was being allowed to select what you wanted for dinner. All of us kids chose corn-on-the-cob as a first course, even though all you could get in Ireland was the frozen stuff. Clare and Edward's meal of choice was steak. Gerald's was breaded chicken breast with a grilled rasher. Katharine's was sausage, egg, and chips. Mine was prawn cocktail, lamb chops, or paella.

Prawn Cocktail with Marie Rose Sauce

On the occasions that we'd go around the country for a drive, we'd stop in a pub for lunch and I'd always get prawn cocktail. I just loved those plump, rosy delights of the sea and still do. The cocktail is always served with Marie Rose sauce, which is similar to what Americans know as Russian dressing. The sweetness of the ketchup in that sauce probably factored into my liking the dish so much as a youngster; I used to slather the prawns with as much of it as they could hold. (To understand the difference between prawns and shrimp, see Dublin Bay Prawns, page 78.)

Using a candy thermometer to make sure the liquid you cook the prawns in stays at 165°F (and no higher) guards against overcooking, which translates to tough prawns. That is the temperature at which protein starts to coagulate.

{ SERVES 4 }

3 cups court bouillon (page 245)

Kosher salt

16 Dublin Bay prawns or langoustines or large (U10) shrimp, peeled and deveined with tails left intact

Ice

2 large lettuce leaves

1/2 cup Marie Rose Sauce (page 248)

Poach and chill the prawns: In a saucepan, bring the court bouillon to 165°F, measuring the temperature with a candy thermometer. Lightly season the bouillon with salt. Add the prawns and poach them until pink and just cooked through, about 3 minutes. Add just enough ice (a handful) to bring the court bouillon's temperature below 165°F in order to stop the cooking process. Place the saucepan in the refrigerator uncovered and allow the shrimp to cool in the liquid, about 1 hour. Transfer the shrimp to a paper towel–lined plate. Discard the poaching liquid.

Assemble and serve: Cut the lettuce into julienne (thin strips). Divide the lettuce among 4 martini glasses or similar receptacles. Spoon 2 tablespoons of Marie Rose sauce onto the lettuce in each glass and place 4 shrimp attractively around it. Serve immediately. The prawns can be cooked the day before serving and refrigerated.

Pan-Roasted Rack of Lamb with Rosemary Jus

A special treat for me is rack of lamb, so rich and luxurious. The most common way to prepare it is to sear it and finish it in the oven, which is fine. My preferred method is stove-top pan-roasting. (See On Pan-Roasting, page 118.) Be sure to begin with an untrimmed rack; if you prefer for your butcher to French it, ask him to give you all the meat scraps, which you need for the glace (a concentrated meat jus) that is the base for the sauce accompanying this dish. When you buy lamb racks out of the meat case of a grocery store, they are usually trimmed of the fat and shoulder meat. For this reason, it is best to buy the lamb from a butcher.

Today I can't imagine eating the frozen corn on the cob I requested when growing up. As side dishes, I'd recommend Roasted Potatoes (page 182), Creamed Leeks (page 171), and "Marrowfat" Peas (page 172).

⟩ SERVES 4 TO 6 ⟨

LAMB RACK

2 (8-bone, 4½-pound) racks of lamb, chine bones removed by your butcher

6 tablespoons canola oil, plus more as needed

Kosher salt and freshly ground black pepper

2 teaspoons unsalted butter, at room temperature

2 teaspoons chopped garlic

2 teaspoons finely chopped fresh thyme leaves

LAMB GLACE

1 tablespoon canola oil

Lamb scraps (reserved from the whole rack)

½ yellow onion, chopped

1 celery stalk, chopped

1 carrot, peeled and chopped

2 cloves garlic, chopped

¼ cup dry red wine

1 cup lamb demi-glace (page 244)

10 sprigs fresh thyme

½ sprig fresh rosemary

1 large fresh bay leaf

JUS

2 teaspoons cold unsalted butter

1 large shallot, minced

½ teaspoon blanched and finely chopped rosemary leaves (see Notes on Herbs, page 64)

¼ teaspoon kosher salt

⅛ teaspoon freshly ground black pepper

French the racks: Using a boning knife, pull the fat cap off of each rack, trimming the racks down to their loin centers, known as the racks' eyes.

Using a boning knife, remove the shoulder blades from the fat caps and set them aside. Cut out and save any meat in the fat caps, trimming it into approximately 1-inch scraps. French the racks by cutting away all of the meat around and between the ribs to completely denude the bones down to the eyes. Use the butt-end of the knife to scrape any fat or membrane left on the bones. Set all the scraps aside. Discard the fat.

Make lamb glace: In a heavy saucepan over medium-high heat, heat the 1 tablespoon canola oil until it shimmers. Add the trimmed meat scraps, distributing them evenly over the bottom of the pan; let them cook undisturbed for 2 minutes. Turn the scraps over and sear for 2 to 3 minutes more until well browned. Stir in the onion, celery, carrot, and garlic and cook, stirring occasionally, for 3 to 4 minutes, until golden brown. Add the wine and use a flat-edged wooden spatula to scrape any brown bits from the bottom of the pan. Continue to cook until most of the wine has evaporated, about 2 minutes. Stir in the demi-glace,

{continued}

thyme and rosemary sprigs, and bay leaf. Bring the liquid to a simmer and cook for 12 to 15 minutes, skimming often to remove the impurities and fat that rise to the surface. Strain the glace through a fine-mesh sieve into a measuring cup and reserve.

Cook the lamb: In a large slope-sided sauté pan over medium-high heat, heat the 6 tablespoons canola oil until it shimmers. Season the racks well with salt and pepper and sear them, starting with the flesh sides down, for 2 minutes. Turn the racks over and sear for 2 more minutes. Using a meat fork to hold them in place, sear the racks for 2 minutes on both ends. Lower the heat to medium and start a process of cooking and basting the racks, turning them over and over, first on one side, then the other and on both ends, tilting the pan slightly so your spoon can scoop up the oil to baste with. Continue the process of turning and basting for about 15 minutes, until a cake tester inserted into the center of a rack and pressed against your lip feels warm. (If the oil begins to blacken during the process, pour it off and replace it with fresh oil.)

Add the final seasoning: As soon as the lamb is done, quickly add the 2 teaspoons of butter, 2 teaspoons of chopped garlic, and 2 teaspoons of chopped thyme to the pan and baste the racks quickly for several seconds, taking care to cook the garlic but not burn it, adjusting the heat if necessary. Transfer the racks to a cutting board to rest for 15 minutes.

Make the jus: Heat 1 teaspoon of the butter in a small saucepan over medium-high heat until it bubbles. Add the shallots and let them sweat for 1 minute until translucent. Stir in the reserved lamb glace and bring to a boil. Whisk in the remaining 1 teaspoon of butter and the rosemary, salt, and pepper. Keep warm over very low heat.

Present the dish: Transfer the sauce to a small pitcher or gravy boat. Carve the racks into chops and arrange them on a warm serving platter. Spoon some of the sauce over the chops, and serve with your chosen side dishes.

ON PAN-ROASTING

Searing and finishing in the oven is a common way to cook small items, like a steak, a piece of fish, a chunk of pork belly, or a rack of lamb, but not necessarily the ideal method of preparation. The method of pan-roasting I employ yields more consistent and often better results, which is why it is a preferred method in some of the world's best kitchens.

With pan-roasting, all the work is done on the stove top. You use a fair amount of oil and cook the items over medium to medium-high heat, turning them frequently and continually basting them with the hot oil so they cook and brown evenly. The technique requires a bit of dexterity and patience, but what you

wind up with is more succulent because the cooking is more even. The heat source is direct instead of emanating from the bottom of the oven.

As you go through the process, the oil may burn. It can be a challenge to maintain the heat in such a way to keep that from happening; it takes a little practice. Should the oil burn, simply dispose of it, wipe the pan clean, and continue with fresh oil.

Adding garlic and herbs for the final stage of basting imparts an extra level of complexity that you don't get from oven roasting. The flavor-infused oil finds its way into the meat or fish but remains forward on the palate.

Ramiro's Paella Valenciana

This paella is another one of those dishes that, though not Irish, is such an important part of my food history that I can't imagine not including it.

When I was about six years old my parents took us to visit a business colleague of my father's named Ramiro Ivorra. He (my father) was a travel agent. This gentleman's family lived in the mountains above Alicante in southeastern Spain. Ramiro's abuela (grandmother) made paella. The men went out in the fields to hunt rabbits while she made the rest of the preparations. I remember how the paella tasted. I also remember, traumatically, how the rabbits were killed and how the air smelled.

Paella had a special place in my heart, so it was often a birthday dinner request. My Da liked to make it for the family, especially when Ramiro showed up for a visit, usually unannounced and always very late at night. He'd come with plenty of bounty and we kids would all get out of bed to partake in it, gorging ourselves on massive Seville oranges.

My brother Gerald likes to tell the story of how he was once peeling the garlic for the paella and rubbed his eyes, which started stinging so much he thought he was going blind and so screamed bloody murder. Da thought he was trying to get out of going to Mass and sent Gerald to the garage for an hour and then to bed without dinner—and Mass.

Paella is a superlative example of the best type of food: simple country cooking, peasant style, with layers and layers of complex flavors. It is loaded with so many goodies, you don't need anything to accompany it, except for plenty of well-chilled, white Spanish wine. Fresh langoustines are difficult to find, but head-on shrimp are more readily available. If you absolutely must, use very large unpeeled shrimp.

Paella cannot be made ahead of time. Allow about an hour and a half for all the prep and the cooking. You will need a 17-inch paella pan (see Resources, page 263).

∗{ SERVES 8 TO 10 }∗

1 (3-pound) whole rabbit

Kosher salt

2 tablespoons canola oil

1/2 cup extra-virgin olive oil

3 tomatoes, peeled, cored, and chopped

20 cloves garlic, chopped

1 cup chopped fresh parsley

2 tablespoons saffron threads

20 littleneck clams, well rinsed

4 cups Spanish short-grain rice, such as Bomba or Calasparra (see Resources, page 263)

6 cups chicken stock (page 239)

2 large, fresh bay leaves

1 pound fresh squid, cleaned and cut into 1-inch pieces (2 cups)

3 dozen mussels, well rinsed and debearded (see Mussel Prep, page 35)

10 fresh whole langoustines, U8 live head-on shrimp, or U10 unpeeled shrimp

3 lemons, cut into wedges, for garnish

Cut up the rabbit: Cut the rabbit into 14 bone-in pieces: 8 breast, 2 whole front legs, 2 back legs, and 2 back thighs. Using a boning knife, remove the front legs and leave them whole. (They are much smaller than the back legs.) Remove the back legs and separate the legs and thighs. Using a chef's knife or cleaver (best), cut the rabbit's body crosswise into 4 pieces, then cut each piece in half lengthwise.

{continued}

Brown the rabbit: Season the rabbit pieces well with salt. In a large slope-sided sauté pan over medium-high heat, heat the canola oil until it shimmers. Add the rabbit pieces and sauté for 5 minutes on each side, until nicely browned. Transfer them to a platter.

Compose the paella: In a 17-inch paella pan over high heat, heat the olive oil until it shimmers. Stir in the tomatoes, garlic, and parsley. Cook for 3 to 4 minutes, stirring constantly, until most of the water has evaporated from the tomatoes. Stir in the saffron and let it cook for 1 minute to diffuse its color. Stir in the clams and cook for 1 minute. Add the rice and cook for 2 minutes, stirring constantly. Pour in the chicken stock and add the bay leaves,

squid, and rabbit pieces with any of their collected juices, stirring well to combine. Lower the heat to medium. Dot the surface of the mixture with the mussels, standing them hinge-down in the rice. Cover the surface with the langoustines or shrimp.

Cook the paella: Cover the pan loosely with heavy-duty aluminum foil and cook the paella undisturbed for 25 to 30 minutes, using tongs to turn the langoustines over halfway through. The paella is done when the liquid has been absorbed, the rice is al dente, the seafood is cooked, and a light crust has formed on the bottom of the pan.

Present the dish: Dot the paella with the lemon wedges and serve piping hot from the pan.

HALLOWEEN

~

HALLOWEEN happens in the middle of the autumn, a time of year when we'd get all kinds of fruits that we just didn't see the rest of the year in the markets—exotic things like pineapple, pomegranate, coconut, and kiwi fruit. My parents, ever the fans of rare gustatory treats, would buy a big quantity of them, along with Brazil nuts, hazelnuts, and almonds all in the shell, and we'd break out the nutcrackers.

Halloween is a big deal in Irish history and folklore. It has been celebrated since ancient times. Samhain (pronounced SOW-an), the festival marking the harvest, is mentioned in some of the earliest Irish literature. The celebration was significant because it was the time to prepare for winter, but there was also a mystical aspect. It was believed that during Samhain the souls of the dead could return to Earth.

A lot of pagan holidays were converted into Christian holidays such as Christmas and Easter, around which huge celebrations took place. In Ireland, Halloween is a prime example; everybody participates in it to the max. There was a huge party in our house every year that required days of preparation: cleaning the house, acquiring all the foodstuffs, prepping them, getting dressed and made up, setting up the Halloween games. It was also a big day of anticipation, because we'd have to wait for Da to get home from work to have dinner. By that time, we were totally wound up.

Before the party, we'd have our traditional Halloween dinner—Boiling Bacon with Parsley Sauce (page 122), Colcannon (mashed potatoes and kale, page 181), lots of side dishes, and Barmbrack (page 225) for dessert and then a party afterward. Our parents used to wrap coins in foil and put them in the colcannon and all us kids wound up 73 pence richer at dinner.

After dinner, Da would make us up as ghosts, witches, and ghouls and we'd get all dressed up and go out door-to-door, knocking on the neighbors' doors and pleading, "Help the Halloween party," the Irish equivalent of "Trick or treat?" They would give out fruit or nuts, never candy as in the States. Eventually, we'd make it back to the house where we'd play games, like bobbing for apples or dunk your head for a coin, and plunder our stash late into the evening. As we got older, we'd skip the door-to-door part and go to a bonfire instead, where we'd light illegal fireworks until it was time to reconvene at the house for the party.

Boiling Bacon with Parsley Sauce

We'd always have boiling bacon for Halloween, but it's good on any winter day. Because there was a lot of other preparation to do on Halloween, it was an ideal dish to make—you just put the pork belly in a pot on the stove and let it simmer away. I'm including a related recipe for Corned Beef (page 124) because it goes well with the same sauce and accompaniments: Boiled Russet Potatoes (page 177), Braised York Cabbage (page 163), Colcannon (page 181), and always Barmbrack (page 225) for dessert.

Before it is boiled, the bacon needs to brine for 3 days, so plan accordingly. You can boil the bacon up to 3 days before serving and reheat it by simmering it in water until it's warm all the way through, about 20 minutes. Then broil it just before serving. Make or reheat the parsley sauce while the bacon broils.

❧ SERVES 6 ❧

1 (2 1/2-pound rectangle) pork belly, preferably Kurobuta or Berkshire, rind removed
2 quarts Curing Brine for Pork (page 238)
1 1/2 cups warm Parsley Sauce, for serving (page 253)

Brine the bacon: Place the pork belly in a 2 1/2-gallon zip-top bag placed in a large bowl. Pour the brine into the bag. Seal the bag, removing as much air as possible so that the pork is completely submerged. Refrigerate the pork in the bag for 3 days.

Boil the pork: Remove the pork from the brine; discard the brine and thoroughly rinse the pork under cold running water. In a large pot, cover the pork with cold water and boil it over high heat for 3 hours, or until fork tender. Add water as needed throughout the process so the pork remains covered at all times.

Broil the bacon: Heat the broiler, positioning the rack 8 inches from the heating element. Remove the bacon from the pot, blot it dry with paper towels, and place it on a rimmed baking sheet. Broil it for several minutes until the top is dark brown and crisp. Be patient with the broiling. It doesn't have to be high temperature or close to the heat: you want a nice, even caramelization and crunchiness on the top.

Present the dish: Spoon the warm parsley sauce into a small bowl. Transfer the bacon to a cutting board and slice it 1/2 inch thick, cutting crosswise. Arrange the bacon on a serving platter or individual plates; serve with the sauce on the side, along with your chosen side dishes.

Corned Beef

This brined and boiled beef is similar to Boiling Bacon (page 122) and goes well with the same accompaniments, but of course, it's beef, not pork. The beef has to be started 17 days before you want to eat it. Once it's cooked, you can store it refrigerated in its cooking liquid for up to 3 days and reheat it by simmering it in water until it's warm all the way through, about 20 minutes.

{ SERVES 8 TO 10 }

BRINE

2 quarts water

¾ cup kosher salt

1 tablespoon pink curing salt, such as sel rose or Insta Cure #1 (see Resources, page 263)

½ cup light brown sugar

3 tablespoons prepared pickling spice

2 quarts ice water

1 (5-pound) beef brisket, with the deckle intact

RUB

3 large fresh bay leaves, torn into small pieces

9 cloves garlic, crushed

3 tablespoons yellow mustard seed

2 tablespoons coarsely ground black pepper

½ teaspoon ground cinnamon

½ teaspoon ground allspice

¼ teaspoon freshly grated nutmeg

¼ teaspoon ground cayenne pepper

¼ teaspoon ground coriander

2 cups warm Parsley Sauce, for serving (page 253)

Brine the meat: In a saucepan over high heat, heat the water, kosher salt, curing salt, brown sugar, and pickling spice, stirring until the salt is dissolved. Add the ice water. Place the beef in a 2-gallon zip-top bag. Place the bag in a stockpot and pour the brine into it, over the meat. Seal the bag, squeezing as much air out of it as possible so the meat remains completely submerged. Refrigerate the beef in the bag for 10 days.

Rinse the beef: Remove the beef from the brine; discard the brine. Thoroughly rinse the beef under cold running water, removing all of the spices, and blot it dry on paper towels.

Season the beef with the rub: Combine all of the rub ingredients in a small bowl. Spread the rub over the beef with your hands, covering all surfaces, and place the beef in a 2-gallon zip-top bag; seal the bag, squeezing out as much of the air as

possible. Place the bag on a baking dish and refrigerate for a week, turning the bag over once a day. This is known as dry brining—you will notice each day that more liquid leaches from the beef.

Cook the beef: On the day you wish to serve the beef, place it in a large pot with all of the accumulated juices in the bag. Add water as needed to cover the meat and bring to a boil over high heat. Lower the heat to medium, cover the pot, and let the beef simmer for 3 hours, until fork tender but not falling apart.

Present the dish: Spoon the warm parsley sauce into a small bowl. Drain the beef and transfer it to a cutting board. Let it rest for 15 minutes and then slice it ½ inch thick, cutting lengthwise, against the grain. Arrange the meat on a serving platter or individual plates; serve with the sauce on the side, along with your chosen side dishes.

CHRISTMAS EVE AND CHRISTMAS DAY

I REMEMBER DISTINCTLY how at 5:30 p.m. on Christmas Eve, as soon as the day's work was done, everybody in Ireland would pile in to their local pub, celebrating the holiday and the fact that they were all on a break—practically the whole country shut down for the ensuing twelve days of Christmas. Good luck finding a seat if you didn't get there early. But forget finding a restaurant open for supper on Christmas Eve. This was a time to be with family.

There was always a strange hush or calmness in our house on Christmas Eve because all the shopping had been done, most of the food had been prepared, and Da had closed up the office for the holiday season.

When we were grown up enough, we'd go to Midnight Mass after dinner, which was a simple affair, say Shepherd's Pie (page 65) or Beef Stew (page 72), because the next day would be the opposite. After Mass, we'd come home for Spiced Beef Sandwiches (page 129) and a glass of beer and then hit the hay. More likely than not, I'd be dreaming of the various desserts we'd been prepping for weeks: Christmas pudding, Christmas cake, and my beloved mince pies. (See Chapter Nine.)

At the crack of dawn on Christmas Day, we were up to see what Santa had left us. We'd have a big breakfast, then go visit the aunts and uncles, Nana and Granda (my Da's parents), and Granny and Granda (my mother's parents) before heading home for dinner.

In Ireland, everybody has both roast turkey and ham for Christmas dinner. The day was always stressful because Da wanted all of the dishes to come out at the same time. When the turkey came out of the oven, there would be the inevitable Christmas argument between Da and Mam. Da would get in a dither worrying about how all of the various components of the meal would come together. The more Mam tried to calm him, the more heated the debate became. The scene was totally needless, really. The turkey could rest for at least an hour and still be hot, leaving plenty of time to get everything else together.

One year when I was about fourteen, Da bought a turkey that was not plucked or gutted. On Christmas Eve, he got me into the kitchen to do the dirty work. It was hanging off the door and my arm was stuck up it pulling out the innards. It was all I could do to keep from retching.

On Saint Stephen's Day, the day after Christmas, we always went to Anthony and Eithne's, my dad's brother and his wife. The grown-ups ate fancy fillet steak, the kids ate Christmas leftovers while watching the annual airing of Willy Wonka and the Chocolate Factory, and everything was good.

Spiced Beef Sandwiches

Spiced beef is a big Dublin tradition at Christmastime. It is served after Midnight Mass on Christmas Eve, thinly sliced and piled between two slices of white bread such as my Batch Loaf (page 194) and always accompanied by hot English mustard. The beef has to cure for a week to attain its flavor and is always served cold, so plan accordingly.

{ SERVES 8 }

2 packed tablespoons light brown sugar

2 tablespoons Dublin Spice (see Dublin Spice, below)

1½ teaspoons kosher salt

2 teaspoons pink curing salt, such as Sel Rose or Insta Cure #1 (see Resources, page 263)

1 (3-pound) eye of round roast

1 (12-ounce) bottle Guinness

Pullman bread (page 196) or Batch Loaf (page 194), cut into 16 slices

English mustard (such as Colman's), for serving

Season the beef: In a small bowl, combine the sugar, spices, kosher salt, and curing salt. With your hands, rub the spice mix all over the meat, creating a thick coating. Place the meat in a 2-gallon zip-top bag. Refrigerate for 1 week, rolling the meat in the accumulated juices once a day.

Cook the beef: Transfer the meat (do not rinse it) to a pot. Add the Guinness and enough water to cover the meat. Bring to a boil over medium-high heat. Lower the heat to medium, cover the pot,

and simmer for 3 hours, until fork tender but not falling apart. Remove the pot from the heat and let the beef cool completely in its cooking liquid. Drain the meat and place it in a clean food storage container; refrigerate it for at least 4 hours before serving. Tightly wrapped in plastic wrap, the beef can be refrigerated for up to 3 days.

Present the dish: Spread the bread slices with mustard and make sandwiches with the beef, thinly sliced.

DUBLIN SPICE

Dublin Spice is the mix used for spiced beef, which is really a Dublin tradition. No two people use the same recipe probably, but this is the combination I like: in a spice grinder, grind 2 tablespoons juniper berries into a fine powder. Transfer it to a small bowl and combine with 3 tablespoons ground black pepper, 2 tablespoons ground allspice, and 2 tablespoons ground cloves. Store in an airtight container for up to 3 months. Makes about ½ cup.

Roast Turkey with Stuffing and Gravy

We don't have Thanksgiving in Ireland, but we do serve roast turkey for Christmas dinner, as well as for other big family affairs because it feeds a lot of people. Next to the turkey, there'd also be a Baked Cured Ham (page 132).

This is a foolproof way to make a beautifully browned roast turkey. Get rid of that plastic pop-up thing on the bird if it has one. You really don't need to use a meat thermometer at all—this recipe works perfectly if you cook the turkey for 15 minutes per pound, plus an additional 15 minutes. For a 15-pound turkey, that means 240 minutes, or 4 hours total cooking time: 3 hours at 300°F and 1 hour at 400°F. (If your bird is a different weight, add or subtract minutes to the 300°F roasting time.)

You can make stock out of the neck and gizzard and use it for gravy, filling in with chicken stock if need be. If there are leftovers, be sure to remove the stuffing from the bird completely before refrigerating. Save the carcass for stock or soup.

Serve the roast turkey with Boiled Russet Potatoes and Roasted Potatoes (pages 177 and 182), Glazed Baby Carrots (page 166), and Brussels Sprouts with Bacon (page 165).

} SERVES 8 TO 10 {

STUFFING AND TURKEY

1 teaspoon canola oil

8 ounces thick-sliced streaky (American) bacon, diced (see On Irish Bacon, page 15)

1 large russet potato, peeled, diced, and held in cold water

1 large yellow onion, diced

1 (1-pound) sourdough bread loaf, cut into 1/2-inch cubes (about 10 cups)

1/4 cup chopped fresh parsley leaves

3 tablespoons chopped fresh sage leaves

2 tablespoons chopped fresh rosemary leaves (see Notes on Herbs, page 64)

2 tablespoons chopped fresh thyme leaves

1 teaspoon kosher salt

1/2 teaspoon freshly ground black pepper

4 cups chicken stock (page 239)

5 large eggs, lightly beaten

1 (15-pound) turkey, preferably purchased from a farmers' market

8 slices thick-sliced streaky (American) bacon

GRAVY

1/4 cup all-purpose flour

3 cups chicken stock (page 239)

2 cloves garlic, crushed

1/2 teaspoon kosher salt

Make the stuffing: In a large slope-sided sauté pan over medium-high heat, heat the oil until it shimmers. Cook the diced bacon, stirring frequently until the fat is partially rendered and the bacon is lightly browned, about 10 minutes. Drain the potatoes and add them, along with the onions, to the pan; cook, stirring frequently, until the onions are translucent and the potatoes are just cooked through, about 10 minutes. Transfer the mixture to a large bowl and stir in the bread, parsley, sage, rosemary, thyme, salt, pepper, 2 cups of the stock, and the eggs, combining them well.

Stuff the turkey: Preheat the oven to 300°F. Place a V-shaped roasting rack in a large flameproof roasting pan. Fill the turkey's cavity with the stuffing. Tie the legs together tightly with kitchen twine. Place the turkey, breast up, on the rack. Arrange the bacon slices over the breast, covering it completely, then cover with aluminum foil.

Roast the turkey: Pour the remaining 2 cups of stock into the pan. Bake the turkey for 3 hours. Remove the foil, saving it for tenting later. Remove and discard the bacon. Increase the temperature to 400°F and roast for 1 hour more. The turkey should be a deep golden brown and a metal cake tester inserted into the thickest part of the thigh should feel hot to the touch when pressed against your lip. (An internal temperature of 165°F if using a meat thermometer.) Transfer the turkey to a cutting board and cover loosely with the aluminum foil to rest for at least 20 minutes.

Make the gravy: Meanwhile, pour the pan juices into a fat separator or measuring cup. Return ¼ cup of fat to the roasting pan and skim off and discard the rest, leaving only the pan juices. Place the pan over medium heat and use a flat-edged wooden spatula to stir the flour into the fat. Add the stock slowly, scraping up all the browned bits from the bottom of the pan and stirring well so no lumps form. Add the pan juices, garlic, and salt and simmer for several minutes until the gravy is thickened and the flour is cooked. Strain the gravy through a fine-mesh sieve into a saucepan and keep it warm, covered, over very low heat, stirring occasionally.

Present the dish: When you are ready to eat, transfer the turkey to a platter. Pour the gravy into a gravy boat. Carve the turkey at table, removing the legs whole and cutting the drumsticks from the thighs, then slicing along both sides of the breast. Pass the gravy and your chosen side dishes to your guests.

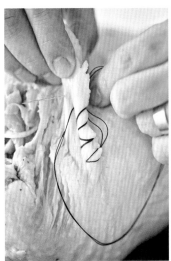

Baked Cured Ham

Just as Roast Leg of Pork (page 112) was a mainstay of Easter dinner, ham that we cured ourselves was always served on our Christmas table alongside the turkey and all its trimmings (see Roast Turkey with Stuffing and Gravy, page 130). I can't really say why we'd have ham instead of roast pork; it was just what we did on Christmas.

A leg of pork is a large cut (they can run upwards of 24 pounds), is relatively inexpensive, and feeds a lot of people. It's something we almost always had in the house because it's great cold and makes a great sandwich. A ham cured this way may not be pink all the way through, and that's fine. If you plan to cure often, I recommend you buy a meat injector (see Resources, page 263) to inject the brine into the center of the meat.

The pork leg must be brined for 14 days before roasting, so plan accordingly.

} SERVES 12 {

1 (12-pound), hind pork leg, preferably Kurobuta or Berkshire, rind removed
10 quarts Curing Brine for Pork (page 238)
English mustard (such as Colman's), for serving

Brine the ham: In a 16- to 22-quart, nonreactive stockpot or foodsafe bucket, submerge the pork leg in the brine. Cover it with a plate to help keep it submerged. Refrigerate it in the pot for 14 days.

Rinse the ham: Remove the pork leg from the brine; discard the brine. Thoroughly rinse the leg under cold running water. Blot it dry on paper towels.

Roast the ham: Preheat the oven to 275°F. Place the ham skin-side up on a V-shaped roasting rack set over a baking sheet. Bake for about 4 hours (allow 20 minutes per pound), until a meat thermometer inserted into the thickest part of the meat (but not touching the bone) registers 165°F. When the ham is done, transfer it to a cutting board and let it rest for 30 minutes before carving.

Present the dish: Spoon the mustard into a small serving bowl. Carve the ham at the table, arranging the slices on a serving platter or individual plates. Pass the mustard and your chosen side dishes to the diners.

CHAPTER SIX

From Restaurant Eve

The recipes in this chapter are for dishes from the repertoire at Restaurant Eve. Many of them are certainly more involved than other recipes in this book and present a challenge for the home cook.

In a restaurant setting, we have a team of trained chefs working on various components of a dish at the same time. The home cook is generally on his or her own. I offer these recipes for two reasons: to illustrate the complexity behind food that appears to be simple and to offer something for those experienced cooks who enjoy a good challenge. It's always a good idea to read all the way through a recipe before beginning, but in this chapter, I think it's a must.

A bit of history about the journey that led to Restaurant Eve: Growing up in Ireland, where food was such a central part of my family's life, my parents instilled in me the importance of sourcing the best seasonal ingredients. This appreciation was always going to be the driving force behind any restaurant of my own. After almost ten years of learning the craft of cooking, particularly French technique, I felt that I finally had the wherewithal to go out on my own.

When Meshelle and I first started thinking about a project, the original concept was to open an Irish guesthouse in the Virginia hunt country. That rural but gentrified location seemed a fitting backdrop to merge my more refined cooking skills with the finest ingredients the Mid-Atlantic region had to offer and interpret the foods I grew up with in Ireland.

None of the properties we looked at were ever really realistic; as it turned out, they were way out of our price range. So we decided to look for a small space for a restaurant in Old Town Alexandria. In 2002, Meshelle found the perfect spot, an early-nineteenth-century townhouse that had been converted to commercial use and housed an existing, but failing, restaurant.

Now an inn was one thing; a restaurant was quite another. You could get away with serving Irish breakfast, modernized steak and kidney pie, and Christmas pudding in a bucolic setting with guest rooms, but I wasn't confident that an Irish fine-dining restaurant would have credibility without the country inn trappings. Irish cooking just didn't have a great reputation in the United States and therefore we put it on the back burner.

We designed Restaurant Eve as two restaurants in one space. The Bistro, where we served rustic, modern American dishes, and The Tasting Room, where we offered multicourse tasting menus in a more formal setting.

The reviews were good from the start. So good, in fact, that I felt more confident about introducing great Irish ingredients to the menu, both those I made myself based on traditional recipes (white pudding, black pudding, brown bread, Irish sausage, etc.) and those we could import from Ireland, such as Kerrygold butter and great farmhouse cheeses. This is how Irish-inspired dishes made their way onto the menu at Restaurant Eve. The recipes that follow are just a taste of them and represent the full range of the dining experience we offer at Restaurant Eve in the order they would be served, from Caesar salad to Irish coffee.

Irish Caesar Salad

This is a salad we sometimes offer for Lickety Split, a prix-fixe two-course lunch we offer at the bar of Restaurant Eve for diners on the go. We use Cashel Blue cheese and brown bread as a riff on what has become an American classic. Feel free to make the brown bread topping crouton size. At the restaurant, we use fine bread crumbs.

{ SERVES 4 }

DRESSING

1 large egg

2 cloves garlic, crushed

2 tablespoons freshly squeezed lemon juice

6 anchovy fillets

1/2 cup canola oil

1/2 cup extra-virgin olive oil

Kosher salt

SALAD

2 small slices Brown Bread (page 192)

2 large heads romaine lettuce, dark outer leaves discarded, cleaned, and cut crosswise into 2-inch pieces

4 ounces Cashel Blue cheese, crumbled (see Resources, page 263)

1 teaspoon freshly ground pepper

Make the dressing: Combine the egg, garlic, lemon juice, and anchovies in the bowl of a food processor. With the machine running, add the oils in a thin stream through the small tube in the bowl's lid to create an emulsion. Add salt to taste.

Make the bread crumbs: Preheat a toaster or conventional oven to 350°F. Crumble the bread into fine crumbs and place them on a small baking sheet. Bake them lightly for several minutes, stirring occasionally, until they are crunchy.

Assemble the salad: In a large bowl, combine the lettuce, cheese, and 1 cup of the dressing, tossing to coat the leaves well. Mound the salad on 4 plates and sprinkle them with the bread crumbs and ground pepper. (Leftover dressing can be stored in the refrigerator for up to 3 days.)

Irish BLT

Growing up in Ireland, it was rare to have sandwiches in our household, other than for school or on Christmas Eve, when we'd have Spiced Beef Sandwiches (page 129). My Da was never a fan of them for some reason, but I like a good sandwich, and there are few better than a BLT. By the way, eating a sandwich without a glass of milk should be illegal.

I developed this BLT version (made with Restaurant Eve's Pork Loin Bacon, page 14) to serve in the summertime at Restaurant Eve, when tomatoes are in season. Make sure you have good ventilation when you make it; I prepared it once in the studio of Martha Stewart's radio show and filled the whole place with smoke when I fried the bacon slices.

The tomato marmalade can be made well ahead of time. Although the bacon for the sandwich can be eaten cold and therefore cooked ahead of time, the sandwich is so much better made with bacon hot from the skillet.

{ 1 SANDWICH }

2 teaspoons unsalted butter, at room temperature

2 (1/2-inch-thick) slices Pullman Loaf (page 196) or any good-quality sandwich bread made without sweeteners

1 teaspoon canola oil

3 (1/4-inch-thick) slices Restaurant Eve's Pork Loin Bacon (page 14)

1 teaspoon Basic Mayonnaise (page 247)

A few Bibb or leaf lettuce leaves

2 tablespoons Tomato Marmalade (page 256)

Toast the bread: Butter the bread thinly and evenly on all sides. Heat a slope-sided sauté pan over medium-high heat until a drop of water sizzles and disappears instantly. Arrange the bread in the pan and toast until golden brown on both sides, turning frequently to achieve even toasting without burning. Set aside.

Cook the bacon: In a nonstick slope-sided sauté pan over medium-high heat, heat the oil until it shimmers. Sauté the bacon slices for about a minute on each side, until they are golden brown and cooked through. Transfer the bacon to a paper towel–lined plate.

Assemble the sandwich: Spread 1/2 teaspoon of the mayonnaise on one side of each slice of toasted bread. Place even layers of lettuce and bacon on one piece (the bottom) and spread the tomato marmalade on the other piece (the top). Put the sandwich together and cut in half diagonally.

Braised Lamb Shoulder Sandwiches with Harissa Mayonnaise

For this complex but spectacular sandwich, a rich, buttery lamb stew, called a daube in French, is piled on a potato roll with spicy harissa mayonnaise, caramelized onions, and greens. Before making the daube, see Emulsions Made with Cold Butter, page 142, and Making Sauces for Meat, page 142.

We bake our own Potato Rolls (page 197) at Restaurant Eve, but feel free to substitute any high-quality soft roll. A lamb shoulder runs about 6 pounds, so you will have more meat than necessary. Freeze the unused meat for another use.

The harissa mayonnaise can be made up to 2 days ahead of time. The lamb can be cubed and the reduction made the day before. Make the caramelized onions while the braising liquid is reducing. Assemble the sandwiches when ready to eat.

{ MAKES 4 SANDWICHES, PLUS ADDITIONAL MEAT }

MIREPOIX

4 large onions, peeled and quartered

3 carrots, peeled and cut into 3-inch pieces

3 heads garlic, halved crosswise

2 tablespoons extra-virgin olive oil

LAMB BRAISE

1 (6-pound) square-cut, bone-in lamb shoulder

Kosher salt and freshly ground black pepper

1 tablespoon canola oil

2 bay leaves

1 teaspoon black peppercorns

1/2 bunch fresh thyme

6 large sprigs fresh rosemary

4 quarts chicken stock (page 239)

LAMB REDUCTION

2 tablespoons unsalted butter

2 tablespoons chopped garlic

2 large shallots, finely chopped

10 cups braising liquid (from cooking the lamb)

LAMB DAUBE

1 1/2 cups Lamb Reduction

1 cup cold unsalted butter, cut into 1/2-inch cubes

1 teaspoon chopped fresh thyme leaves

1/2 teaspoon blanched and finely chopped rosemary leaves (see Notes on Herbs, page 64)

Kosher salt and freshly ground black pepper

SANDWICHES

4 Potato Rolls, halved (page 197)

8 teaspoons unsalted butter, at room temperature

8 teaspoons Harissa Mayonnaise (page 250)

1 cup mixed salad greens

Lamb Daube

1/2 cup Caramelized Onions (page 257)

Make the mirepoix: Preheat the oven to 400°F. In a large flameproof roasting pan, mix the onions, carrots, and garlic heads with the oil. Roast the vegetables for 1 hour until they are lightly browned.

Remove from the oven and set aside. Lower the heat to 300°F.

Braise the lamb: Season the shoulder well on all sides with salt and pepper. In a large slope-sided

sauté pan over medium-high heat, heat the oil until it shimmers. Sear the shoulder for a couple of minutes on all sides until golden brown. Place the shoulder on top of the mirepoix and distribute the bay leaves, peppercorns, thyme, and rosemary around it. Pour enough chicken stock into the pan to come halfway up the lamb. Cover the pan with heavy-duty aluminum foil and roast the lamb until it is fork tender but not falling apart, 3 to 4 hours, basting every hour. Remove the pan from the oven, let it cool to room temperature, and refrigerate overnight still covered. (It will be much easier to cut the lamb into nice, neat cubes when it's cold.)

Cut the lamb: The next day, the cooking liquid and a layer of fat will have congealed around the lamb. Remove and discard the congealed fat on top of the cooking liquid. Lift the lamb from the congealed liquid and transfer to a cutting board. Pull the meat off the bone, removing and discarding any bits of cartilage, fat, and tendon; you want pure, clean meat. Cut the meat into $1/2$-inch cubes, taking care not to overhandle it so it remains in chunks. You will have between $1^1/2$ to $1^3/4$ pounds of meat, or about 5 cups. Reserve 2 cups of it for the sandwiches and store the rest for another use.

Strain the braising liquid: Place the roasting pan over medium heat to melt the congealed cooking liquid. Using a mesh spider, remove and discard as many solids as you can from the pan. Strain the cooking liquid first through a wide-mesh sieve, then a fine one, and reserve it, making sure that all the fat has been skimmed off the top. Discard any remaining solids. (See Straining Stock and Braising Liquids, page 147.) There should be about 10 cups of liquid.

Make the reduction: In a large stockpot over medium heat, heat the butter until it bubbles. Add the garlic and shallots and let them sweat until tender, about 5 minutes. Pour the braising liquid into the pot. Bring it to a boil over medium-high heat, then lower the heat to medium. Simmer the liquid, skimming off any fat or scum every so often, for 75 to 90 minutes, until it has reduced to a syrupy consistency. Strain into a small saucepan through a fine-mesh sieve and keep warm over low heat. There should be about $1^1/2$ cups.

Make the daube: Raise the heat under the lamb reduction to medium. Gently whisk in the butter, 1 tablespoon at a time. Add the thyme and rosemary. Season to taste with salt and pepper. Fold the 2 cups of lamb cubes into the sauce and keep the daube warm over very low heat.

Assemble the sandwiches: Butter both halves of each roll generously with the butter, spreading a thin, even coat from side to side. Toast the roll halves on a griddle or in a hot slope-sided sauté pan over medium heat until golden, about 1 to 2 minutes, turning them over so they have some crunch on both sides. Blot the buttered sides of the rolls on paper towels after toasting. Spread 1 teaspoon of harissa mayonnaise on each half of all 4 rolls. Put a small handful of greens on the bottom half of each sandwich. Top each greens mound with $1/2$ cup of the daube, one-quarter of the onions, and finally the top of the roll. Serve immediately.

EMULSIONS MADE WITH COLD BUTTER

Often used in classical French cooking, delicate butter emulsions are a rich, refined, and subtle way to thicken sauces and create glazes. In them, butter is employed as the thickening agent rather than starches such as flour or cornstarch, which can leave an aftertaste. In this book, certain meat sauces, such as the ones in Pork Belly with Braised Cabbage and Poached Apples (page 148) and Pan-Roasted Loin of Venison (page 152) are enriched with a butter emulsion, and vegetables such as Glazed Baby Carrots (page 166) and "Marrowfat" Peas (page 172) use a butter emulsion in their glaze. It is useful to understand the chemistry that makes these emulsions work.

When cold butter is slowly stirred into a hot liquid, be it water leaching from vegetables as they're cooking or a reduction of wine and stock or demi-glace, the fat molecules and milk solids in the butter suspend themselves evenly in the liquid, binding everything together in what is known as an emulsion. The butter must be cold and the sauce hot; if either or both of those components are at room temperature, the butter will melt and separate from the liquid, creating a greasy, broken sauce. Once a butter emulsion is achieved, it is sensitive to high heat, because as everyone knows, oil and water tend to repel each other. This is why dishes using these emulsions should be served as quickly as possible. You can keep them warm over very low heat for a short period of time, but bear in mind that they are temperamental.

MAKING SAUCES FOR MEAT

For me, what separates great restaurants from good restaurants is the art of making sauce. Over the years, I've taught hundreds of people how to do it. It's one of those things where people tend to revert to a lazy method, just throwing in things such as random vegetable scraps or meat trimmings. They are not thinking about what they want their end product to be or not taking the necessary time to develop the sauce through a variety of steps along the way.

The correct method involves browning and caramelizing scraps of meat trimmed from the meat for which the sauce is being made (chefs refer to this concentration of flavors as an essence); adding to them some stock or demi-glace and acid (such as red wine, other liquors, or vinegars) with a combination of aromatic vegetables known as a mirepoix,

and cooking the mixture until it is reduced; straining the reduction; and then thickening the sauce by introducing cold cubes of butter into it, as explained in Emulsions Made with Cold Butter, above. At this point, final seasoning additions are made, be they chopped fresh herbs or small amounts of the acid, spice, salt, and pepper already used.

Nothing is arbitrary in sauce making. The meat scraps must be cut into small, evenly sized pieces to extract the most flavor from them. The aromatics must reflect the overall profile of the dish. The stock and demi-glace used must be of the highest quality, as must the butter used to thicken the sauce. Most importantly, you must take time with each step if you want the end result to be superlative. I encourage home cooks to aspire to this level of excellence.

Foie Gras with Black Pudding and Pears

In the cuisine of many continental European countries, black pudding is featured as a main ingredient, such as the Spanish morcilla and French boudin noir. In Ireland, I've only ever seen it at breakfast time as a side dish or occasionally as a first course, such as Black Pudding and Onions (page 47), so I love the idea of pairing this earthy ingredient with a luxurious ingredient like foie gras. It's really a perfect marriage of classic French and traditional Irish cooking.

⁂❦ SERVES 4 AS A FIRST COURSE ❧⁂

SAUCE

3 slices (about 3 ounces) thick-cut streaky (American) bacon, cut into 4 by 1/2-inch strips (lardons) (see On Irish Bacon, page 15)

2 large shallots, minced

2 pears, such as Anjou or Bosc, peeled, cored, and cut into 1/2-inch cubes

1/2 cup Calvados

1/2 cup veal demi-glace (page 244)

1 tablespoon cold unsalted butter

1 tablespoon chopped fresh thyme leaves

1 teaspoon freshly squeezed lemon juice

Kosher salt and freshly ground black pepper

PUDDING

1 tablespoon canola oil

4 ounces Black Pudding (page 22), casing removed, cut crosswise into 1-inch slices

4 (1 1/2-inch-thick) slices Grade-A foie gras (2 ounces each, see Resources, page 263)

Kosher salt and freshly ground black pepper

Micro arugula, for garnish (optional)

Make the sauce: In a slope-sided sauté pan over medium heat, lightly brown the bacon, stirring often, about 5 minutes. Stir in the shallots with a flat-edged wooden spoon and let them sweat for 30 seconds. Stir in the pears and sauté for 30 seconds. Add the Calvados, scraping up the brown bits from the bottom of the pan with the edge of the spoon. Stir in the demi-glace and bring to a boil. Stir in the butter and let the sauce cook for 1 minute to slightly reduce. Stir in the thyme and lemon juice. Season to taste with salt and pepper. Keep warm covered over very low heat, stirring occasionally.

Brown the black pudding: Heat the oil in another slope-sided sauté pan over medium-high heat until it shimmers. Brown the black pudding slices for 30 seconds on each side to give them a nice sear. Transfer them to a cutting board, quarter them, and stir them into the sauce. (Move the slope-sided sauté pan off the heat while you do this.)

Sear the foie gras: Using a sharp paring knife, lightly score the foie gras slices in a 1/2-inch grid on both sides and season them with salt and pepper. Return the slope-sided sauté pan to medium-high heat and sauté the foie gras for about 2 minutes on each side, until medium rare. (The slices should feel like a rare steak when you poke them with your finger.)

Present the dish: Divide the sauce equally among 4 pasta bowls and place a slice of foie gras in each one. Garnish with the micro arugula if you wish.

Kerrygold Butter–Poached Lobster with Parsnips

Cooking lobster in two steps, first just enough to be able to remove it from the shell, and then poaching gently in an emulsion of butter and water (known as beurre monté) imparts a smooth, silky mouthfeel and ensures that the meat will not be rubbery. Although clarified butter is a well-known condiment for lobster, it can be unctuous and leave your palate greasy. A much worthier foil is a butter emulsion such as the one in this recipe, made with lobster stock. (See Emulsions Made with Cold Butter, page 142.)

In the Restaurant Eve kitchen several years ago, I gathered our team of chefs to blind-taste some of the world's great butters. Unanimously, Ireland's own Kerrygold was the top choice. It's made with milk from grass-fed cows raised on co-ops of small farms. Its sweetness enhances breads and potatoes beautifully.

The lobster can be cooked and shelled the day before serving. The parsnips can be blanched and the lobster stock made the day before, too. Warm the stock in a saucepan over low heat for a few minutes before using it to finish the parsnips. You will need poultry shears and a very large stockpot for cooking the lobsters.

⟨ SERVES 4 ⟩

LOBSTER

4 (1½-pound) live lobsters

1 gallon plus 3 tablespoons water

¼ cup distilled white vinegar

1 pound cold unsalted Kerrygold butter, cut into 1-inch cubes (see Resources, page 263)

Micro cilantro, for garnish (see Resources, page 263)

LOBSTER STOCK

¼ cup unsalted Kerrygold butter

1 celery stalk, coarsely chopped

2 shallots, coarsely chopped

½ bulb fennel, coarsely chopped

2 carrots, peeled and coarsely chopped

1 tablespoon tomato paste

1 sprig fresh thyme

1 fresh bay leaf

1 sprig fresh tarragon

PARSNIPS

½ pound parsnips, trimmed, peeled, and cut into ½-inch pieces

2 teaspoons kosher salt

2 tablespoons sugar

13 tablespoons cold unsalted Kerrygold butter, cut into 1-inch cubes

1 teaspoon minced fresh ginger

½ cup lobster stock

Claw meat (reserved from the cooked lobsters)

1 tablespoon freshly squeezed lime juice

1 tablespoon chopped cilantro

Cook the lobsters: With your hands, pull the tail sections and whole claws off the lobsters' bodies. Set aside the bodies. In a large stockpot, bring 1 gallon of the water and the vinegar to a rolling boil. Add the tails and claws. After 2 minutes, remove the tails. After 5 additional minutes, remove the claws.

Remove the meat: While the lobsters are still warm, remove the meat from their shells. Using poultry shears, slit the underside of each tail shell and pull out the meat, then, using a chef's knife, halve the meat lengthwise and remove the center vein from both sides. Place the claws between two kitchen towels and whack them with the back of a sturdy knife. Then use the shears to cut through the shells lengthwise, far enough so you can pop out the claw meat. Remove the cartilage from the centers of the claws and then dice the claw meat into 1/2-inch pieces. Reserve all shells for the sauce. Cover the tail and claw meat separately and refrigerate both.

Make the lobster stock: Use poultry shears to split the reserved lobster bodies in half lengthwise. Inside the head on both sides, you will see feathery gills. Cut away and discard them. Use a cleaver or chef's knife to chop the bodies into approximately 2-inch pieces. In a large, heavy saucepan over medium heat, melt the 1/4 cup butter. Stir in the celery, shallots, fennel, and carrots and let them sweat until soft but not at all brown, about 5 minutes. Stir in the lobster shells (including the tail and claw shells) and tomato paste. Add enough water to cover the shells by 1 inch. Increase the heat to medium-high and bring the liquid to a simmer. Lower the heat to medium and maintain the simmer for 45 minutes. Throughout the simmering, skim and discard any foam or impurities that rise to the top. Add the thyme, bay leaf, and tarragon and cook for another 10 minutes. Strain the stock through a large-mesh sieve into a large container. Clean the pot and strain the stock into it through a fine-mesh strainer. Simmer the stock over medium-high heat until it is reduced to 1/2 cup, about 90 minutes.

Meanwhile, blanch the parsnips: Put the parsnips, salt, and sugar in a heavy saucepan, cover with cold water, and bring to a boil over high heat. Lower the heat to medium and simmer until the parsnips are tender but still firm, about 5 minutes. Transfer the pan to the sink and run cold water into it in a thin stream for about 6 minutes to slowly stop the cooking process and cool the parsnips completely. Drain the parsnips. If more than a few minutes remain to complete the stock, refrigerate the parsnips.

Finish the parsnips: In a slope-sided sauté pan over medium heat, melt 1 tablespoon of the 13 tablespoons of butter. Stir in the ginger and cook until tender, about 3 minutes. Add the blanched parsnips and lobster stock. Increase the heat to medium-high and bring to a boil. Stir in the remaining 12 tablespoons of butter. Once it is incorporated, add the claw meat, lime juice, and cilantro. Keep warm over very low heat.

Poach the lobster tails: Run a bamboo skewer lengthwise through each tail half to keep them from curling when poaching. In a medium saucepan over medium-high heat, bring the remaining 3 tablespoons of water to a boil. Lower the heat to medium and whisk in the cubes of the pound of butter one by one until completely incorporated. Then decrease the heat to low, add the reserved lobster tails, and poach them until a cake tester inserted into the center of one and pressed to your lips feels warm, about 8 minutes. (Be careful not to overcook the lobster or it will be tough.)

Present the dish: Divide the parsnip mixture among 4 pasta bowls and top each with 2 lobster tail halves. Garnish with micro cilantro and serve immediately.

Pan-Roasted Rockfish with Mushroom Reduction and Mock Risotto

There isn't anything more synonymous with the Chesapeake Bay region than rockfish, also known as striped bass. The trick to making it really special is to get the skin nice and crisp and retain the delicateness of the flesh by pan-roasting it. (See On Pan-Roasting, page 118.) The risotto is actually a potato dish; the starch in the potato thickens the stock and creates a texture similar to that of the famous rice dish. Mushroom stock, reduced into a flavorful sauce, melds with the risotto once the dish is finished.

{ SERVES 4 }

MUSHROOM REDUCTION

4 cups mushroom stock (page 242)

$1/4$ cup cold unsalted butter, cut into $1/2$-inch cubes

Salt

RISOTTO

5 tablespoons cold unsalted butter, cut into $1/2$-inch cubes

$1/2$ yellow onion, minced

$1/2$ cup washed, dried, and minced chanterelle mushrooms

1 small russet potato, peeled and cut into $1/4$-inch cubes (1 cup)

$1^1/2$ cups chicken stock (page 239)

1 teaspoon chopped fresh thyme leaves

$1/2$ cup minced fresh chives

$1/4$ cup grated Parmesan cheese

$1/2$ teaspoon kosher salt

FISH

2 tablespoons canola oil

4 (6-ounce) skin-on rockfish fillets, well scaled, with pinbones removed

1 tablespoon unsalted butter

1 teaspoon chopped fresh thyme leaves

1 clove garlic, minced

Make the reduction: In a saucepan over medium-high heat, simmer the stock until it is reduced to $1/2$ cup, about 40 minutes. Whisk in the butter. Season with salt to taste. Keep warm covered over low heat, stirring occasionally to keep a skin from forming.

Make the risotto: In a slope-sided sauté pan over medium-high heat, melt 1 tablespoon of the butter. Stir in the onions and let them sweat for 2 minutes, stirring occasionally, until translucent but not at all brown. Add the chanterelles and cook for several more minutes, until all their moisture has evaporated. Add the potatoes and $1/4$ cup of the stock. Stir the potatoes until the stock is almost gone. Continue adding stock in $1/4$-cup increments, stirring constantly and cooking until the liquid reduces and becomes thick before making the next addition. Once all the stock has been added, lower the heat to medium-low and stir in the remaining 4 tablespoons of butter until melted. Add the thyme, chives, cheese, and salt. The potatoes should be tender and the risotto should be creamy. Keep warm over low heat.

Pan-roast the fish: In a large slope-sided sauté pan or cast-iron skillet over medium-high heat, heat the oil until it shimmers. Place the fillets in the pan skin-side down and sear until well browned and crisp, about 5 minutes. Turn the fillets over and cook for another several minutes. From time to time as the fish cooks, grab the handle of the skillet and tilt it downward so the oil pools. Use a dessert spoon to baste the fillets over and over with the oil. The fish is done when a cake tester inserted into the center of a fillet feels warm when touched to your lip. (See Testing Meat and Fish for Doneness, page 89.) As soon as the fish is cooked, add the butter, thyme, and garlic to the pan and baste the pieces over and over for 30 seconds.

Present the dish: Remove the pan from the heat. Divide the risotto among 4 soup plates. Top each with a rockfish fillet and spoon the mushroom reduction equally over the top. Serve immediately.

STRAINING STOCK AND BRAISING LIQUIDS

Before straining braising liquids, stocks, or reductions, first use tongs to remove and discard meat, bones, vegetables, etc., and then use a mesh spider to rid the liquid of as many of the remaining solids as you can. Next, strain the liquid twice: the first time through a coarse-mesh sieve to get rid of most of the extraneous pieces you missed and then a second time through a fine-mesh sieve. If you were only to use a fine-mesh sieve, the holes would clog quickly and the straining process would take a lot longer.

Pork Belly with Braised Cabbage and Poached Apples

This dish, designed for The Bistro at Restaurant Eve, transforms humble pork belly into something truly elegant. It takes times to produce, four days from start to finish, but for three of those you can go about your life while the pork brines. The result absolutely makes the effort worthwhile.

This recipe calls for preparing the apples sous-vide, meaning to vacuum seal them in plastic and cook them in a water bath. This method allows the apples to cook in their own natural juice and sugar, concentrating their flavor. This is how we do it at Restaurant Eve. But don't worry if you don't have the special gear for doing this; I've provided instructions for poaching the apples on the stove top as an alternative. Whichever method you use, prepare the apples while the cabbage is cooking. For sous-vide cooking, you will need a vacuum sealer, a vacuum seal bag, and a circulator attached to a deep hotel pan (see Resources, page 263).

{ SERVES 6 AS A MAIN COURSE }

PORK

1 (4-pound) pork belly, Kurobuta or Berkshire preferred, rind removed

4 quarts Curing Brine for Pork (page 238)

6 apples, such as Bramley, Ida Red, Granny Smith, or Pink Lady

2 heads garlic, halved crosswise

2 small yellow onions, quartered

2 medium carrots, cut into 1-inch pieces

3 small leeks, white and light green parts only, coarsely chopped and well washed (see How to Clean Leeks, page 32)

1/2 small bunch fresh thyme

1/2 small bunch fresh rosemary

3 fresh bay leaves

1 teaspoon black peppercorns

2 cups veal demi-glace (page 244)

2 tablespoons extra-virgin olive oil

2 cloves garlic, chopped

1 teaspoon chopped fresh thyme leaves

1/2 cup micro greens, such as mizuna, for garnish (see Resources, page 263)

CABBAGE

1/2 teaspoon whole allspice

1/2 teaspoon juniper berries

2 teaspoons black peppercorns

12 slices (about 12 ounces) thick streaky (American) bacon, cut into 4 by 1/2-inch strips (lardons) (see On Irish Bacon, page 15)

2 large yellow onions, halved lengthwise and then cut lengthwise into thin strips (julienne)

30 cloves garlic, chopped

2 pounds Savoy or York cabbage, quartered and cut crosswise into 1/4-inch slices

1 cup chicken stock (page 239)

Kosher salt

6 large fresh bay leaves

1/2 cup unsalted butter, cut into pieces, at room temperature

1 teaspoon chopped fresh thyme leaves

SAUCE

2 tablespoons canola oil

Scraps from the cooked pork belly, cut into 1-inch chunks

1 small leek, white and light green parts only, chopped and well washed

1 small yellow onion, chopped

1 carrot, chopped

1/2 cup apple cider vinegar

1 cup veal demi-glace (page 244)

2 large fresh bay leaves

1/2 to 1 cup braising liquid (reserved from cooking the pork)

1/2 small bunch fresh thyme sprigs

2 sprigs fresh rosemary

1 cup apple peelings (from the poached apples)

2 teaspoons unsalted butter

1 large shallot, chopped

Brine the pork belly: In a large, nonreactive stockpot, submerge the pork belly in the brine. Cover it with a plate to help keep it submerged; refrigerate for 3 days.

Rinse the pork belly: Remove the belly from the brine; discard the brine and thoroughly rinse the belly in cold running water. Blot on paper towels.

Prep the apples: (To poach them instead, see recipe below.) Peel, core, and quarter the apples; reserve 1 cup of peels for the sauce. Using a paring knife, trim the apple quarters into pretty, barrel-shaped pieces by making vertical cuts from top to bottom, turning the apple slightly after each cut. The resultant pieces will be nicely faceted.

Sous-vide the apples: Fill a large bowl with ice water. Place the apples in a gallon-size plastic cooking pouch and vacuum seal it on maximum pressure. Attach a circulator to a deep hotel pan filled with water and set it to 181°F. When it reaches temperature, cook the apples for 10 minutes. Submerge the packet in the ice water for 30 minutes, and then refrigerate it for up to 2 days.

Braise the pork belly: Preheat the oven to 300°F. Trim the belly so that it is a perfect rectangle. Cut the trimmings into 2-inch pieces and place them in the bottom of a large flameproof roasting pan along with the garlic, onions, carrots, leeks, thyme and rosemary sprigs, bay leaves, and peppercorns. Place the belly on top skin-side up. Pour the demi-glace over it. Cover the pan with aluminum foil and bake until the belly is fork tender (about 3½ hours), basting it with pan juices every 30 minutes. Remove the foil, increase the oven heat to 400°F, and roast the belly for 30 minutes more, basting after 20 minutes. Remove the pan from the oven, let it cool it to room temperature, then cover it and refrigerate overnight.

Portion the pork and strain the braising liquid: The next day, the cooking liquid and a layer of fat will have congealed around the belly. Lift the belly from the congealed liquid and transfer to a cutting board. Remove the layer of congealed fat and save it for another use, such as sautéing vegetables, or discard it. Place the roasting pan over medium heat to melt the congealed cooking liquid. Using a mesh spider, remove and discard as many solids as you can from the pan. Strain the cooking liquid first through a coarse-mesh sieve, then a fine one, and reserve it, making sure that all the fat has been skimmed off the top. Discard any remaining solids. (See Straining Stock and Braising Liquids, page 147.) Cut the pork belly into 6 equally sized squares, reserving all the trimmings for the sauce.

Make the cabbage: In a spice grinder, finely grind the allspice, juniper berries, and peppercorns and set aside. In a large casserole over medium heat, sauté the bacon until it is light brown and the fat has rendered from it, about 5 minutes. Add the onions and garlic, stirring to combine. Cook until the onions are tender, but not browned, about 10 minutes. Add the cabbage and cook until it begins to soften, about 10 minutes. Stir in the chicken stock. Season with salt to taste. Add the bay leaves. Cut a piece of parchment paper to fit over the cabbage, inside the pot, and make a 1-inch hole in the center of it. Cover the cabbage with the parchment round, but no lid, and cook, stirring occasionally, for 1 hour. Then keep warm, over low heat.

While the cabbage is cooking, make the sauce base: In a medium saucepan over medium-high heat, heat the oil until it shimmers. Add the pork scraps and sauté until they begin to brown, about 5 minutes. Add the leek, onion, and carrot. Using a wooden spatula, stir the vegetables, scraping up any brown bits from the bottom of the pan. Let the vegetables cook for several minutes, stirring and scraping often. Add the vinegar and scrape some more; cook for 5 minutes to let the vinegar reduce. Add the demi-glace, bay leaves, and enough braising

{continued}

liquid to flavor the sauce but not make it too salty, up to 1 cup. Let the sauce simmer, but not boil, for 10 minutes, skimming impurities and fat from the surface every couple of minutes. Add the thyme and simmer another 5 minutes. Add the rosemary and apple peelings. Cook the sauce until it begins to be viscous and slightly syrupy, about 15 minutes. Continue to skim the sauce throughout the process. Pass the sauce through a fine-mesh sieve, discarding the solids. (At Restaurant Eve, we strain 8 times because we are obsessive about removing impurities, but once is sufficient for home cooks.) Keep the base warm in a covered saucepan over low heat, stirring occasionally, to keep a skin from forming.

Brown the pork: In a large slope-sided sauté pan over medium heat, heat the oil until it shimmers. Place the belly pieces skin-side down in the pan and brown for 2 minutes. Turn the pieces over and cook for another 2 minutes. In this way, brown the pieces on each remaining side. Then continue to cook, turning them over every couple of minutes and basting them with the fat that renders from them, until they are brown, crispy, and warm in the center, about 15 minutes total. (A cake tester inserted into the center and pressed to your lips should feel warm.) Add the garlic and thyme to the pan and baste the belly pieces with the flavored fat for 30 seconds. Keep warm over low heat.

Reheat the apples: Cut open the refrigerated bag and transfer the apples and their collected juices to a saucepan. Cook over medium heat, stirring often, until warmed through, about 3 minutes.

Finish the cabbage: Stir the butter and thyme into the cabbage. Add more salt if you wish.

Finish the sauce: In a small slope-sided sauté pan over medium-high heat, heat 1 teaspoon of the butter until it bubbles. Add the shallot, and cook, stirring often, until soft, about 2 minutes. Stir in the sauce base and remaining 1 teaspoon butter. Remove from the heat.

Present the dish: Divide the cabbage into neat piles among 6 large, warm dinner plates. Top each pile with a piece of pork belly, placing 4 apple pieces around it. Drizzle the sauce over and around each belly piece. Top with the micro greens and serve immediately.

Poached Apples

6 apples, such as Bramley, Ida Red, Granny Smith, or Pink Lady

1 cup sugar

1 cup water

Poach the apples: Prep the apples as directed. In a medium saucepan, bring the sugar and water to a boil over medium-high heat, stirring to dissolve the sugar. Lower the heat to medium to maintain a simmer, add the apples, and cook until they are just tender, about 5 minutes. Transfer the apples with the syrup to a bowl and refrigerate until ready to use.

To serve: To reheat for serving, pour $1/4$ cup of the syrup into a saucepan and warm over medium heat. Using a slotted spoon, transfer the apples to the pan and cook, stirring often, until the apples are warmed through, about 3 minutes.

Pan-Roasted Loin of Venison au Jus with Carrot Purée, Glazed Baby Carrots, and Brown Bread Cream

In the short time of fall when venison is available from Shaffer Farm in Central Pennsylvania, we feature it in The Tasting Room. Theirs is by far the most flavorful venison I've ever had. (See Resources, page 263.) Carrots are in season at the same time, so they make a natural accompaniment. Brown bread cream, simply Brown Bread (page 192) puréed with heavy cream, is something I came up with out of the blue one day. It adds a nice, rich counterpoint to the bold flavor of the meat.

The dish has several steps, so read through it carefully first and organize yourself. Brown bread cream is served at room temperature, so it can be made several hours in advance. The carrots can be cooked the day before and finished with the venison.

The method for cooking the venison is known as pan-roasting. (See On Pan-Roasting, page 118.) You will need a tamis (see Resources, page 263) or fine-mesh sieve for the carrot purée.

⟩ SERVES 6 ⟨

VENISON

1 (3-pound) whole venison loin

2 tablespoons canola oil

Kosher salt and freshly ground black pepper

2 teaspoons unsalted butter

2 teaspoons chopped garlic

2 teaspoons finely chopped fresh thyme leaves

Dublin Spice, for garnish (see Dublin Spice, page 129)

VENISON *GLACE*

1 tablespoon canola oil

Venison scraps (reserved from the loin)

1/2 yellow onion, chopped

1 celery stalk, chopped

1 carrot, peeled and chopped

2 cloves garlic, chopped

1/4 cup dry red wine

1 cup veal demi-glace (page 244)

1/2 sprig fresh rosemary

1 large fresh bay leaf

10 sprigs fresh thyme

BROWN BREAD CREAM

1/8 loaf Brown Bread (page 192), broken into cubes (about 1 cup)

1 1/2 cups heavy cream

1/2 teaspoon kosher salt

CARROT PURÉE

2 cups carrot juice, preferably freshly extracted

3 medium carrots, peeled and chopped (about 2 cups)

1/2 teaspoon kosher salt

Glazed Baby Carrots (page 166)

JUS

2 teaspoons unsalted butter

1 large shallot, minced

Venison *Glace*

1 teaspoon chopped fresh thyme leaves

1/4 teaspoon kosher salt

1/8 teaspoon freshly ground black pepper

Trim the meat: Cut away the flap of meat around the pure meat center of the loin (known as the eye) and trim the flap into roughly 1-inch scraps. Set them aside. Using the tip of a sharp paring or boning knife, remove and discard all of the silverskin until you have a neat, perfectly cleaned eye. Set the loin aside.

{continued}

Make the venison glace: In a heavy saucepan over medium-high heat, heat the 1 tablespoon of canola oil until it shimmers. Add the meat scraps, distributing them evenly over the bottom of the pan; let them cook undisturbed for 2 minutes until they become well seared. Turn the scraps over and sear for 2 to 3 minutes more until well browned. Stir in the onion, celery, carrot, and garlic and cook, stirring occasionally, for 3 to 4 minutes, until golden brown. Add the wine and use a flat-edged wooden spatula to scrape up any brown bits from the bottom of the pan. Continue to cook until most of the wine has evaporated, about 2 minutes. Stir in the demi-glace, rosemary, bay leaf, and thyme. Bring the liquid a simmer and cook for 12 to 15 minutes, skimming often to remove the impurities and fat that rise to the surface. Strain the sauce through a fine-mesh sieve into a measuring cup and reserve. Discard the solids.

Make the brown bread cream: Place the bread cubes, cream, and salt in a saucepan and bring to a boil over high heat. Transfer the mixture to a blender and purée until smooth. Spoon the cream into a bowl and set it aside at room temperature.

Make the carrot purée: Cook the carrot juice, carrots, and salt in a saucepan over medium-high heat until the carrots are completely soft, 20 to 25 minutes. Transfer to a food processor and purée until smooth. Using a rubber spatula, press the purée into a bowl through a tamis or fine-mesh sieve. Keep the purée warm uncovered over very low heat.

Make the Glazed Baby Carrots (page 162) and keep warm over very low heat, uncovered.

Pan-roast the venison: In a large slope-sided sauté pan over medium-high heat, heat the 2 tablespoons of oil until it shimmers. Season the loin well with salt and pepper and sear it for 2 minutes on each side. Reduce the heat to medium and start a process of cooking and basting the loin, turning it over and over, first on one side, then the other, tilting the pan slightly so your spoon can scoop up the oil. Continue turning and basting for about 7 minutes, until a cake tester inserted into the center of the loin and pressed against your lip feels warm, for medium rare. (See Testing Meat and Fish for Doneness, page 89.) (If the oil begins to blacken during the cooking process, pour it off and replace it with fresh oil.) As soon as the venison is done, quickly add the butter, chopped garlic, and chopped thyme to the pan and baste the loin quickly for several seconds, taking care to cook the garlic but not burn it, adjusting the heat if necessary. Transfer the venison to a cutting board to rest for 15 minutes.

Make the jus: Heat 1 teaspoon of the butter in a small saucepan over medium-high heat until it bubbles. Add the shallots and let them sweat for 1 minute, until translucent. Stir in the reserved venison *glace* and bring to a boil. Whisk in the remaining 1 teaspoon butter, the thyme, salt, and pepper. Keep warm over very low heat while you assemble the dish.

Present the dish: Slice the loin crosswise into 12 even slices. Divide the carrot purée evenly among 6 deep-welled soup plates or pasta bowls. Overlap 2 slices of meat partially over the purée. Spoon the Brown Bread Cream on the side of the purée and attractively arrange the baby carrots next to it. Spoon the jus over the meat, then sprinkle it with some Dublin spice. Serve immediately.

Irish Coffee

In Ireland, serving Irish coffee with a stirring implement is considered an insult because it shouldn't require stirring—it should be perfectly sweetened already and have a layer of softly whipped cream on top that lasts down to the final mouthful. It should resemble a glass of Guinness: richly dark with a creamy head on top.

The place where most people go wrong with Irish coffee is that they don't sweeten it enough. Also, many bartenders think they're doing you a favor by putting more whiskey in it. They're not. It throws off the balance completely. You will need four 8-ounce Irish coffee glasses.

✽⟩ SERVES 4 ⟨✽

$1/2$ cup heavy cream
3 cups strong black coffee, hot
4 ounces Irish whiskey
8 teaspoons packed light brown sugar

Whip the cream: In a small stainless steel bowl, beat the cream with a small whisk until thickened but still pourable. Transfer it to a pouring receptacle with a lip, such as a measuring cup.

Mix the coffee: Pour $3/4$ cup of coffee and 1 ounce of whiskey into each glass; add 2 teaspoons of sugar. Using a dinner teaspoon, stir each glass vigorously to dissolve the sugar.

Finish and serve: To float a $1/2$-inch layer of cream on each coffee, hold the tip of the teaspoon wrong side up just over the surface of the coffee and pour the cream down it. Serve immediately.

Cashel Blue and Toasted Pecan Terrine with Frisée and Apple Jam

Ireland has a long history of cheese making, mostly cheddar. In the seventies, a few small producers starting making artisanal cheeses, largely from unpasteurized cow's milk. Cheesemakers Jane and Louis Grubb created Cashel Blue, one of the best blue cheeses in the world, near the town of Cashel in County Tipperary in southwestern Ireland. It has just the right balance of salty, sweet, and creamy without being overwhelmingly pungent.

In 1997, a great cheese shop called Sheridan's opened in Dublin's city center. The Celtic Tiger was at its height, the economy was booming, and modern Irish cuisine was evolving. The Irish had developed an appetite for much more sophisticated foods, and Sheridan's found a niche selling and promoting the new farmhouse cheeses being created in the countryside, such as washed rind varieties like Milleens, Durrus, and Gubbeen. They carried some of the great cheeses from other countries, especially France, and my father became a regular there. Whenever we were having a shindig, he'd come home loaded up with French and Irish cheeses, but eventually he let the French ones go to the wayside.

"Why bother?" he'd ask. "These cheeses are better than those French snobs, anyway."

I couldn't agree more about the quality of Irish farmhouse cheese. In The Tasting Room at Restaurant Eve, we always offer a composed cheese course featuring a variety of them. Cashel Blue cheese is the centerpiece of this dish, its saltiness and slight tang balanced with apple jam. A small, simply dressed salad completes the course.

The apple jam and the terrine, which is great to serve on a cocktail party buffet, both keep well for several days in the refrigerator.

{ SERVES 12 }

TERRINE

1 cup coarsely chopped pecans

1 pound Cashel Blue cheese, crumbled (see Resources, page 263)

JAM

2 small apples, such as Bramley, Ida Red, Granny Smith, or Pink Lady, peeled, cored, and coarsely chopped

1/2 cup sugar

1/2 cup honey

1/2 cup freshly squeezed lemon juice

SALAD

6 ounces (about 8 cups) frisée

2 tablespoons finely minced shallot

2 teaspoons extra-virgin olive oil

1/4 teaspoon kosher salt

Toast the pecans: Preheat the oven to 300°F. Line a 9-inch loaf pan with plastic wrap, leaving a generous overlap. Spread the pecans on a pie pan and lightly toast them in the oven for 10 minutes, then allow them to cool.

Make the terrine: Combine the cheese and pecans in a large bowl and pack the mixture firmly into the loaf pan. Fold the overlapping plastic wrap over to cover completely and refrigerate overnight or for up to 3 days.

Make the jam: Combine the apples, sugar, honey, and lemon juice in a saucepan and cook over medium-high heat until the apples are syrupy, about 5 minutes. Lower the heat to medium and continue cooking for another 10 minutes, stirring often, until the apples are completely soft and caramelized. Remove from the heat and mash the apples into jam with the back of a fork. Let cool.

Present the dish: Unmold the terrine and cut it into 12 half-inch slices. Gently separate the frisée leaves and put them in a small bowl. Add the shallot, olive oil, and salt and toss to mix. For each serving, center a slice of terrine on a dinner plate and place a small mound of salad and a dollop of apple jam next to it.

CHAPTER SEVEN

From Da's Garden

It is said that the kitchen is the heart of a house, and while it was a very important part of the one we grew up in on Watson Road, the garden was really the heart. It was Da's pride and joy. Never was he happier than when he was working the garden or regaling neighbors and friends with stories during the bacchanalias we'd host there in the summer months.

Da started the garden behind the house pretty much immediately after we moved in in 1975 and spent all of his off time on it, whether it was planning what he was going to grow, going to a horse farm to secure manure, or planting and weeding. Everything else in our life revolved around its cultivation because the garden produced the highest quality food, and that is what we lived for. Having toiled for many years in that garden, I have the utmost respect for food and what it takes to produce it.

Da grew a wide variety of fruits and vegetables; really, anything that he could get to grow. One of the first big projects was building a path for easier access to the beds he was planting. The cobblestones came from Marylebone Lane, a very old part of Dublin, and my father bribed a guy to bring them to us. They were precious and, in Mam's words, "definitely not meant to be sold to people like us."

Then Da planted a row of raspberry bushes as a border between where we socialized and where the beds were. He was very concerned that we have a good variety and that the crops be rotated properly to preserve the land. As staples, there were potatoes, leeks, onions, peas, carrots, beets, radishes, celery, rhubarb, apples, and pears. Over the years we planted lots of other things, such as cabbage, brussels sprouts, asparagus, gooseberries, strawberries, and plums.

Nothing in my culinary career has given me as much of an appreciation for the quality of freshly cultivated vegetables as the food from Da's garden did. Even the freshest peas from a local farm will never, in my mind, taste as sweet as those picked, shucked, and eaten right off the vines in Da's garden.

Chilled Asparagus with Parmesan–Black Pepper Vinaigrette and Poached Egg

Fresh asparagus is one of the first indicators of spring, a really exciting time for us because the winter season is long in Virginia. We love asparagus prepared this way because the poached egg's yolk melds beautifully with the vinaigrette and adds an extra touch of richness, and besides, the salad looks so pretty.

The asparagus can be blanched the day before and refrigerated. The vinaigrette can be made up to 3 days in advance.

{ SERVES 4 }

1 pound medium asparagus, peeled and trimmed to even lengths

6 quarts water, for poaching the eggs

1/4 cup white vinegar

1 1/2 cups table salt

4 large eggs

1/2 cup Parmesan–Black Pepper Vinaigrette (page 246)

Chunk of Parmigiano-Reggiano cheese, to shave for garnish

Chive flowers, for garnish (optional)

Blanch the asparagus: Refer to How to Blanch Green Vegetables on page 162 to cook the asparagus for 4 to 5 minutes, until they are bright green and very slightly al dente. Shock them in an ice water bath and then blot them dry. Divide them evenly among 4 dinner plates, arranging them in a flat layer with the tips facing in one direction.

Poach the eggs: Line a dinner plate with paper towels. In an 8-quart stockpot over high heat, bring the water, vinegar, and salt to a simmer (165°F). Holding them at the surface, crack the eggs into the water one at a time, placing them equidistant from each other. They will slowly descend to the bottom and the whites will start to cook and envelop them. After 30 seconds, use a rubber spatula to gently release the eggs from the bottom of the pot. They will gradually rise to the surface, getting lighter as they cook. After 2 minutes total cooking time (the white should be set and the yolks runny), use a slotted spoon to transfer the eggs to the towel-lined plate.

Trim the eggs to be pretty: Using a paring knife, trim away any extraneous wisps of egg white so that your eggs are neatly oval shaped.

Assemble and serve: Center an egg on top of the asparagus on each plate and drizzle the Parmesan–Black Pepper Vinaigrette over them. Using a vegetable peeler, shave ribbons of the cheese over each salad and then garnish them with the chive flowers if you wish.

Blanching is a process in which you cook vegetables in boiling, salted water until al dente, plunge them into ice water to stop the cooking process, removing them immediately once they are cool, and then dry them on kitchen or paper towels. At this point, they can be stored refrigerated in airtight containers or zip-top bags for a day.

Blanched vegetables can quickly be reheated without danger of overcooking, so you can add them to another recipe at the last minute and enjoy their best flavor and texture. The salt is important; it has a chemical reaction to chlorophyll in green vegetables to maintain bright color, provided you use the correct ratio of salt to water. Whenever I tell home cooks how much salt is needed, that the water should taste like the sea, they are always incredulous—until they see the result. But still, when the vegetables are used in a recipe, they often require more salt in the final step before serving.

A bonus: your kids will be more inclined to eat vegetables if they are cooked correctly and taste good.

1. Fill an 8-quart stockpot with 6 quarts of water and stir in 1 1/2 cups table salt. (The proper proportions are 1/4 cup table salt per 1 quart water.) Bring the water to a boil over high heat. (The salt will dissolve.)

2. Have ready a large bowl of ice water and a medium strainer. (A mesh spider may work better depending on the shape of the vegetable you are blanching.) Set these items near the stove top.

3. Make sure the water is at a full rolling boil, then add the vegetables in small batches (no more than a single layer of the vegetable on the water's surface) to ensure that the water returns to a boil as quickly as possible. Once it does, cook the vegetables and monitor them as they cook by tasting a piece from

time to time until it is al dente, cooked through but still retaining a slight crunch. (In this book, the approximate cooking times are listed in individual recipes.)

4. Remove the vegetables from the water with the strainer or spider and plunge them into the ice water (chefs call this step "shocking the vegetables"). Only leave them in there long enough to cool completely; do not make the mistake of leaving the successive batches in the cold water until all the vegetables are blanched because they will get soggy. Lift the vegetables out of the ice water with the strainer or spider, transfer to clean kitchen towels, and blot dry.

5. Blanch the remaining vegetables in the same way, allowing the water to return to a rolling boil between each batch.

6. Once all the vegetables are blanched and patted dry, package and refrigerate them immediately.

Braised York Cabbage

In the States, it is usually hard to find York cabbage, which is dark green and mineral-intense, nothing much like the flavorless white cabbage you find in grocery stores. Collard greens are the closest approximation to York cabbage and work perfectly well in this buttery, garlicky recipe. The greens can be blanched the day before, but put the dish together when ready to serve.

} SERVES 4 {

6 quarts water

1¹/₂ cups table salt

8 cups coarsely chopped York cabbage leaves or collard greens

6 tablespoons unsalted butter

6 cloves garlic, chopped

1 large shallot, chopped

¹/₄ cup chicken stock (page 239)

1 teaspoon kosher salt

1 teaspoon freshly ground pepper

Blanch the cabbage: Refer to How to Blanch Green Vegetables, opposite, to cook the greens in the water and salt for 3 to 4 minutes. Shock them in an ice water bath, drain, and then blot them dry.

Prepare the dish: In a slope-sided sauté pan over medium-high heat, heat 2 tablespoons of the butter until it foams. Stir in the garlic and shallot and sauté for 2 minutes until tender. Add the cabbage and cook for 1 minute. Stir in the stock, salt, and pepper and let the greens simmer for 1 minute. Stir in the remaining 4 tablespoons of butter and continue cooking until the stock and butter mixture has thickened and coats the greens nicely, about 7 minutes. Serve hot.

A GENERAL RULE FOR COOKING VEGETABLES

To cook vegetables that grow on top of the ground, say, asparagus or peas, add them to water that is boiling. To cook vegetables that grow under the ground (potatoes, turnips, rutabagas, for example), start the cooking process in cold water. The exception is new potatoes, which are added to boiling water. Why? Because that's the rule.

Brussels Sprouts with Bacon

Even as a child, my sister Katharine was a huge fan of brussels sprouts, so they were always part of our traditional Christmas meal. The trick is to not overcook them when you blanch them. If you wish, you can blanch the sprouts a day ahead and finish the dish when ready to serve.

} SERVES 4 {

6 quarts water

1¹/₂ cups table salt

1 pound brussels sprouts, trimmed, halved, and rinsed

¹/₄ pound streaky (American) bacon, diced (see On Irish Bacon, page 15)

1 yellow onion, diced

2 tablespoons unsalted butter

2 tablespoons chicken stock (page 239)

1 tablespoon chopped fresh thyme leaves

Kosher salt and freshly ground black pepper

Blanch the brussels sprouts: Refer to How to Blanch Green Vegetables on page 162 to cook the sprouts in the water and salt for 2 to 3 minutes until they are bright green and very slightly al dente; shock them in an ice water bath, drain, and then pat them dry.

Prepare the dish: In a slope-sided sauté pan over medium heat, cook the bacon, stirring often, until it is lightly browned on all sides, about 3 minutes. Add the onion and sauté until lightly browned and tender, another 3 minutes. Add the brussels sprouts and cook for 2 minutes to warm through. Stir in the butter, stock, and thyme. Season to taste with salt and freshly ground pepper. Serve immediately.

Glazed Baby Carrots

At Restaurant Eve we cook most root vegetables, including carrots, sous-vide (cooked slowly in vacuum-sealed bags in a water bath). The process cooks the vegetables in their own natural sugar and water, thereby concentrating their flavor. Since most households don't have sous-vide capability, I'm offering this method of glazing, adding sugar to the cooking water to replace the natural sugar that leaches out and then enriching the glaze with butter. (See Emulsions Made with Cold Butter, page 142.)

You can blanch the carrots the day before, but finish the dish when ready to serve.

{ SERVES 4 }

24 baby carrots, trimmed and peeled
1 tablespoon kosher salt
3 tablespoons sugar
2 tablespoons unsalted butter

Cook the carrots: Place the carrots, salt, and sugar in a heavy saucepan. Add water to barely cover the carrots and bring to a boil over high heat. Lower the heat to medium and simmer until the carrots are tender but still firm, about 5 minutes. Transfer the pan to the sink and run cold water into it in a thin stream for about 6 minutes to slowly stop the cooking process and cool the carrots completely.

Make the buttery glaze: Drain the carrots so that they still retain a bit of water and return them to the saucepan. Over high heat, stir in the butter until it melts completely, then lower the heat to medium. The idea is to create an emulsion by letting the butter thicken the remaining sugary water and coat the carrots; stop cooking as soon as this happens so the coating doesn't separate. Add more salt if you wish and serve immediately.

Cauliflower Baked in Cheddar Cheese Sauce

My siblings and I always favored this side dish, which is something that my Da would make. It's a really good one for kids. It's so cheesy that it got my son, Eamonn, to eat cauliflower, which he now loves. If you like, you can do all the prep for this dish a day ahead, refrigerate it, and then bake it so it's hot for your meal.

{ SERVES 6 TO 8 }

1 head (about 2 pounds) cauliflower, outer leaves removed and cored

1/4 cup unsalted butter

1/4 cup all-purpose flour

1/8 teaspoon fine sea salt

2 cups whole milk, plus more if needed

1 1/4 cups (10 ounces) grated cheddar cheese

Freshly ground black pepper

Steam the cauliflower: Arrange a footed steamer rack in a large pot. Pour in water until you see it starting to come through the bottom of the rack. Bring the water to a boil over high heat. Set the whole cauliflower on the rack, cover the pot, and steam the cauliflower until it's tender, about 10 minutes.

Break apart the cauliflower: Transfer the cauliflower to a bowl. Once it is cool enough to handle, use your hands to gently break 1 1/2-inch florets from the thick central stalk. Arrange them in one layer in a 9 by 13-inch baking dish. Set aside. Discard the stalk.

Make the cheese sauce: Preheat the oven to 375°F. Melt the butter in a large, heavy saucepan over medium heat. Turn the heat to low, add the flour and salt, and whisk until both are incorporated and the mixture turns golden brown, about 2 minutes. Raise the heat to medium and add the milk, whisking constantly, until the mixture reaches a boil and a smooth white sauce forms, about 3 minutes. The sauce should be thick and glossy, but still runny. If it is too thick, gradually whisk in additional milk to achieve the desired consistency. Add 1 cup of the cheese and whisk until melted and incorporated.

Finish the dish: Pour the cheese sauce over the cauliflower, making sure to cover all the florets. Sprinkle the remaining 1/4 cup of cheese over the top and season with pepper. Bake until the cauliflower is golden brown and the cheese sauce is bubbling, about 30 minutes.

Cauliflower with Toasted Garlic and Black Pepper

When my Da was a young man in his twenties, he lived in London for a while in a flat with three other fellows. One of them was Indian, and he taught my dad how to make this dish. It's one of the best ways to eat cauliflower, especially when it's fresh from the farm. It is absolutely crucial that the pepper be freshly ground to bring out its maximum heat. If you happen to have leftovers, this dish is also delicious cold.

⟩ SERVES 4 ⟨

3 tablespoons canola oil
1 head (about 2 pounds) cauliflower, outer leaves removed, cored and cut into 1^1/$_2$-inch florets
12 cloves garlic, thinly sliced
^{1}/$_2$ teaspoon kosher salt
1 teaspoon freshly ground black pepper

In a large slope-sided sauté pan over medium heat, heat the oil until it shimmers. Add the cauliflower and sauté, stirring often, until the florets are golden brown and tender but still firm, about 15 minutes.

Stir in the garlic, salt, and pepper. Cook for about 2 minutes until the garlic is golden brown, stirring constantly. Serve immediately.

Braised Celery with Cashel Blue Cheese

Cashel Blue was the first artisanal blue cheese made in Ireland. It's a great introduction to blue cheese because it is rich, creamy, and nutty without being overpowering. For this recipe you can use any blue cheese you wish, but Cashel Blue is tops, in my opinion.

You can blanch the celery pieces a day ahead. You could also make the entire dish the day ahead and then reheat it by heating ½ cup of milk in a saucepan over medium heat and stirring in the celery in batches, warming each one through before adding the next.

} SERVES 4 TO 6 {

6 quarts water

1½ cups table salt

1 bunch celery, leaves and bottom trimmed, cut into 2-inch pieces

6 tablespoons unsalted butter

½ cup all-purpose flour

⅛ teaspoon fine sea salt

3 cups warm (110°F) whole milk

8 ounces crumbled Cashel Blue cheese (see Resources, page 263)

Kosher salt and freshly ground black pepper

Blanch the celery: Refer to How to Blanch Green Vegetables on page 162 to cook the celery pieces in the water and salt for 4 minutes, until they are bright green and very slightly al dente. Shock them in an ice water bath, drain, and then pat them dry.

Make the cheese sauce: Melt the butter in a heavy saucepan over medium heat. Turn the heat to low, add the flour and salt, and whisk until both are incorporated and the mixture turns golden brown, about 2 minutes. Raise the heat to medium and add the milk, whisking constantly. Bring the sauce to a boil and cook until it thickens, about 3 minutes, whisking continually to keep lumps from forming. Whisk in the cheese until it is melted and incorporated. The sauce should be thick and glossy, but still runny. If it is too thick, whisk in additional milk to achieve the desired consistency. Stir in the celery pieces and heat through. Season to taste with salt and pepper. Serve immediately.

Creamed Leeks

Leeks are hearty vegetables that grow through the winter in Ireland. I remember digging them out of the garden on freezing, rainy winter days. We'd trim the tops and bottoms at the back door and put them right in the shite bucket.

This is a great dish to serve with Roast Prime Rib of Beef (page 105); magic happens on the plate when the meat's gravy mixes with the leeks' cream.

{ SERVES 4 }

1 tablespoon unsalted butter

4 leeks, white and light green parts only, halved lengthwise, cut diagonally into $^1/_2$-inch slices,
and washed well (see How to Clean Leeks, page 32) (about 4 cups)

1 teaspoon kosher salt

1 cup heavy cream

Pinch of freshly grated nutmeg

Melt the butter in a flameproof casserole over medium-high heat. Stir in the leeks and salt, and let the leeks sweat uncovered, stirring occasionally, until tender but still bright green, about 5 minutes.

Stir in the cream and nutmeg. Lower the heat to medium and cook the leeks for 5 more minutes, until the sauce is thickened and the leeks are completely soft but still bright. Serve immediately.

"Marrowfat" Peas

Marrowfat is the name we Irish give to mature shelling peas left on the vine to dry. To prepare these old peas, you soak them in water overnight like beans and then boil them to death with baking soda before smashing them into what we call mushy peas, a dish I never cared for. But don't worry, this is a recipe for fresh, tender garden peas, refined and made all the richer with little, intact pieces of beef marrow—hence my little bit of irony in referring to them as marrowfat peas.

You can blanch the peas a day ahead, but put this recipe together when just ready to serve.

} SERVES 6 {

6 quarts water

1¹/₂ cups table salt

2 cups fresh, shelled peas

2 (4-inch) beef marrowbones

5 tablespoons cold unsalted butter, cut into pieces

3 large shallots, minced

¹/₄ cup chicken stock (page 239)

¹/₂ teaspoon kosher salt

¹/₄ teaspoon freshly ground black pepper

1 teaspoon chopped fresh thyme leaves

Blanch the peas: Refer to How to Blanch Green Vegetables on page 162 to cook the peas in the water and salt for 3 minutes. Shock them in an ice water bath, drain, and then blot them dry.

Prepare the marrow: Fill a large bowl with ice water. Bring a medium pot of water to a boil and cook the bones in it for 3 minutes. Transfer them to the ice water to cool. Blot the bones dry on paper towels. Use a chopstick or other narrow implement to remove the marrow from the bones, then cut it into approximately ¹/₂-inch pieces.

Prepare the dish: In a slope-sided sauté pan over medium heat, heat 1 tablespoon of the butter until it bubbles. Stir in the shallots and let them sweat for 30 seconds, until translucent. Stir in the peas, stock, and marrow. Increase the heat to high and add the remaining 4 tablespoons of butter, stirring constantly until it melts and the sauce thickens, about 2 minutes. Stir in the salt, pepper, and thyme. Serve hot.

Roasted Root Vegetable Purée

Nothing says winter more than root vegetables. Don't cook the vegetables to mush—they should be just fork tender so that the purée will have good body and flavor. If you like, this dish can be prepared a day ahead and reheated in a saucepan over low heat, stirring often, until warmed through. If you do this, add the final portion of butter when ready to serve.

{ SERVES 6 TO 8 }

2 carrots, peeled and cut into
2-inch pieces

1 parsnip, peeled and cut into
2-inch pieces

1 celery root, peeled and cut into
1-inch pieces

1 teaspoon kosher salt

1/2 cup unsalted butter, at room
temperature, cut into pieces

Freshly ground black pepper

Cook the vegetables: Place the carrots, parsnip, celery root, and salt in a large saucepan and cover them with cold water. Bring to a boil over high heat and cook for 30 minutes or until they are fork tender.

Make the purée: Drain the vegetables and transfer them to a food processor. Add 6 tablespoons of the butter and process until the mixture is smooth, scraping down the sides of the bowl from time to time. Spoon the purée into a serving bowl and season with pepper. Nestle the remaining 2 tablespoons of butter in the center and serve immediately.

Creamed Spinach

When I was in my superhero phase (it's still going on, actually), I thought I was Popeye. Because of that, I love spinach, the way you can almost feel the iron in your teeth. Creaming spinach is a great way to introduce it to children.

You can make this dish a day ahead if you like. To reheat, heat ½ cup of milk in a saucepan over medium heat and stir in the spinach in batches, warming each one through before adding the next.

{ SERVES 6 }

2 tablespoons unsalted butter

2 tablespoons all-purpose flour

½ teaspoon kosher salt

2 cups warm (110°F) whole milk

¼ teaspoon freshly grated nutmeg

2 pounds (about 5 cups packed) fresh spinach

¼ teaspoon freshly ground black pepper

Make the sauce: Melt the butter in a large, heavy slope-sided sauté pan over medium heat. Turn the heat to low, add the flour and salt, and whisk until both are incorporated and the mixture turns golden brown, about 2 minutes. Raise the heat to medium and add the milk, whisking constantly. Bring the sauce to a boil and cook until it thickens, about 3 minutes, whisking continually to keep lumps from forming. Stir in the nutmeg.

Make the spinach: Add the spinach in batches (the pan will likely not be large enough to handle all the spinach at once), stirring until each addition has wilted enough to make room for another one. Stir in the pepper and let the spinach boil, stirring occasionally, for about 5 minutes to evaporate the water released by the spinach and reduce the sauce. Serve hot.

POTATOES

POTATOES, spuds, murphys, balls of flour, praties . . . whatever we called them, they were always a central part of our diet. Mam served them with almost every meal, except when we were having an ethnic meal, like curry, which my sister Clare hated and would always be in tears over. On really special occasions like Christmas or Easter, we'd have two or three preparations of potatoes. The first restaurant I worked at in Dublin, they served lasagna with a side of chips equal to the lasagna portion. And if it ever came without them, there would have been a riot.

Here is a brief, if oversimplified, synopsis of Ireland's long history with the potato. Sir Walter Raleigh originally introduced them in the sixteenth century. One of the most famous episodes in Irish history is known as the Great Potato Famine; it occurred from 1845 to 1848 at a time when Ireland was under British rule and was largely rural. Most of Ireland's vast, fertile countryside was designated as grazing land to raise beef for consumers in England. By decree, crops grown by tenant farmers went to the landlord, except potatoes, which therefore became the mainstay of the Irish diet and created a monoculture. In 1845, the crop caught a blight and was decimated over the next three years and starvation ensued. It is estimated that over a million people starved to death; several million others emigrated.

The species of potato grown at that time was known as the Lumper, which became virtually extinct but is now gradually being reintroduced. The potatoes we ate growing up were called Pinks, Golden Wonders, Queens, and Roosters. We grew them every year. We'd lay out newspaper on the living room floor by the window and spread out the seed to sprout so it was ready for planting. Da always used the trench method. We'd plant the sprouted seeds in trenches and keep piling soil on top of them as they grew (this is known as hilling). The soil remained loose that way, allowing them to grow but protecting them from the sun, which could turn them green and toxic.

Harvesting potatoes is like treasure hunting. You put your fork in the ground, turn the soil over, and out they come, apples of the earth.

Boiled Russet Potatoes

In Ireland, potato lovers are often divided into two categories: those that like what we call "soapy" potatoes and those who like floury potatoes. It's the difference between waxiness and starchiness, the latter producing a fluffier potato. I like to use russet potatoes because it's a good all-purpose variety with a good balance of soap and flour. Serve these potatoes with the cold butter on the side, and with salt.

{ SERVES 4 TO 6 }

4 russet potatoes, peeled and quartered
1 tablespoon kosher salt, plus more for serving
$^1/_2$ cup cold unsalted butter, cut into $^1/_2$-inch cubes

Cook the potatoes: Place the quartered potatoes and salt in a pot and cover them with cold water. Bring the water to a boil, then lower the heat to medium and allow the potatoes to simmer uncovered until cooked through, about 40 minutes. To tell if they are cooked, take a piece out and cut it in half to see if it's soft in the center.

Drain and serve: Meanwhile, warm a serving bowl by filling it with hot water or placing it in a low-temperature oven. When the potatoes are done, drain them in a colander and transfer to the (dried) serving bowl. Pass the butter and additional salt at the table.

Boiled New Potatoes

For me, one of the most exciting times of the year is when the first new potatoes come in, in the late spring and early summer in our region. Few things evoke memories of Ireland more than the sensation I get from boiling up the first potatoes of the season, pulling one out of the pot, breaking it in half with my fingers, and eating it piping hot with not a thing on it but a knob of cold butter and a sprinkling of sea salt.

{ SERVES 4 }

8 golf ball–size new potatoes, skins on and scrubbed free of dirt
1 tablespoon cold unsalted butter
1 tablespoon chopped parsley

In a medium saucepan over medium-high heat, bring 2 quarts of lightly salted water to a boil. Add the potatoes and cook them for 20 minutes, or until a cake tester inserts into them easily. Drain the potatoes and return them to the pot. Add the butter and parsley and gently stir to coat completely. Serve immediately.

This being an Irish cookbook, there are ample recipes that include mashed potatoes as a component, so making them correctly is vital.

To achieve good, creamy mashed potatoes rather than waterlogged and soggy ones, it's important not to cut the potatoes into too-small pieces before boiling them. Quartered potatoes are perfect—they should be equally sized for even cooking. Russets make excellent mashed potatoes, as do Yukon Golds, even though they are a bit waxier than russets.

You want to cook potatoes until completely tender, but they can be deceptive. The only real way to tell if they are cooked through is to take a piece out and cut into the middle of it. It should have a smooth texture and have no trace of crunch.

For lump-free mashed potatoes, pass them through a food mill or ricer (be sure to have one on hand) while hot.

When using mashed potatoes as a topping for a baked dish like Shepherd's Pie (page 65) or Fish and Seafood Pie (page 84), you have to add a little egg yolk so they brown nicely, and they must have a stiffer consistency so they don't deflate when they are baked.

The mashed potatoes recipe on page 181 in this chapter is another matter entirely. They are not what you'd ordinarily find in Ireland because I load them up with butter and cream. I adhere to Julia Child's oft-quoted rule, "If you're afraid of butter, use cream," because what she really means by that is don't be afraid of butter or cream.

Mashed Potatoes

This isn't exactly the way my mother would have made mashed potatoes: my method is certainly much richer than she would allow. They are quite decadent and therefore thoroughly tasty.

This recipe is also the base for colcannon, a mixture of mashed potatoes and kale; the method for making it follows. The mashed potatoes used for Shepherd's Pie (page 65) and Fish and Seafood Pie (page 84) are not the same as these because those dishes require something with a completely different consistency. See On Making Mashed Potatoes, page 179. It's a good idea to have a food mill or potato ricer on hand.

{ SERVES 4 TO 6 }

4 russet potatoes, peeled and quartered
1 tablespoon plus 1 teaspoon kosher salt
1 cup cold unsalted butter, cut into 1/2-inch cubes
1/4 cup heavy cream

Cook the potatoes: Place the quartered potatoes and the 1 tablespoon of salt in a pot and cover them with cold water. Bring the water to a boil, then lower the heat to medium and allow the potatoes to simmer uncovered until cooked through, about 40 minutes. To tell if they are cooked, take a piece out and cut it in half to see if it's soft in the center.

Mash the potatoes: Drain the potatoes in a colander and then pass them back into the pot through a food mill or ricer. Place the pot over medium-high heat and whisk in the butter until it is completely incorporated. Whisk in the cream and the remaining 1 teaspoon salt. Work quickly so the potatoes do not cool and become gummy and starchy. Serve immediately.

Colcannon

Prepare the mashed potatoes as above. While the potatoes are boiling, sauté 1 large chopped yellow onion in 2 tablespoons of canola oil for 1 minute, until translucent but still firm. Stir in 3 cups of coarsely chopped kale that has been blanched for 5 to 6 minutes (see How to Blanch Green Vegetables, page 162) and cook for 1 minute to warm it through. When the potatoes are mashed, fold the kale and onion mixture into them.

Roasted Potatoes

These are the potatoes we serve with Roast Prime Rib of Beef (page 105). If you do the same, you will have beef fat on hand. If you don't, just use canola oil.

{ SERVES 6 }

6 russet potatoes, peeled and halved crosswise into lemon-size pieces
1 tablespoon kosher salt
½ cup rendered beef fat or canola oil

Parboil the potatoes: Preheat the oven to 400°F. Place the potatoes in a large pot and add enough cold water to cover by 1 inch. Add the salt and bring the potatoes just to a boil, uncovered, over high heat. Drain the potatoes and pat them dry.

Roast the potatoes: Pour the fat into a pie plate or similar shallow dish. Roll the potatoes in the fat and then arrange them in a single layer in a roasting pan or on a baking sheet. Bake the potatoes for 25 minutes, then turn them over. Bake for 25 minutes longer, until they are very soft and golden brown.

Lyonnaise Potatoes

We never had these potatoes in Ireland, but I had them often during my adolescence as an exchange student in France. The duck fat is what makes them luxurious—and addictive. You can bake the potatoes ahead of time, but the dish should be made when you are ready to serve it. Be gentle as you stir: the objective throughout the cooking is to keep the potatoes as intact as possible.

{ SERVES 4 }

2 russet potatoes, unpeeled, scrubbed and patted dry

1/4 cup rendered duck fat (see Resources, page 263)

1 large yellow onion, halved lengthwise and sliced crosswise into 1/2-inch slices

1 teaspoon kosher salt

8 cloves garlic, thinly sliced

1 tablespoon chopped fresh thyme leaves

Bake the potatoes: Preheat the oven to 350°F. Bake the potatoes directly on the oven rack for 40 minutes (the flesh will still be firm). When the potatoes are cool enough to handle, peel them, halve them lengthwise, and cut them crosswise into 1/2-inch slices.

Sauté the potatoes: In a large slope-sided sauté pan or cast-iron skillet over high heat, heat the duck fat until it shimmers. Spread the potato slices in a flat layer on the bottom of the pan and let them cook undisturbed for about 3 minutes on each side, until nicely browned. Add the onion, and use a flat-edged wooden spoon to gently mix with the potatoes. Cook for about 5 minutes, stirring from time to time so the potatoes cook evenly (or lift the pan by its handle and jerk it to jumble them), until the onions are slightly softened but still a bit firm and the potatoes are cooked through. Season with salt, stir in the garlic and thyme, and serve hot.

Broiled Potatoes with Aioli

This is something we'd always have at Da's backyard parties growing up because you can make a lot of them easily and they are always well received.

⟩ SERVES 4 ⟨

2 russet potatoes, unpeeled and scrubbed well
¼ cup extra-virgin olive oil
Kosher salt
Aioli (page 251), for serving

Bake the potatoes: Preheat the oven to 350°F. Wrap the potatoes individually in aluminum foil and prick them all over with a fork, through the foil. Bake for 45 to 60 minutes, until a fork goes in easily.

Dress and broil the potatoes: Set the broiler on high. Slice the potatoes in half lengthwise, through the foil. Place them on a baking sheet flesh side up and drizzle 1 tablespoon of the oil over each half. Broil in the upper third of the oven until the tops are golden brown, about 7 minutes (keep an eye on them so they don't burn). Serve the potatoes hot, still in their foil sleeves, sprinkling each with salt and then topping with a dollop of aioli.

Potato Gratin

Gratin potatoes are rich and creamy and so always welcomed at special occasion dinners. Don't go overboard with the nutmeg. As Chef Patrick O'Connell of The Inn at Little Washington likes to say, "If you can taste the nutmeg, you've used too much." Two things are important to know for preparing this: do not begin by slicing all the potatoes at once and soaking them in water; they'll lose their starch. Instead, slice and add them to the cream one at a time. And you can't make this dish ahead of time, because the butterfat will separate when you reheat it.

✲⟩ SERVES 6 TO 8 ⟨✲

1 clove garlic, halved crosswise
3 cups heavy cream
1 teaspoon kosher salt
Pinch of freshly grated nutmeg
6 russet potatoes, peeled and placed whole in cold water

Prepare the cream mixture: Preheat the oven to 325°F. Rub the inside of a 2-quart gratin dish with one of the garlic halves. Rub the inside of a large, heavy slope-sided sauté pan with the other garlic half and add the cream, salt, and nutmeg; bring to a boil over medium-high heat.

Prepare the potatoes: Using a mandoline, Japanese slicer, or very sharp knife, slice 1 potato crosswise into ¼-inch disks. Add those slices to the pan with the cream mixture, overlapping them like shingles. This will help create a layered effect and keep them from sticking together in stacks. Repeat with the remaining 5 potatoes, gently shaking the pan back and forth from tine to time throughout the process. As soon as all the potatoes are added, turn the heat off and spoon the sliced potatoes into the prepared gratin dish, maintaining overlapping slices as best you can. Pour any remaining cream over the potatoes.

Bake the gratin: Line a rimmed baking sheet with aluminum foil and place the gratin dish on top of it in case any cream boils over. Bake for 45 minutes, until the gratin is golden brown and bubbling and a sharp knife inserts easily into the center of the potato slices. Serve hot.

Peggy's Bread

Mass-produced bread from the grocery store was fine for our school sandwiches, but Da wouldn't eat that stuff, ever. We had some kind of bread with every meal—sometimes three kinds.

Where the best bread in Dublin came from was a very common topic of conversation and speculation in our household. For years Mam and Da used to go to a bakery near my Nana's house in the city, and then they discovered Peggy's in Glasthule, which was closer to our house. That's where they bought their bread for at least twenty years, and continue to do so, even though they now live twenty miles away.

One year I sent our baker at Society Fair to Peggy's to learn how to make the Irish breads from Billy, the baker there. Billy had one of those huge mixing machines and would stick his hand down in it to move the dough around while the machine was running. God knows how he managed to keep that arm.

In the world of food, there isn't much better than freshly baked bread, the smell of it baking in the oven, the texture of a good, crunchy crust and a pillowy center, the richness of the butter melted into the crumb. The recipes here represent a good swath of the traditional breads I grew up with. I titled the chapter Peggy's Bread to pay respect to those who continue to honor the traditions of the craft of bread making.

THE IRISH YEAST CO

Irish Soda Bread

The history of Irish soda bread is a relatively new one. Bicarbonate of soda was introduced there in the mid-nineteenth century. As did sourdough breads in the United States, soda bread became prevalent because yeast was costly. Some of the country people make soda bread with raisins, but I prefer to keep it savory. For tips on baking soda bread, see On Irish Quick Breads, below.

❧ MAKES 1 (1-POUND) LOAF ❧

4 cups all-purpose flour
1 teaspoon baking soda
1 teaspoon kosher salt
1/2 cup cold unsalted butter, diced, plus more for serving
2 1/4 cups buttermilk

Make the dough: Preheat the oven to 400°F. Lightly dust a baking sheet with flour. In a large bowl, whisk together the flour, baking soda, and salt. Using your fingertips, rub the butter pieces into the flour mixture until it resembles coarse meal. Make a well in the center of the flour mixture, pour in the buttermilk, and work it into the dough with your hands just until it is incorporated. Do not overmix the dough.

Bake the bread: Turn the dough out onto a lightly floured surface and form it into a round loaf about 8 inches in diameter. Place it on the baking sheet and, using a sharp knife, cut a cross into its top 1/2 inch deep. Bake for 1 hour, until well browned. Transfer the bread to a wire rack and let it rest for at least 20 minutes before serving with lots of butter.

ON IRISH QUICK BREADS

Brown Bread (page 192) and Irish Soda Bread (above) are simple, no-yeast quick breads that are easy to make and go with everything. We always left pints of milk out to sour for a couple of days, which you can use instead of buttermilk. It is very important not to overmix the dough or the bread will be very tough.

Most households in Ireland have their own recipe for quick breads passed down through the generations—yeast would have been too expensive for people in the countryside in the time of the British occupation. These breads are good for a couple of days stored in a bread bin but are best eaten fresh. They do not freeze well.

Brown Bread

Apart from potatoes, nothing is more synonymous with the food of Ireland than brown bread. You find it served there with just about anything, from breakfast to Christmas dinner. For tips on baking brown bread, see On Irish Quick Breads, page 191.

{ MAKES 1 (1-POUND) LOAF }

2 cups Irish-style wholemeal flour
(see Resources, page 263)

2 cups all-purpose flour

1 teaspoon baking soda

1 teaspoon kosher salt

1/2 cup cold unsalted butter, diced, plus
more for serving

1 3/4 cups buttermilk

1 large egg, lightly beaten

Make the dough: Preheat the oven to 400°F. Lightly dust a baking sheet with flour. In a large bowl, whisk together the flours, baking soda, and salt. Using your fingertips, rub the butter pieces into the flour mixture until it resembles coarse meal. Make a well in the center of the mixture and pour in the buttermilk and egg; work them into the dough with your hands just until they are incorporated. Do not overmix the dough.

Bake the bread: Turn the dough out onto a lightly floured surface and form it into a round loaf about 8 inches in diameter. Place it on the baking sheet and, using a sharp knife, cut a cross into its top about 1/2 inch deep. Bake for 40 minutes, until well browned. Transfer the bread to a wire rack and let it rest for at least 20 minutes before serving with lots of butter.

Batch Loaf

This is one of the great breads of the world in my opinion, right up there with baguettes and ciabatta. It's called a batch loaf because you bake several of them together in one pan. When they bake, they rise and touch each other like Parker House rolls do. This bread is great for sandwiches; cut into 1/2-inch-thick slices, toasted, and served with strawberry jam, it's one of the best things you'll ever eat. However you use it, serve it with lots of butter.

Don't be afraid to let the crust get darker than you think it should be; the contrast between the bitterness of the burnt crust and the sweetness of the white bread is really quite fantastic.

The recipe calls for 10 cups of flour, which is more than a home mixer can handle at once, so you have to make the dough in 2 batches unless you have a commercial mixer.

You will need a 9 by 13 by 6-inch baking pan (half hotel pan; see Resources, page 263).

{ MAKES 4 (1-POUND) LOAVES }

10 cups bread flour
2 tablespoons kosher salt
1 tablespoon active dry yeast
2 tablespoons canola oil
1 quart water

Make the dough: Place half of the ingredients in the bowl of a stand mixer fitted with the dough hook. Mix on the lowest speed for about 3 minutes and then on the next highest speed for another 3 minutes, until the dough comes together and pulls away from the bowl. It will be slightly sticky. Transfer the dough to a large, lightly oiled bowl and cover with plastic wrap. Repeat the process with the remaining ingredients and place the second batch in the bowl next to the first. Cover the bowl again and let it rise in a warm part of the kitchen for 1 1/2 to 2 hours, until doubled in size.

Let the dough rise a second time: Spray a 9 by 13 by 6-inch baking pan with cooking spray. Turn the dough out onto a lightly floured surface and divide it into 4 pieces. With floured hands, shape each piece into a ball about the size of a grapefruit.

Place them in the bottom of the pan. They should fit perfectly, touching each other and the sides of the pan. Cover the pan with plastic wrap and let the dough double in size again, about 30 minutes. Meanwhile, preheat the oven to 475°F.

Bake the bread: Dip your thumb into a glass of water and push it all the way down into the center of one loaf; repeat the dipping and indenting for each of the other loaves. Bake the bread for 40 minutes, until it forms a dark, slightly burnt crust (lay a piece of foil over the pan halfway through if you object to that) and an instant-read thermometer inserted into the center of a loaf registers an internal temperature of 200°F. Let the bread rest in the pan for an hour before breaking the four loaves apart. This bread is good for about 2 days if stored in a bread bin.

Pullman Loaf

Every day that I was in school I had a sandwich for lunch made with Johnson Mooney and O'Brien's sliced white pan bread, which is the Irish version of Wonder bread, though it is way better. Pullman loaf is sometimes called pan bread or sandwich bread. This recipe calls for 11 cups of flour, which is more than a home mixer can handle at once, so you have to make the dough in two batches unless you have a commercial mixer. You will need a loaf pan that is 4 by 16 inches and 4 inches deep.

⟩ MAKES 1 (4 1/4-POUND) LOAF ⟨

5 1/2 cups all-purpose flour
5 1/2 cups bread flour
2 teaspoons kosher salt
2 teaspoons active dry yeast
1 quart water

Make the dough: Place half of the ingredients in the bowl of a stand mixer fitted with the dough hook. Mix on the lowest speed for 5 minutes and then on the next highest speed for 1 minute. The dough should be smooth and slightly tacky. If it is extremely tacky, beat in a bit more flour, adding it gradually until your fingers pull away from the dough with just a bit of adhesion when you touch it. Transfer the dough to a large, lightly oiled bowl and cover with plastic wrap. Repeat the process with the remaining ingredients and place the second batch in the bowl next to the first. Cover the bowl again and let it rise in a warm part of the kitchen for 1 1/2 to 2 hours, until doubled in size.

Let the bread rise a second time: Lightly coat the 4 by 4 by 16-inch loaf pan with nonstick cooking spray. Turn the dough out onto a lightly floured surface. Flatten it with the palms of your hands to form a 14 by 8-inch rectangle with the long side facing you. Fold the top edge up and over toward you and align it to the middle of the dough. Use a pastry brush to sweep off any flour on the folded section. (You don't want raw flour inside the shaped dough.) Fold the bottom half of the dough up and align the long edge with the first fold. Crimp the dough with your fingertips to seal the seam at the top fold. Place the dough in the pan seam-side down. Cover the pan loosely with plastic wrap. Let the dough rise until it comes about 1/2 inch above the rim, about 45 minutes. Meanwhile, preheat the oven to 350°F.

Bake the bread: Bake the bread for about 40 minutes, until it is golden brown and an instant-read thermometer inserted into the center registers 180°F. Turn it out onto a wire rack and let it rest for at least 30 minutes before serving. If stored in a bread bin, this bread lasts for about 2 days for sandwiches and perhaps a third day for toast.

Potato Rolls

Considering that I'm Irish, it makes sense for me to make these rolls because bread and potatoes are practically all you ever see in Ireland. The potato liquid in the dough imparts a suppleness and subtle flavor that you don't find in a water-based dough. A well-made potato roll makes a good sandwich even better, especially hamburgers. We use potato rolls for the Braised Lamb Shoulder Sandwich (page 140) at Restaurant Eve. You could fashion a smaller version into dinner rolls and place them side by side in the pan for that nice texture contrast that occurs when they bake nestled against each other and you pull them apart, like with the Batch Loaf (page 194).

⟨ MAKES 8 TO 10 (4-INCH) ROLLS ⟩

1 medium russet potato, peeled and quartered

2 1/2 teaspoons kosher salt

1 cup water

2 tablespoons unsalted butter, at room temperature, cut into pieces

1 large egg yolk

3 1/2 cups all-purpose flour

1 tablespoon active dry yeast

Make the mashed potatoes: Place the quartered potato and 1/2 teaspoon of the salt in a small pot and cover with cold water. Bring the water to a boil, then lower the heat to medium and allow the potatoes to simmer uncovered until cooked through, about 40 minutes. To tell if they are cooked, take a piece out and cut it in half to see if it's soft in the center. Drain the potatoes, reserving the cooking liquid. Transfer the potatoes to a blender and purée. Add the water and purée until smooth, about 30 seconds. Blend in the butter. Allow the mixture to cool for 1 minute, then blend in the egg yolk. Let the mixture cool in the blender jar for 15 minutes.

Make the dough: Place the flour, the remaining 2 teaspoons of salt, the yeast, and the reserved potato liquid in the bowl of a stand mixer fitted with the dough hook. Mix on the lowest speed for 4 minutes. Set the mixer on the next highest speed and mix for another 4 minutes, until the dough pulls away from the sides of the bowl. (It will be quite sticky.) Transfer the dough to a large, lightly oiled bowl and cover with plastic wrap; let it rise in

a warm part of the kitchen for 1 1/2 to 2 hours, until doubled in size.

Form the rolls: Line a baking sheet with parchment paper. To form each roll, tear a 4-ounce piece of dough from the bowl (about the size of a lemon) and place it on a lightly floured work surface. Cup one of your hands over the dough piece and roll in a circular motion to form it into a ball, then continue to roll it with just the palm of your hand until it forms a perfect sphere. Place the balls on the baking sheet, spacing them 2 inches apart. Cover the dough balls loosely with plastic wrap and let them rise for 15 minutes. Meanwhile, preheat the oven to 350°F.

Bake the rolls: Bake the rolls for 15 minutes, until golden brown. Transfer them to a wire rack and let them rest for 10 minutes if serving warm or let them cool completely to use for sandwiches. These rolls will keep for up to 2 days when stored in a bread bin.

Fruit and Nut "Bread"

I wanted a bread that was chock-full of fruit from edge to edge to serve with the cheese board in The Bistro at Restaurant Eve. Our baker kept making these beautiful loaves with fruit, but I wanted fruit with bread, so I showed him how to do it one day. I made it up, really, but we ate so many things with dried fruit at home in Ireland that it wasn't difficult to create what I wanted.

The bread is very dense and is supposed to be. The scant batter is just enough to hold the fruit and nuts together without crumbling. Don't expect the bread to rise; the yeast isn't there for leavening, it's there for its yeasty flavor. It's okay if the edges of the bread are dark; that provides a nice bitter contrast to the sweetness of the fruit.

Note: To skin hazelnuts, spread them in a pie pan and toast in a 350°F oven for 8 to 10 minutes, then rub them vigorously between 2 slightly damp kitchen towels. The warmth of the nuts will help steam the skins off.

This bread can be stored in a bread bin for up to 3 days and it freezes well for up to 3 months.

❊⟩ MAKES 1 (2½-POUND) LOAF ⟨❊

½ cup diced Mixed Candied Citrus Peel (page 224)

1 cup dried currants

1 cup sultanas (golden raisins)

1 cup raisins

1 cup sulfured dried apricots, halved

½ cup whole, skinned hazelnuts (see recipe note)

½ cup pecan halves

½ cup walnut halves

1½ cups all-purpose flour

½ teaspoon kosher salt

1½ teaspoons active dry yeast

1 cup warm (110°F) whole milk

Make the dough: Preheat the oven to 325°F. Combine the peel, fruit, and nuts in a large bowl. Add the flour, salt, and yeast and stir to coat the fruit and nuts well. Stir in the milk, mixing well. It will not really resemble a batter.

Bake the bread: Spoon the batter into an 8½ by 4¼-inch loaf pan, pressing firmly. (No need to prep the pan.) Cover with aluminum foil and bake for 45 minutes. Remove the foil and bake for another 10 minutes, until the loaf is nicely browned and has reached an internal temperature of 180°F measured on an instant-read thermometer. Let the loaf cool in the pan on a wire rack for 15 minutes. Run a thin-bladed knife between the loaf and the pan and turn the bread out onto a wire rack to cool completely.

Scones

Scones, traditionally served with afternoon tea or breakfast, are not something Mam made very often. I don't know why, really. We offer them every morning at Society Fair, and they invariably sell out. Scones are at their best right out of the oven. If you have them later, they really should be toasted before you serve them.

} MAKES 12 SCONES {

4½ cups all-purpose flour

½ cup granulated sugar

1 tablespoon baking powder

½ teaspoon baking soda

¼ teaspoon kosher salt

Zest of 1 orange

1½ cups cold unsalted butter, cut into ½-inch cubes

⅔ cup dried currants, soaked in warm water for 30 minutes and drained

¾ cup buttermilk

¼ cup unsalted butter, melted

Turbinado (raw) sugar, for sprinkling

Make the dough: In a large bowl, whisk together the flour, granulated sugar, baking powder, baking soda, and salt. Using your fingertips, rub the orange zest and butter pieces into the flour until it resembles coarse meal. Make a well in the center of the dry ingredients. Add the currants and buttermilk and fold them in with a rubber spatula. The dough will look slightly dry.

Flatten the dough: Turn out the dough onto a lightly floured surface and with your fingertips press it into a 1-inch-thick round disk. Fold the dough in half and again press it into a 1-inch-thick disk. Fold and press one more time. Lightly grease a baking sheet.

Cut out the scones: Dip a 3½-inch round biscuit cutter in flour before each cut, then press straight down and do not twist. Twisting will impede the scones' ability to rise. Cut as many scones out of the disk as you can and place them on the baking sheet, spacing them 1 inch apart. Gently continue to reshape and cut the dough scraps, handling it as little as possible, until the dough is all gone. You should have 12 scones. Refrigerate them for 1 hour.

Bake the scones: Preheat the oven to 350°F. Brush the tops of the scones with the melted butter and sprinkle them with the turbinado sugar. Bake for 10 minutes, then turn the baking sheet around and bake for another 5 minutes, until the scones are evenly browned. Transfer them to a wire rack; if serving warm, let them rest for 5 minutes first; otherwise, allow them to cool completely.

CHAPTER NINE

All Things Sweet

Ireland is blessed with a climate that is ideal for farming, its largest industry. Everyone who wishes has access to the finest flour, butter, and eggs, all essential ingredients in baking. I was lucky to grow up in a family of bakers and frequently enjoyed their output.

Before we kids were old enough for Mam to go back to work, she used to bake a lot. There was always something going on . . . buns, pies, cakes. Both of her sisters, Ann and Joan, baked too. My Auntie Ann's Pavlova (page 220), the best ever, defies the rules of meringue making. Aunt Joan baked complex, award-winning cakes. Between the three of them, you'd have thought they were getting ready for a big bake sale going on at the church every day.

When people reminisce about their childhoods, they often think of the desserts their mothers made; indeed, desserts figure prominently in my memories of home. We all talk about how our mother's this or that is the best in the world, but in my case it's true. Mam's Apple Pie (page 209) is legendary. Its pastry is better than any puff pastry any fancy pastry chef can make.

We had dessert every day in our household, whether it was as simple as an ice cream wafer or a delicious apple picked from one of the trees in Da's garden. When I was in boarding school, the cakes my mother sent helped me survive the homesickness. When we got home from school, the mere smell of buns (cupcakes to Americans) gave us the energy we needed to do our homework. (I haven't included a recipe for them because I can't make them as well as Mam does, nor can I seem to get her porter cake right.)

The dessert recipes, especially the pastry, were the hardest ones to write because I didn't feel I had a right to translate my mother's or my aunties' delicate touch. As you can see, I worked through it.

Mam's Quick Puff Pastry Dough

This is Mam's recipe for pie dough. It's got a unique texture—crisp, but with a little chew to it—that makes it ideal for apple pie, in my opinion. I refer to it as quick puff pastry because the traditional way of making puff pastry requires two overnight restings for the dough and six turns (repeated rolling, folding, and rotating) to make 700 layers, though I'm not sure anyone ever counted the layers. This version is made and rolled in less than an hour, and it's far superior to any pastry dough you can buy ready made, even the best all-butter options. If you lose track of which way you've rotated the dough with each turn, just remember the open edge of your layered pastry should face north or south before you roll it out again.

The recipe calls for a pound of cold unsalted butter formed into a rough 5-inch square 1 inch thick. This is achieved most easily by laying 4 slender sticks of butter side by side with no space in between. Butter sticks in the United States come in two different sizes—one is longer and more slender than the other. The slender type seems to be more common in the East, the stubbier size in the West. If you are not using the slender sticks, place the butter between sheets of plastic wrap and use a rolling pin to gently beat the butter into the desired size. If the butter has become a bit soft during this process, refrigerate the square for 10 minutes or so until it is solid again.

I always make this size batch because I like having portions on hand in the freezer; they really come in handy in a pinch. Feel free to halve the recipe if you wish, though, adjusting the butter square to 2 1/2 inches and the rolled dough square to 10 inches.

*{ **MAKES 4 PORTIONS OF PASTRY, EACH SUFFICIENT FOR 1 (9- TO 12-INCH) PIECRUST** }*

3 1/2 cups pastry flour, plus more for dusting

A pinch of fine sea salt

1 1/2 cups cold water, plus 1 to 2 tablespoons more as necessary

1 pound cold unsalted butter, formed into a rough 5-inch square, 1 inch thick (see recipe note)

Start the dough: Place the flour and salt in a large bowl, combining them with your fingers. Make a well in the center. Pour the 1 1/2 cups water into the well. Using a butter knife, stir the flour into the water. (You want to avoid overworking the dough and developing its gluten.) The object here is to get all of the dry flour away from the edge of the bowl and have it come together and adhere into a single mass; if this doesn't occur, add a little water, sprinkling it on a bit at a time. Once all the flour has come together, the dough is ready to be rolled.

Turn it out onto a lightly floured surface and roll it into a 15 by 9-inch rectangle.

Add the butter: Lay the butter square in the center of the rectangle. Fold one long edge of the dough up and over the butter, aligning it 1 inch beyond the center. Fold the opposite edge of the dough over the butter to overlap about 1 inch in the center. Fold the short edges up so that one just overlaps the other. Wrap it in plastic wrap, turn it seam-side down, and let it rest in the refrigerator for 10 minutes.

{continued}

Roll out the dough: Return the dough (unwrapped) to the lightly floured surface. Use the side of a rolling pin to gently beat down the butter until it softens enough to roll out. Then roll the dough into an approximately 14-inch square. Fold the square horizontally in thirds by first lifting the bottom edge and folding it away from you and then lifting the top edge and folding it toward you. Then, starting with the left edge, fold it vertically in thirds. Wrap it with plastic wrap, rotate it 90 degrees, and let it rest in the refrigerator in this orientation for 10 minutes.

Roll out the dough two more times: Return the dough to the floured surface, making sure to orient it the way it was when you put it in the refrigerator. Roll the dough again into a 14-inch square and fold it first horizontally and then vertically in thirds as before. Wrap in plastic wrap, rotate 90 degrees, and refrigerate for 10 minutes. Repeat this rolling and folding process once more. Cut the dough into quarters. Wrap each portion in plastic wrap and then aluminum foil. The dough can be refrigerated for up to 2 days or frozen for up to 3 months. Defrost it in the refrigerator before using.

~·{ Pastry That Doesn't Grow on Trees }·~

You know how everyone says their mother makes the best apple pie? Well, my Mam does make the best apple pie—and I can't make it as well as she can. I've never made apple pie at Restaurant Eve, partially out of reverence and partially because I fear that I'll never get it right.

My parents knew a couple, Monica and Neil Sheridan. Monica is actually mentioned in Colman Andrews' book, *The Country Cooking of Ireland*, six or seven times. She had a cooking show in Ireland in the sixties. She was kind of similar to Julia Child in that she was rambunctious, always had a glass of wine in her hand, and preferred the pleasurable side of cooking to the chore side of it.

The Sheridans were elderly and not in the best physical shape when my parents befriended them. Monica died a few years before Neil did, so Mam and Da would have him over for dinner often. Neil was a writer (a friend of James Joyce, in fact), so he had a clever way with words. He came over for lunch one Sunday and we were having apple pie. Everyone, as usual, was humming about how delicious the apple pie was—Neil, in particular.

So Da said, "You know, Neil, it's the apples from my tree that make this pie so delicious."

Neil didn't skip a beat. He turned to Mam and quipped, "Angela, you tell him that pastry like that doesn't grow on trees."

Mam's Apple Pie

Da grew apples in his garden on Watson Road, and when they were in season was naturally when there would be the best pies. He grew Bramleys, which we call sour apples. They are fist-sized, squat-shaped, and tart—similar in taste to Granny Smith, but more tart. In America, I like the Pink Lady, because they are nice and tart, but with a touch of sugar. I like my apples a little on the sweet side.

Mam always assembles the pie long before making dinner so that it is cold going into the oven, which is vital. If there are any pastry scraps, reroll them into a rectangle, wrap with plastic wrap, and freeze for future use, such as for sausage roll (otherwise known as pigs in a blanket). She never uses any spice in her apple pie; for her, it's all about the apples and the pastry, and I agree. Mam always bakes her pie on a 10-inch rimmed, ovenproof dinner plate, but of course, it will taste just as fine made in a large, shallow glass or ceramic pie plate.

⟫ SERVES 8 ⟪

½ batch Mam's Quick Puff Pastry Dough (page 204) or 2 (14-ounce) packages prepared all-butter puff pastry

4 large apples (2 pounds), such as Bramley, Ida Red, Granny Smith, or Pink Lady, peeled, cored, quartered lengthwise, and cut into ¼-inch slices (about 3 cups)

¼ to ½ cup sugar

Roll out the bottom crust: On a lightly floured surface, roll half of the dough into a circle approximately 11 inches in diameter and ¼ inch thick. (Sprinkle some flour on the dough if it seems to want to stick to the rolling pin.) Loosely roll the dough onto the rolling pin, then unroll it onto the dinner plate or 10-inch pie plate. Using a sharp paring knife, trim the pastry so that it is flush with the edge of the plate.

Fill the pie shell with apples: Pile the apples onto the center of the pastry, but not all the way to the edge of the plate; leave a 1-inch border of pastry. Sprinkle the apples with the sugar (the exact amount depends on the tartness of the apples and your preference). Place the pie in the refrigerator.

Roll out the top crust: Roll the remaining half of the dough into a 12-inch-diameter circle on a lightly floured surface. Remove the pie from the refrigerator and lay the rolled-out dough on top of it nice and snugly so that the edge of the top crust is exactly on top of the edge of the bottom crust. Using your fingers, press down along the rim to join the dough layers. Let the piecrust conform to the shape of the apple mound. Trim the crust flush with the edge of the plate. Crimp or flute the edge decoratively to seal the layers. Use a paring knife to cut small slits all over the top at 1½-inch intervals.

Chill the pie: Refrigerate the pie for at least 1 hour or up to 4. THE PIE MUST BE ICE COLD WHEN IT IS PUT IN THE OVEN. Meanwhile, set a rack in the middle of the oven and preheat to 400°F. Line a baking sheet with aluminum foil.

Bake the pie: Place the pie on the prepared baking sheet and bake for 35 to 40 minutes, until the crust is deep golden brown. Transfer the pie to a wire rack to rest for 10 minutes before serving. The pie will keep for 2 days refrigerated. Not that there will be any leftovers.

Apple Crumble

This is the Irish equivalent to American apple crisp. Mam often made this when apples were in peak season in the fall. Because the fruit was so good, she never mucked it up with any spice. So resist the urge to use cinnamon, please. Served hot with vanilla ice cream, there is nothing better.

Crumble is best served fresh from the oven, but you could make it as much as a day ahead and reheat it gently in a 300°F oven for 15 to 20 minutes.

} SERVES 8 {

FILLING

10 apples (4 pounds), such as Bramley, Ida Red, Granny Smith, or Pink Lady, peeled, cored, and cut into 1-inch chunks

2 cups sugar

1/2 cup all-purpose flour

1/4 cup freshly squeezed lemon juice

TOPPING

2 1/4 cups all-purpose flour

3/4 cup rolled oats (not instant)

1/2 cup cold unsalted butter, cut into 1-inch cubes

1/2 cup sugar

Prepare the filling: Preheat the oven to 375°F. Mix the apples well with the sugar, flour, and lemon juice in a large bowl. Spread them in a 9 by 13-inch baking dish.

Make the topping: Place the flour, oats, butter, and sugar in a large bowl and use the tips of your fingers to work the butter into the dry ingredients until the mixture resembles coarse meal.

Bake the crumble: Spoon the topping evenly over the apple filling and bake the crumble for 1 hour, until nicely browned and bubbling. Let the crumble rest for just a few minutes before serving piping hot.

Bakewell Tart

This jam-filled dessert is a pie shell with cake batter baked on top of it, so you can say it's the best of both worlds. Mam always made jam anytime the fruit was in season, and when we were lucky, she made Bakewell tart with some of it. If there was any leftover batter, Mam would put some raisins in it and bake buns—what we call cupcakes in America. When she was done, we used to fight about who got to lick the leftover batter on the spoon.

The tart is a really simple dessert to make, but make sure that the butter and eggs are at room temperature—if the eggs are cold, they will curdle the batter.

} SERVES 8 {

¼ batch Mam's Quick Puff Pastry Dough (page 204) or 1 (14-ounce) package prepared all-butter puff pastry

1 cup unsalted butter, at room temperature

1 cup sugar

4 large eggs, at room temperature

½ teaspoon pure vanilla extract

1 cup all-purpose flour

½ cup jam, such as raspberry, blackberry, or strawberry

Custard Sauce (page 214)

Roll out the dough: On a well-floured surface, roll the dough into a ¼-inch-thick, 15-inch-diameter circle. Loosely roll the dough onto the rolling pin, then unroll it into a 9-inch pie pan or fluted tart pan with a removable bottom. Press the dough into the bottom and sides of the pan, making sure the dough comes all the way to the rim. Using a paring knife, trim the dough, leaving a 1-inch overhang all around. (It will shrink a bit as it chills.) Cover the pan with plastic wrap and refrigerate for 30 minutes. Meanwhile, preheat the oven to 350°F.

Make the batter: In the bowl of a stand mixer fitted with the paddle attachment, cream the butter and sugar on high speed until white, light, and fluffy, about 10 minutes. Scrape the bowl down from time to time. Lower the speed to medium and beat the eggs one at a time, completely incorporating each one before adding the next and scraping the bowl down occasionally. Beat in the vanilla. Using a rubber spatula, fold in the flour by hand. (See Folding Flour into Batter, page 214.)

Assemble the tart: Remove the pie pan from the refrigerator and trim the dough flush with the rim of the pan. Spread the jam evenly in the pie shell and spoon the cake batter over it. Bake for 10 minutes, then lower the heat to 300°F and bake for another 50 to 60 minutes, until the tart is nicely browned and a cake tester inserted into the middle comes out clean.

Present the dish: When the tart is done, transfer it to a wire rack and let it rest for 10 minutes. Serve with warm custard sauce. The tart will keep for up to 2 days; gently reheat it covered at 300°F until warm, about 10 minutes.

Custard Sauce

This basic custard sauce, also known as crème anglaise, is to my mind the perfect finish for the Bakewell Tart (page 212), but in truth, it goes well as a sauce with just about any dessert. The recipe calls for only half a vanilla bean. You should cut the bean crosswise and use the half you need and wrap the other half tightly in plastic wrap for later use. By halving the bean crosswise, you expose less of its aromatic center and therefore help retain the flavoring potential of the reserved piece.

⟩ MAKES 1 1/2 CUPS ⟨

1 cup heavy cream
1/2 vanilla bean, cut crosswise and then split lengthwise
4 large egg yolks, at room temperature
1/4 cup sugar

Infuse the cream: In a saucepan over medium-high heat, heat the cream with the vanilla bean until small bubbles form around the inside of the pan. Remove the pan from the heat and let it sit for 20 minutes to infuse the cream with the vanilla. Using a paring knife, scrape the seeds from the pod and add them to the cream; discard the pod. Keep the cream warm over low heat.

Cook the sauce: Stir the egg yolks and sugar in a bowl until combined. Slowly whisk in the cream, then return the mixture to the pan. Cook over medium heat, stirring constantly, until the custard coats the back of a spoon, about 10 minutes. Strain the sauce through a fine-mesh sieve into a sauceboat. If you are not planning to serve the custard right away or prefer it cold, strain it into a bowl, cover it with plastic wrap pressed directly onto the surface (to keep a skin from forming), and refrigerate for up to 2 days. To reheat custard sauce, cook it over very low heat in a small saucepan for several minutes, stirring constantly until just warmed through. Cooking over high heat could cause the sauce to curdle.

FOLDING FLOUR INTO BATTER

It is a good idea when making batters to fold the flour in by hand. Using a rubber spatula to continually turn the bowl and bring batter up from the bottom and over the dry ingredients has a twofold effect. It maintains air in the batter and guards against overmixing. The goal is to fold just until the point that the dry ingredients have been absorbed and are no longer visible. This helps prevent an overabundance of gluten, the protein in wheat, from developing, which can impede the cake's ability to rise well. Folding flour in by hand yields a much more tender crumb.

Almond Cake

My Da particularly enjoys almond cake. I can still clearly see him in his armchair in front of the TV after dinner with a cup of coffee and a piece of this rich, sweet cake. This cake is best when fresh but will keep for up to 2 days.

Be sure to buy unsweetened almond paste, not marzipan.

} SERVES 8 TO 10 {

1 cup unsalted butter, at room temperature

1 cup sugar

8 ounces almond paste

4 large eggs, at room temperature

1^1/$_2$ cups all-purpose flour

^{3}/$_4$ cup sliced blanched almonds

^{1}/$_2$ cup apricot jam, for glazing

Prep the oven and pan: Preheat the oven to 350°F. Butter a 9-inch round cake pan, lightly dust it with flour, then knock out any excess.

Make the batter: In the bowl of a stand mixer fitted with the paddle attachment, cream the butter, sugar, and almond paste on high speed for 10 minutes, until light and fluffy, scraping down the sides of the bowl occasionally. Lower the speed to medium and beat the eggs into the batter one at a time, completely incorporating one before adding another. Using a rubber spatula, fold in the flour by hand. (See Folding Flour into Batter, opposite.)

Bake the cake: Spread the batter evenly in the prepared pan. Scatter the almonds evenly over the top. Bake for 50 minutes, until a cake tester inserted into the middle comes out clean. Let the cake cool in the pan for 10 minutes, then invert it onto a plate and reinvert it onto a wire rack (so the almond side is up) to cool completely.

Glaze the cake: Stir the jam in a small saucepan over medium heat until it is completely melted. Brush the top of the cake with it.

Pineapple Upside-Down Cake

My sister Katharine is a huge pineapple fan. One night when she and her family came to our house in Virginia for dinner, I realized I hadn't made anything for dessert. So I whipped up this recipe, which has become a staple in our family. It's one of the few recipes I passed to my mother rather than the other way around.

The trick to making a cake with a rich, custardy texture is to use as little flour as possible and to fold it in by hand; this prevents the gluten in the flour from developing and keeps the cake tender.

As a time-saver, you can caramelize the pineapple and have it in the pan ahead of time. Just make sure it is cool before adding the batter. Or you could assemble the whole cake ready for the oven a few hours ahead of time and pop it in the oven just before dinner. Again, make sure the caramel is cool before adding the batter.

Serve this cake hot out of the oven with vanilla ice cream.

{ SERVES 8 TO 10 }

1 pineapple, peeled

3 cups sugar

1 pound unsalted butter, at room temperature

8 large eggs

1 cup all-purpose flour

Vanilla ice cream, for serving

Cut the pineapple: Quarter the pineapple lengthwise. Remove and discard the core from the quarters, halve them lengthwise, and then cut each eighth crosswise into $1/2$-inch slices.

Prepare the caramel: Spread 1 cup of the sugar on the bottom of a well-seasoned 9-inch cast-iron skillet and place it over medium heat. Let the sugar cook for a few minutes, until you see a ring of clear syrup around the edge of the pan. Stir the sugar until it begins to caramelize (take on a golden hue), breaking up any clumps of sugar crystals that may form. Continue stirring until the sugar is completely dissolved and the caramel is deep brown.

Cook the pineapple: Stir the pineapple into the skillet. The caramel will come together in a mass, but will turn to liquid again as the water in the pineapple boils and melts it. Continue cooking the pineapple, stirring occasionally, until most of its water evaporates and the caramel becomes a thin syrup, about 10 minutes. Remove the skillet from the heat and set aside to cool.

Prepare the batter: Preheat the oven to 350°F. In the bowl of a stand mixer fitted with the paddle attachment, cream the butter and the remaining 2 cups sugar on high speed until white, light, and fluffy, about 10 minutes. Scrape down the sides of the bowl from time to time. Lower the speed to medium and add the eggs one at a time, completely incorporating each one before adding the next and scraping the bowl down occasionally. Remove the bowl from the mixer and, using a rubber spatula, fold the flour into the batter by hand. (See Folding Flour into Batter, page 214.)

Bake the cake: Spoon the batter into the skillet, spreading it over the pineapple. Bake the cake for 1 hour, until a toothpick inserted into the middle comes out clean. Remove the skillet from the oven and immediately invert the cake onto a cake plate. Use a rubber spatula to scrape off any caramel or pineapple left in the pan and spread them onto the top of the cake. Serve hot with vanilla ice cream.

Lemon Cake

My Auntie Joan, my mother's sister, and her husband Larry live on the north side of Dublin. A few times a year growing up we'd go out to their house for dinner, which was always a treat because they had children our age and Auntie Joan was known for her baking skills. The cake part of this recipe comes from her; I added a glaze to it. It's a nice, rich, buttery cake that's great with a cup of tea.

*⟨ **SERVES 12 TO 16** ⟩*

CAKE

2 cups all-purpose flour

1 tablespoon baking powder

1 cup unsalted butter, at room temperature

1 cup granulated sugar

1 tablespoon freshly grated lemon zest

3 large eggs, at room temperature

1 cup buttermilk

½ cup freshly squeezed lemon juice

SYRUP

½ cup freshly squeezed lemon juice

¼ cup water

2 cups granulated sugar

GLAZE

2 tablespoons freshly squeezed lemon juice

1 cup confectioners' sugar

Prep the oven and pan: Preheat the oven to 350°F. Butter a 10-cup Bundt pan, lightly dust with flour, then knock out any excess.

Make the batter: In a small bowl, whisk together the flour and baking powder. In the bowl of a stand mixer fitted with the paddle attachment, cream the butter, granulated sugar, and lemon zest on high speed for 10 minutes, until light and fluffy, scraping down the sides of the bowl occasionally. Lower the speed to medium and beat the eggs into the batter one at a time, completely incorporating one before adding another. Scrape down the sides of the bowl, then continue beating, adding the buttermilk and lemon juice until incorporated. Remove the bowl from the mixer. Using a rubber spatula, fold in the flour mixture by hand. (See Folding Flour into Batter, page 214.)

Bake the cake: Transfer the batter to the prepared pan and bake for 50 minutes, until a cake tester inserted halfway between the side and the tube comes out clean.

Meanwhile, make the syrup: When about 10 minutes of baking time remains, heat the lemon juice, water, and granulated sugar in a small pan over medium heat until the sugar is dissolved. When the cake is done, turn it out onto a wire rack set over a baking sheet. Pour the syrup evenly over the warm cake and then allow the cake to cool completely.

Glaze the cake: Stir the lemon juice and confectioners' sugar in a small bowl until smooth. Transfer the cake to a serving plate. Drizzle half the glaze over the top of the cake, let it set for 10 minutes, and then drizzle the remaining glaze over it. Serve with a cuppa. The cake keeps nicely on a covered cake plate for up to 2 days.

Auntie Ann's Pavlova

Pavlova is my all-time favorite dessert. My Auntie Ann's is the best. When I'd come home from America to visit, Mam would always ask her sister to make pavlova. This is her recipe, which I decorate with whatever fruit is in season—berries, peaches, kiwi, pineapple. I could eat this whole thing myself, no problem.

From a pastry chef's perspective, this recipe for pavlova is odd because you don't dissolve the sugar in the meringue. The recipe was probably invented by accident when someone turned up the oven too high for a meringue. What you want is a crisp, light-brown shell with a creamy, marshmallow-y consistency in the center. The key to getting it right is to get the oven hot, then turn it down low as soon as you put the meringue in. Do not open the door during the baking process—that could deflate the meringue.

You can bake the meringue the day before serving and store it covered in a cool, dry place.

❋} SERVES 8 {❋

1 cup plus 2 tablespoons sugar

1½ teaspoons cornstarch

4 large eggs whites, at room temperature

1 teaspoon distilled white vinegar

1½ cups cold heavy cream, for serving

About 3 cups fresh fruit, such as sliced strawberries, raspberries, or blueberries, and sliced tropical fruit, such as mango, kiwi, and pineapple

Prep the oven and pan: Preheat the oven to 425°F. Line a baking sheet with parchment paper and trace an 8-inch circle on it using a plate or cake pan as a template.

Make the meringue: In a small bowl, mix ½ cup of the sugar with the cornstarch. In a stand mixer fitted with the whisk attachment, beat the egg whites on high speed until stiff peaks form, about 3 minutes. Remove the bowl from the mixer and, using a rubber spatula, fold in the remaining ½ cup plus 2 tablespoons of sugar until it is completely incorporated. Fold in the cornstarch/sugar mixture. Fold in the vinegar.

Bake the meringue: Using a spatula, pile the meringue into the center of the circle traced on the parchment, pushing out from the center until the meringue fills the outlined space. The mound does not have to be precise; the meringue should be about 2 inches high. Put the meringue in the oven and lower the heat to 275°F. Bake for 1 hour. Turn the oven off and leave the meringue inside to cool completely, about 1 hour. Do not open the oven door during the baking and cooling.

Make the whipped cream: Place the cream in a chilled mixing bowl. Using a hand-held mixer, beat the cream on medium-high speed until soft peaks form, about 2 minutes.

Present the dish: To serve, transfer the meringue to a serving plate. Top it with the whipped cream and fresh fruit.

~∗{ Tuck! }∗~

When I was about eleven, my parents sent me to a boarding school called Coláiste na Rinne, in the south of Ireland. This was so that I could make the transition from elementary school, which was taught in English, to the Irish-language high school they wanted me to attend.

That place was like being in prison at first. Lights were switched out at 8 p.m. and if you were caught talking after then, you were sent to the office for "six of the best on the hands." You can use your imagination as to what that means. You would see a line of boys outside the office crying every morning, knowing what was about to happen to them next. It was something right out of Dickens.

After a while, we figured out that the school's drainpipes were made from cast iron and were always really cold, so you could numb your fingers before you received your punishment and it didn't hurt as much. So we turned it into a competition to see who could get sent the most.

In the dining room, students were divided by how you took your tea, so, for instance, those who took milk sat together. The food was some of the worst I have ever eaten, so when we were home, we'd sew plastic bags into our jacket pockets so we could get rid of Friday's fish after dinner and not ruin our clothes.

One of the only bright spots of that experience was receiving a care package our parents sent once a month or so. This was known as tuck, named after lidded boxes used in times gone by to send food to boarding school students.

For tuck, Mam would usually include either a porter cake, which is a big, rich fruit cake, or a Biscuit Cake (opposite), the entirety of which I would eat in one day. Part of the reason for that was how much I love those cakes; the rest was purely a practical matter—we were only allowed to eat our tuck goodies on Saturday afternoons.

Biscuit Cake

With no baking required, this is so simple to make, like an American icebox cake, and it's a great treat for kids. Mam used to send this to me at boarding school because she knew how much I loved it. (See Tuck!, opposite.) Years later, I discovered that biscuit cake is actually called Royal Wedding cake, and is commonly served at weddings in England. It can be glazed with chocolate if you would like to make it prettier. If you're not familiar with them, digestive biscuits are similar to the graham crackers Americans are used to.

The eggs in this cake aren't cooked, so be sure to use the freshest eggs possible or use pasteurized eggs if you are concerned about them.

❧ SERVES 12 ❧

1 cup unsalted butter, at room temperature, cut into pieces

$1/4$ cup sugar

$1/4$ cup semisweet chocolate chips

2 tablespoons cocoa powder

2 large eggs, lightly beaten

1 pound digestive biscuits (see Resources, page 263), crumbled

Prep the pan: Line a 6-cup terrine mold or loaf pan with plastic wrap, allowing several inches to hang over each side.

Make the batter: In a large bowl set over a pan of simmering water, stir together the butter, sugar, chocolate chips, and cocoa until the mixture is completely melted. Remove the bowl from the heat and let the chocolate mixture cool completely.

Beat in the eggs. Fold the biscuits into the chocolate and pack the mixture into the prepared mold. Cover it with the excess plastic wrap and refrigerate for several hours, preferably overnight. (Or up to 2 days.)

Present the dish: To serve, unmold the terrine and cut it into slices. It's rich enough to stand on its own.

Mixed Candied Citrus Peel

Because this process is time-consuming, you may as well make a big batch. This recipe candies the peel in large pieces, which gives you the option of cutting it to the size you want when you need it, whether in strips or little cubes.

{ MAKES ABOUT 2 POUNDS, OR 6 CUPS OF DICED PEEL }

1 large grapefruit, ends trimmed, halved lengthwise

3 oranges, ends trimmed, halved lengthwise

3 lemons, ends trimmed, halved lengthwise

3 limes, ends trimmed, halved lengthwise

6 cups sugar

1 quart water

Prepare the peels: Using a spoon, scoop the pulp and membranes from all of the fruit halves. (You can juice it by squeezing it with your hand; reserve the juice for another use.) Cut the fruit peel halves into quarters.

Boil the peels: Place the peels in a saucepan, cover them with water and bring to a boil. Using tongs or a spider, transfer the peels to a bowl, then discard the water. Repeat this process once.

Make the syrup: Return the empty pan to the stove and add 4 cups of the sugar and the 1 quart of water. Bring to a boil, stirring to dissolve the sugar. Add the peels and lower the heat to medium; simmer for about an hour, until the peels are tender. Using tongs, transfer the peels, separating the pieces, to a wire rack set over a baking sheet. Let

them dry for 1 hour. Discard the cooking syrup, which will be quite bitter.

Coat the peels with sugar: Pour the remaining 2 cups of sugar into a large bowl and, working in batches, toss the peel in it to coat each piece completely, returning the coated pieces to the wire rack. Set the sugar aside and let the coated peel dry for another hour. Repeat the coating and then let the peel dry again, this time overnight. Coat the peel with sugar one more time and then let it dry for another 12 to 24 hours.

Store the peels: To store, layer the citrus pieces (chop them first if you prefer) with the sugar left over from coating them (plus more if necessary) in an airtight container and refrigerate for up to 3 weeks.

Auntie Joan's Barmbrack

Barmbrack is a Halloween tradition in Ireland. The fruit represents charms that ward off evil spirits. Traditionally, the cake is baked with a ring in it, which was considered good luck for whoever wound up with it. This is another of my Auntie Joan's recipes. The brandy she uses in it adds a nice complexity. We eat it with cold rather than room-temperature butter because of the texture, which is similar to hard sauce.

You can make the cake the day before serving, and it is great sliced and toasted.

⧽ SERVES 12 TO 16 ⧼

3/4 cup dried currants

3/4 cup raisins

3/4 cup sultanas (golden raisins)

3/4 cup (about 4 ounces) Mixed Candied Citrus Peel (opposite), cut into 1/2-inch squares

1 cup brewed Irish breakfast tea, at room temperature

1/2 cup brandy, plus more for sprinkling

3/4 cup packed brown sugar

1/2 teaspoon Mixed Spice (see below)

1 large egg, lightly beaten

1 3/4 cups all-purpose flour

1/2 teaspoon baking soda

Cold unsalted butter, for serving

Macerate the dried fruit: In a large bowl, stir together the currants, raisins, sultanas, citrus peel, tea, brandy, brown sugar, and mixed spice. Cover and let stand overnight at room temperature.

Prep the oven and pan: Preheat the oven to 350°F. Grease an 8-inch-diameter by 3-inch-tall round cake pan and line the bottom with a parchment paper circle.

Make the batter: Stir the egg into the fruit mixture. In a small bowl, whisk together the flour and the baking soda. Using a rubber spatula, gently fold the flour mixture into the fruit until the batter is combined, being careful not to overmix (see Folding Flour into Batter, page 214).

Bake the cake: Spread the batter evenly into the prepared pan and bake for 60 minutes, until a cake tester inserted into the middle comes out clean. Remove the pan from the oven and sprinkle some brandy over the top. Let the cake cool in the pan for 10 minutes, then turn it out onto a wire rack to cool completely. Serve with lots of butter.

MIXED SPICE

Mixed spice is a combination of spices often found in Irish baking because it complements dried fruit so well. Dried fruit is another ingredient that figures prominently in Irish baking. No doubt cooks have personal preferences of combinations; this is mine: In a small bowl, mix together 1 tablespoon of ground cinnamon, 1 tablespoon of ground allspice, 1 tablespoon of freshly grated nutmeg, and 1 tablespoon of ground cloves. Store in an airtight container for up to 3 months. Makes about 1/4 cup.

Mincemeat

Either you're a fan of mincemeat or you're not. I am. I offer a large-batch recipe that yields 12 cups because it takes time and effort to make, so you may as well make a lot of it. You may not necessarily need that much, depending on the size batch of Mince Pies (opposite) you make. If you don't use it all, beribboned jars of mincemeat make great gifts throughout the holiday season. Or you can store any remaining jars in a cool, dark place for up to a year.

Note: The recipe classically calls for beef suet, the fat that is closest to the kidneys. I've found it difficult to get suet in small quantities, so we take a whole rib eye or sirloin and clean only the purest white fat off of the surface. We then grind and freeze it, so it can be sliced into pieces that look similar to suet when it's ground.

·} MAKES 12 CUPS {·

1 pound pure white beef fat, cold (see recipe note)

3 cups sugar

2 teaspoons kosher salt

10 tablespoons freshly squeezed lemon juice

Zest of 4 lemons

2 cups sultanas (golden raisins)

2 cups dried currants

1 apple, such as Bramley, Ida Red, Granny Smith, or Pink Lady, peeled, cored, and coarsely grated

1¼ cups raisins

¾ cup brandy

1 teaspoon Mixed Spice (see page 225)

1-inch piece fresh ginger, peeled and grated (about 2 teaspoons)

1½ cups Mixed Candied Citrus Peel (page 224), cut into ½-inch squares (about 8 ounces)

1 teaspoon freshly grated nutmeg

½ pound chopped almonds (2 cups)

1 cup water

Prep the fat: Pass the cold fat through a meat grinder fitted with a coarse grinder plate. (Do not use a food processor; it will break down the fat too much and the friction from the machine will liquefy the fat.) Place the fat in the freezer in a covered container until very firm, at least 2 hours.

Make the mincemeat: Combine all the ingredients except the fat in a large bowl. Remove the fat from the freezer and chop it into pieces the size of raisins. Stir it into the fruit mixture. Cover the bowl with a kitchen towel and keep it in a cool, dark place for at least 6 weeks, stirring once a week. Use what you need and store the rest in jars in a cool dark place for up to a year. (The alcohol and sugar preserve it just fine.)

Mince Pies

Of the Christmas desserts that appear on the traditional Irish table, mince pies take the top prize in my book. The first time I made this recipe, I followed my grandfather's handwritten note that said to use an eighth of a glass of brandy, but I didn't know how big a glass was, so I used the biggest glass I could find, which made for some pretty potent pies.

The pies are best served warm out of the oven with some whipped cream, but they are quite good at room temperature, too. You can assemble the pies several hours ahead and bake them just before dinner, or they can be baked up to 2 days before serving. Homemade Mincemeat (opposite) takes 6 weeks to mature, so plan accordingly.

⟩ MAKES 6 (4-INCH) PIES ⟨

½ batch Mam's Quick Puff Pastry Dough (page 204) or 2 (14-ounce) packages prepared all-butter puff pastry
2 cups homemade Mincemeat (opposite) or store-bought
½ cup cold heavy cream, for serving

Cut the pastry: On a lightly floured surface, roll out the dough to ¼ inch thick, forming a large circle. Using a 4½-inch biscuit cutter, cut out 6 circles of dough for the bottom crusts. Then using a 4-inch biscuit cutter, cut out 6 more circles for the top crusts. One pressing of the dough should more than amply yield 12 cuts.

Make the pies: Line six 4-inch fluted removable-bottom tart pans with a bottom crust, pressing it into the bottom and sides. (The pastry should fit perfectly.) Fill each pan with ⅓ cup of mincemeat. Using the tip of your finger, moisten the pastry all around the edge with water. Then cover each tart with a top crust. Press the edge of the top crust into the moistened edge of the bottom crust to seal the pies. Using the tip of a paring knife, cut

two ½-inch slits near the center of each tart to allow steam to be released. Place the tarts on a baking sheet and refrigerate them for at least 1 hour or up to 4 hours. THE PIES MUST BE ICE COLD WHEN THEY ARE PUT IN THE OVEN.

Bake the pies: Preheat the oven to 350°F. Arrange the pies on one rack in the oven and bake for 20 minutes, until golden brown. Transfer them to a wire rack to cool for 10 minutes.

Make the whipped cream: Place the cream in a chilled medium mixing bowl. Using a hand-held mixer, beat the cream on medium-high speed until soft peaks form, about 2 minutes. Release the pies from their pans and serve warm with the cream.

~⁕{ The Thrill of Christmas Desserts }⁕~

Nothing evokes Christmas to me more than the various dried-fruit desserts of the season: Christmas Pudding (opposite) and Christmas Cake (page 234). They are some of the things I miss most about home. Because Meshelle wasn't brought up with this sort of thing, they're not really a part of our holiday tradition in Virginia. (Except for the Christmas cake Mam sends every year, which I used to eat with Larousse, our Saint Bernard, before he died.)

Fresh fruit is pretty much abundant in the United States year-round, but it wasn't available much in Ireland in the winter when I was growing up. So almost all of the desserts in the wintertime were made up of dried fruit, which is why you see a lot of ingredients like currants and sultanas at Christmastime.

When we were kids, we would pick a day about six to eight weeks before Christmas to start preparing, because the mincemeat and pudding base had to macerate for so long. In those days, you couldn't just buy blanched almonds, so we would have to blanch our own and peel them. Sometimes Mam and Da put muscatels (dried Muscat grapes) in the fruit mixture, and they had to be cleaned and seeded. That was a full day.

We used to keep the marinating fruit in a plastic baby's bath in the little front room in our house, which for some reason was always cold no matter what we did to it, and I would sneak in there and eat spoonfuls of it fairly regularly.

Of all the Christmas desserts, I love Mince Pies (page 227) the most. When Mam or Aunt Joan made them, I would eat, like, ten or twelve of them. On Christmas day, all of the sweets came at the end of a long banquet when everybody was already stuffed, but that never deterred me. After dinner, my parents and grandparents would go straight to the couch. The four of them would be snoring away within a few minutes, mouths wide open. And I'd still be eating mince pies.

Christmas Pudding

This is a very dense bread pudding made with tons of dried fruit and booze. It's an acquired taste, to be sure, but once you grow accustomed to it, you can't get enough of it. In our family, we were evenly divided between those who loved it and those who didn't. Like it or not, though, turning down the lights and setting fire to the Christmas pudding was always a highlight on that day.

It takes time and effort to make Christmas pudding, so the tradition is to make a lot of them at once. The batter needs to be made at least 2 weeks in advance. If you store it in a cool, dark place, you can make it up to 2 months ahead.

This recipe makes two puddings; each one serves eight. Because the pudding takes so much effort, it's not a bad idea to double the recipe; they make great gifts. Baked puddings not served immediately can be stored in a cool, dark place for up to 2 years. (They get more complex with age.) When we were growing up, Mam would put a pot on each burner and then cook one pudding per pot so each steamed evenly. She filled the stove with them. I suggest you do the same, with two covered pots, each large enough to contain a covered pudding bowl and still leave a couple of inches between the top of the pudding and the pot's lid.

} MAKES 2 PUDDINGS; SERVES 8 EACH {

BATTER

1¹/₂ cups dried currants

1¹/₂ cups sultanas (golden raisins)

3 cups raisins

¹/₂ cup Mixed Candied Citrus Peel (page 224), cut into ¹/₂-inch squares (about 4 ounces)

1 tablespoon blanched almonds, chopped

1 small apple, such as Bramley, Ida Red, Granny Smith, or Pink Lady, peeled and grated

¹/₂ teaspoon kosher salt

1 teaspoon freshly grated nutmeg

¹/₂ teaspoon Mixed Spice (see page 225)

2¹/₂ cups panko bread crumbs

3 large eggs, lightly beaten

¹/₄ cup whole milk

Juice and zest of ¹/₂ orange

1 cup self-rising flour

2 (12-ounce) bottles ale, such as Smithwick's, plus more as needed

2 (12-ounce) bottles stout, such as Guinness, plus more as needed

1¹/₂ cups brandy, Irish whiskey, Calvados, or Grand Marnier

FOR SERVING 1 PUDDING

¹/₂ cup cold heavy cream

¹/₄ cup Irish whiskey

Make the batter: Combine all of the ingredients in a very large bowl. Cover with a kitchen towel and leave in a cool place for 2 to 6 weeks, stirring daily for the first week, and then once a week thereafter. Add more ale and stout as necessary throughout the weeks to maintain a slightly loose texture.

Fill the pudding bowls: Fill two 6-cup ovenproof metal Christmas pudding bowls with lids that clamp on (see Resources, page 263), or similar

6-cup heatproof ceramic bowls, with 4 cups of batter each. Press a circle of parchment or waxed paper onto the batter in each bowl to cover it completely. Place the lids on the pudding bowls. (Or wrap tightly with aluminum foil.) This keeps water from getting inside and making the tops soggy.

Cook the puddings: Place an inverted heatproof plate in each of 2 large pots and then place a pudding on top of it. (This is to keep the pudding

{continued}

bowl from having direct contact with the bottom of the pot.) Fill each pot with enough water to come one-third of the way up the side of the pudding bowl. Cover the pots. Bring the water to a simmer in each one over medium heat and cook the puddings for 6 hours, maintaining a simmer all the way through. Top off the water from time to time as needed. After 6 hours, carefully remove the puddings and transfer to a wire rack.

Present the dish: To serve, place the cream in a chilled medium mixing bowl. Using a hand-held mixer, beat the cream on medium-high speed until soft peaks form, about 2 minutes. Invert a pudding onto a serving plate. Heat the whiskey to warm it, pour it over the pudding, and ignite it. Slice the pudding and serve immediately with the cream on the side.

To store and reheat: Store the puddings, still covered, in a cool, dark place until Christmas Day, or for up to 2 years. Reheat by using the same steaming method as above, but for only about 2 hours, until a cake tester inserted into the center and pressed against your lips is warm. Then invert onto a plate, top with warm whiskey, ignite the whiskey, and serve the pudding with whipped cream.

Christmas Cake

Christmas cake, a rich, dense, dried-fruit cake, was the most decorative of the season's desserts. Prepping the fruit for the array of Christmas desserts began the countdown to Christmas. With the curing of the ham, we knew we were getting even closer, but when Da put the white royal icing on top of the Christmas cake we knew we were almost there. The icing signified the purity of the newborn child.

The cake needs to be baked at least 2 days before serving to allow time for each layer of icing to dry overnight, but Da always made it about 5 days ahead of time. The royal icing acts as a protective coating to help prevent the cake from drying out.

Royal icing is normally made with raw egg whites. If you are concerned about that, use pasteurized egg whites or meringue powder instead.

{ SERVES 16 TO 20 }

CAKE

4 cups dried currants

2$^1\!/_2$ cups sultanas (golden raisins)

1$^1\!/_4$ cups raisins

1 cup chopped blanched almonds

1 cup Mixed Candied Citrus Peel (page 224), cut into $^1\!/_2$-inch squares (about 8 ounces)

Zest of 6 lemons

$^1\!/_4$ cup brandy

1$^1\!/_2$ cups unsalted butter, at room temperature

1$^2\!/_3$ cups packed light brown sugar

7 large eggs, at room temperature

3 cups all-purpose flour

1$^1\!/_2$ teaspoons Mixed Spice (see page 225)

$^3\!/_4$ teaspoon freshly grated nutmeg

ALMOND ICING

4 cups almond flour

1 pound confectioners' sugar, plus more for dusting

3 large eggs, at room temperature

Juice of 1 lemon

ROYAL ICING

1 pound confectioners' sugar

2 large egg whites, at room temperature (or 5 tablespoons meringue powder)

1 tablespoon freshly squeezed lemon juice

Prep the oven and pan: Preheat the oven to 300°F. Butter a 9-inch-diameter by 4-inch-tall cake pan or springform pan and lightly dust with flour, knocking out any excess.

Prepare the batter: In a large bowl, stir together the currants, sultanas, raisins, almonds, mixed peel, lemon zest, and brandy. In a stand mixer fitted with the paddle attachment, cream the butter and brown sugar on high speed until white, light, and fluffy, about 10 minutes. Scrape the bowl down from time to time. Lower the speed to medium and add the eggs one at a time, completely incorporating each one before adding the next and scraping the bowl down occasionally. Fold the flour, mixed spice, and nutmeg into the batter by hand. (This prevents the gluten in the flour from developing and keeps the cake tender; see Folding Flour into Batter, page 214.) Fold the fruit mixture into the batter.

Bake the cake: Spread the batter evenly into the prepared pan. Cover loosely with aluminum foil and bake for 3 to 3$^1\!/_2$ hours, until a cake tester inserted into the middle comes out clean. Let the cake cool in the pan on a wire rack for 20 minutes, then turn it out onto the rack to cool completely.

Make and apply the almond icing: In the bowl of a stand mixer fitted with the paddle attachment, beat the almond flour, confectioners' sugar, eggs, and lemon juice on low speed for 30 seconds (so the sugar doesn't go flying about) and then on medium speed for another 30 seconds to combine completely. It should have a claylike consistency. Working with a small amount at a time, encase the cake completely with the icing by pressing it on with your fingertips, dusting them with confectioners' sugar as you go to keep the icing from sticking to them. Leave the cake on the counter overnight, uncovered, so the icing will dry.

Make the royal icing: In the bowl of a stand mixer fitted with the paddle attachment, beat the confectioners' sugar, egg whites, and lemon juice on low speed until smooth, scraping down the sides of the bowl a few times. The icing should be stiff but spreadable.

Finish the cake: Using an offset spatula, spread the royal icing on the cake to cover the almond icing completely. If you wish, reserve some to pipe decorations on top. Leave the cake on the counter overnight or for up to 4 days, uncovered, so the icing will dry.

CHAPTER TEN

Brine, Stocks, Sauces, and Relishes

Curing Brine for Pork

In the world of processed food, home curing meat is sadly becoming a lost art. Brine curing imparts a distinctive, familiar flavor and is greatly economical because it extends the shelf life of meat. This is a good all-purpose brine, but feel free to experiment with different spices and flavor combinations of your own, as people have done for countless generations.

*{ **MAKES 2 QUARTS** }*

1 quart water

1 cup kosher salt

¹/₂ cup sugar

1 quart water frozen into ice cubes (2 pounds)

1 small head garlic, unpeeled, halved crosswise

1 yellow onion, quartered

2 tablespoons pink curing salt, such as sel rose or Insta Cure #1 (see Resources, page 263)

¹/₂ teaspoon black peppercorns

¹/₂ teaspoon yellow mustard seed

¹/₂ small bunch fresh sage

In a large pot over high heat, bring the 1 quart of water to a boil. Add the kosher salt and sugar, stirring until they are dissolved. Remove from the heat and stir in the ice to completely cool the brine.

Add the garlic, onion, curing salt, peppercorns, mustard seed, and sage. The brine can be kept for several days in the refrigerator.

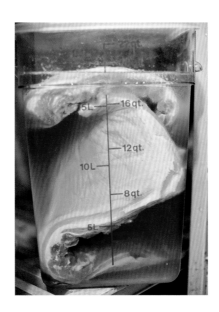

Chicken Stock

Before beginning, see On Making Stock, page 240. Chicken stock is a good all-purpose, neutral stock that is used widely in modern cooking. Using a whole chicken rather than just a carcass or bones results in a more flavorful stock.

⟨ MAKES ABOUT 3 QUARTS ⟩

1 (3-pound) chicken, cut into 12 pieces

3 celery stalks, cut into 2-inch pieces

2 carrots, peeled and cut into 2-inch pieces

1 large white onion, coarsely chopped

10 cloves garlic

1 teaspoon black peppercorns

1 large fresh bay leaf

1 large sprig fresh rosemary

1/2 large bunch fresh thyme

Cook the stock: Place all the ingredients in a stockpot, cover with cold water, and bring to a simmer over high heat. Once the stock begins to simmer, lower the heat to medium and cook for 45 minutes. Skim often to remove any foam and fat that rise to the top, using a large ladle to gently disturb the bones as you do so. This allows any protein that may be trapped between the bones to escape. The vegetables should be soft at this point and the chicken thoroughly cooked.

Strain the stock: Strain the stock through a coarse-mesh sieve into a large heatproof container and then into another through a chinois or fine-mesh sieve. Discard the solids, including the chicken—all the flavor has been leached from it.

Cool the stock: Fill your very clean sink with ice and plunge the pot into it. Let the stock cool completely, then refrigerate it in the coolest part of the refrigerator for several hours until completely chilled. At this point you can freeze if you wish. Chicken stock can be stored in the refrigerator for up to 2 days and frozen for up to 3 months.

Not enough attention is paid to the craft of making stock, which is too bad because stock is the very foundation of many dishes and of most sauces. A well-crafted stock should taste like a soup and be something you wouldn't mind eating on its own. The most important thing to keep in mind is this: don't use the stockpot as a trash receptacle by throwing just any leftover bits of this and that into it. The better the quality of the chicken, fish, veal, aromatics, etc. you start out with, the better the quality of the stock.

No matter what type of stock you are making, you go through three steps. Honor them.

1. Extraction: Extract the maximum amount of flavor from the bones and aromatics. How long you cook them depends on the size that you cut them. Obviously it takes a little time for a wispy fish bone to release its flavor and a great deal of time for a beef bone to do so. The aromatics need to be cut to the size that corresponds to the length of time they will cook.

2. Refinement: This is the process of removing impurities off the surface throughout the entire cooking process (take your time with this and skim, skim, skim!) and then carefully straining the resultant liquid. Even though you can't always see them, there are small bits of coagulated protein throughout the stock, so the more skimming and straining you do the more refined your stock and sauces will be.

3. Concentration: Reduce the stock to the right intensity and consistency. This step may take place as part of your stock-making process or be employed later on in specific recipes. Because you concentrate stock, it's all right to start with too much water in the pot. It's better, in fact, to have too much water than too little—this gives the ingredients room to move around and makes the skimming job easier for you.

Have the right equipment: a heavy stockpot, a wire-mesh spider, a coarse-mesh sieve, a fine-mesh sieve (when conical this is known as a chinois), a large ladle, and an 8-quart heatproof food-safe bucket or similar large receptacle.

Fish Stock

Before beginning, see On Making Stock, opposite. It's crucial not to overcook this stock because you will wind up with a bitter, fishy result. You want it to be fairly neutral so it can take on the profile of whatever dish you are using it in.

Ask your fishmonger for random fish frames cut into 4-inch pieces. Use only those from white fish, like halibut or rockfish. Do not use bones from oily fish, such as mackerel, salmon, or bluefish—they will impart an unpleasant flavor and ruin your stock.

} MAKES ABOUT 2 ½ QUARTS {

5 pounds fish bones (see recipe note)

1½ teaspoons canola oil

2 carrots, peeled and coarsely chopped

2 celery stalks, coarsely chopped

½ yellow onion, coarsely chopped

1 small leek, white and light green parts only, coarsely chopped and well washed (see How to Clean Leeks, page 32)

4 sprigs fresh thyme

1 small sprig fresh rosemary

1 fresh bay leaf

¼ teaspoon black peppercorns

Soak the fish bones: Soak the fish bones in cold water for 4 hours (or overnight), refrigerated. Then drain them and rinse them thoroughly to remove any traces of blood.

Sweat the vegetables: In a stockpot over medium-high heat, heat the oil until it shimmers. Add the carrots, celery, onion, and leek. Let the vegetables sweat for 10 minutes, stirring occasionally, until they are tender but not at all brown.

Cook the stock: Add the bones to the pot and cover with cold water. Add the thyme, rosemary, bay leaf, and peppercorns. Bring to a simmer (do NOT boil) over medium-high heat and cook for 45 minutes.

Skim often to remove any detritus that rises to the top, using a large ladle to gently disturb the bones as you do so. This allows any protein that may be trapped between the bones to escape.

Strain the stock: Using a wire-mesh spider, remove and discard as many of the solids as possible. This makes straining much less cumbersome. Strain the stock through a fine-mesh sieve or chinois.

Cool the stock: Fill your very clean sink with ice and plunge the pot into it. Let the stock cool completely, then refrigerate or freeze it. Fish stock can be stored in the refrigerator for up to 2 days and frozen for up to 3 months.

Mushroom Stock

Before beginning, see On Making Stock, page 240. This is a good vegetarian alternative to meat stock. Feel free to add a variety of dried mushrooms to intensify the flavor, but be sure to strain well; they can be gritty.

{ MAKES ABOUT 2 QUARTS }

1 pound cremini mushrooms, coarsely chopped

1 yellow onion, coarsely chopped

8 cloves garlic

6 cups water

2 large fresh bay leaves

1/2 bunch fresh thyme

4 sprigs fresh rosemary

Pinch of curry powder

In a saucepan over medium-high heat, bring all of the ingredients to a boil. Reduce the heat to medium and simmer uncovered for 40 minutes. Strain through a fine-mesh sieve or chinois and cool completely. Discard the solids. Fill your very clean sink with ice and plunge the pot into it. Let the stock cool completely, then refrigerate or freeze it. Mushroom stock can be refrigerated for up to 2 days and frozen for up to 3 months.

Veal or Lamb Stock

Before beginning, see On Making Stock, page 240. This recipe takes some work over the better part of a day, but having the stock on hand increases the quality of whatever soups, stews, and sauces you are making tenfold. So make it once in a while and freeze it.

While making the stock, adjust your burner heat as needed to keep the liquid at a constant simmer throughout the process; do not ever let the stock boil. Add water as needed to maintain the level of liquid with which you start. Because you don't add the vegetables right away, you can prep them while the stock is simmering.

{ MAKES ABOUT 3 1/2 QUARTS }

5 pounds veal or lamb bones

1/2 cup tomato paste

3 yellow onions, halved

7 carrots, peeled and cut into 3-inch pieces

1/2 bunch celery, leaves discarded, cut into 3-inch pieces

1 small leek, white and light green parts only, halved, cut into 3-inch pieces, and well washed (see How to Clean Leeks, page 32)

3 fresh bay leaves

1/2 teaspoon black peppercorns

1 large bunch fresh thyme

1/4 bunch fresh rosemary

Simmer the bones: Place the bones in a very large stockpot and add enough cold water to cover them by 2 inches. Bring to a simmer over high heat. Lower the heat to medium or medium-high, as needed. Simmer the stock for 2 hours, using a ladle to skim, skim, skim whatever fat and particles rise to the top. Do this very often in the first hour and often in the second hour. From time to time, use the ladle to gently move the bones so that particles trapped among them can rise to the top.

Add the remaining ingredients: Stir in the tomato paste and simmer for another hour, skimming regularly. Then add the onions, carrots, celery, leek, bay leaves, peppercorns, thyme, and rosemary and simmer for another 6 hours, remembering to maintain the water level and skimming regularly.

Strain the stock: Use a wire-mesh spider to remove and discard the solids. Strain the stock into another large pot or bucket. Clean the cooking pot. Set a fine-mesh sieve over it and strain the stock back into it.

Cool the stock: Fill your very clean sink with ice and plunge the pot into it. Let the stock cool completely, then refrigerate it overnight. Remove and discard any congealed fat from the top and strain the stock through a fine-mesh sieve into a clean container. The stock can be stored in the refrigerator for up to 2 days and frozen for up to 3 months.

Veal or Lamb Demi-Glace

Demi-glace is the backbone of meat sauces. Without it, you'd have great difficulty creating the deep, lingering, complex flavor that makes a dish truly great. It used to be that making demi-glace involved roasting bones with tomato paste and incorporating flour into the process, but many modern cooks, I among them, prefer to use a simple stock reduction because the result is more straightforward.

⟩ MAKES ABOUT 7 CUPS ⟨

3 1/2 quarts Veal or Lamb Stock (page 243), skimmed of fat

Reduce the stock: Bring the stock to a boil in a large saucepan over high heat. Lower the temperature to medium, or wherever is necessary to maintain a simmer, and simmer until the stock is reduced by half, 1 1/2 to 2 hours, skimming often.

Strain and cool the demi-glace: Strain into a container through a fine-mesh sieve or chinois. Cool the demi-glace as you did the stock. The demi-glace can be stored in the refrigerator for up to 2 days and frozen for up to 3 months.

Court Bouillon

This is a great all-purpose poaching liquid, especially for high-protein foods like fish, seafood, and chicken. By coagulating protein, citric acid helps the cooking process along. It contains no garlic, as I find that that flavor overpowers fish.

{ MAKES 3 CUPS }

1 large leek, halved, cut into 1-inch pieces, and well washed (see How to Clean Leeks, page 32)

1 carrot, peeled and cut into 1-inch pieces

1 large yellow onion, coarsely chopped

1 lime, quartered

1 navel orange, quartered

1 lemon, quartered

1 cup dry white wine

1 quart cool water

1 fresh bay leaf

$1/2$ teaspoon black peppercorns

$1/4$ bunch fresh thyme

1 sprig fresh rosemary

Cook the bouillon: Place all the ingredients in a large saucepan and bring to a simmer over high heat. Once the liquid begins to simmer, lower the heat to medium and cook for 45 minutes, until the vegetables are soft.

Strain and cool the bouillon: Remove the solids with a wire-mesh spider and discard them. Strain the bouillon through a coarse-mesh sieve and then a fine one. Fill your very clean sink with ice and plunge the pan into it. Let the stock cool completely, then refrigerate or freeze it. Court bouillon can be stored in the refrigerator for up to 2 days and frozen for up to 3 months.

Parmesan–Black Pepper Vinaigrette

This is a variation of Caesar salad dressing, but without the anchovies. It's a nice creamy dressing that goes well with most salads and is a good alternative to dip for crudités.

} MAKES 1¾ CUPS {

1 large egg

4 cloves garlic, crushed

2 tablespoons red wine vinegar

½ cup canola oil

½ cup extra-virgin olive oil

½ cup grated Parmesan cheese

1 teaspoon freshly cracked black pepper

¼ teaspoon kosher salt

Combine the egg, garlic, and vinegar in the bowl of a food processor. With the machine running, add the oils in a thin stream through the small tube in the bowl's lid to create an emulsion. Turn the machine off; add the cheese, pepper, and salt, and then process for another 30 seconds. Store refrigerated in an airtight container for up to 3 days.

Citrus Vinaigrette

Blanching removes the bitterness in the zest used for this dressing, which goes particularly well with seafood-based salads.

} MAKES 1½ CUPS {

1 grapefruit, halved

2 oranges

2 lemons

2 limes

2 quarts water

1 large egg

1 teaspoon sugar

½ teaspoon kosher salt

1 cup canola oil

Prepare the citrus: Grate the zest from one half of the grapefruit and from all of the other citrus; place in a nonreactive saucepan. Squeeze the juice from all of the citrus, straining it into a small bowl, and set aside.

Make the dressing: Add 1 quart of the water to the pan with the zest. Bring to a boil, drain, and repeat the process with the remaining 1 quart water. Return the blanched zest to the saucepan. Add the reserved juices; place over high heat and reduce the liquid by three-quarters, until it is quite syrupy, about 10 minutes. Strain the liquid into a blender; reserve the zest. Add the egg, sugar, and salt to the blender. With the machine running, add the oil in a slow stream until the vinaigrette thickens. Transfer the vinaigrette to a bowl and stir in the reserved zest. Store refrigerated in an airtight container for up to 3 days.

Dill Sauce

This sauce goes beautifully with Gravlax (page 42), but it also goes well with baked or poached salmon or grilled fish such as halibut or swordfish.

⁎⟨ MAKES 1²/₃ CUPS ⟩⁎

¹/₄ cup whole-grain mustard

¹/₄ cup Dijon mustard

¹/₄ cup minced shallot

2 tablespoons Champagne vinegar

2 tablespoons sugar

²/₃ cup canola oil

2 tablespoons chopped fresh dill leaves

Kosher salt

In a small bowl, whisk together the mustards, shallot, vinegar, and sugar until combined. Slowly whisk in the oil. Whisk in the dill and season with salt to taste. If not using immediately, cover and refrigerate for up to 3 days.

Basic Mayonnaise

Beating the egg yolks with acid for several minutes before adding the oil gives your mayonnaise a much lighter consistency and makes it more stable.

⁎⟨ MAKES 2 CUPS ⟩⁎

1¹/₂ tablespoons white vinegar

¹/₂ teaspoon freshly squeezed lemon juice

2 teaspoons water

³/₄ teaspoon sugar

³/₄ teaspoon kosher salt

2 large egg yolks

2 cups canola oil

In a small bowl, stir the vinegar, lemon juice, water, sugar, and salt until completely dissolved. Pour half of this mixture into the bowl of a stand mixer fitted with the paddle attachment; add the egg yolks. Mix on high speed for 5 minutes, until creamy and pale. With the machine running, begin to add the oil in a very slow, steady stream. As soon as the mayonnaise is very thick, almost curdled looking, stop adding the oil and add the rest of the vinegar mixture, pulsing it in. Then add the remaining oil as before. Store refrigerated in airtight containers for up to 3 days.

Marie Rose Sauce

Chef Jeff Buben, for whom I worked at Bistro Bis in Washington, D.C., told me once that the two best things that Ireland gave to the culinary world were Cathal Armstrong and Marie Rose sauce, a riff on what Americans know as Russian dressing and the Irish answer to cocktail sauce. Obviously, I would argue that Ireland gave at least a few other great things to the culinary world, but those two are pretty good.

⟩ MAKES 1¼ CUPS ⟨

1 cup Basic Mayonnaise (page 247)
3 tablespoons ketchup
1 tablespoon freshly squeezed lemon juice
¼ teaspoon cayenne pepper

In a small bowl, whisk together the mayonnaise, ketchup, and lemon juice until blended. Whisk in the cayenne. Store refrigerated in an airtight container for up to 3 days.

Tartar Sauce

The tartness of the cornichons, the saltiness of the capers, the acid of the lemon juice, and the richness of the mayonnaise all conspire to create a perfect foil for seafood in this interpretation of a classic sauce.

⟩ MAKES 1¼ CUPS ⟨

1 cup Basic Mayonnaise (page 247)
2 tablespoons chopped cornichons
2 tablespoons capers, drained and chopped
¼ cup freshly squeezed lemon juice
Kosher salt and freshly ground black pepper

In a small bowl, whisk together the mayonnaise, cornichons, capers, and lemon juice. Season with salt and pepper. Store refrigerated in an airtight container for up to 3 days.

Horseradish and Green Onion Mayonnaise

I came up with this dressing for fried oysters because I don't care for cocktail sauce with oysters. The horseradish part is great, but all that ketchup is too sweet for my palate. This sauce goes nicely with any dish you'd use tartar sauce for.

{ MAKES 2 CUPS }

Juice of 1 lemon

1 large egg

1 large egg yolk

1 tablespoon kosher salt

2 cups canola oil

¼ cup freshly grated horseradish

1 bunch green onions, white and light green parts only, chopped

Place the lemon juice, egg, egg yolk, and salt in the bowl of a food processor and process until smooth. With the machine running, add the oil in a thin stream through the small tube in the bowl's lid until the mixture becomes a thick mayonnaise. Transfer to a bowl and stir in the horseradish and green onions. Store refrigerated in an airtight container for up to 3 days.

Harissa Mayonnaise

I like Le Cabanon harissa in the can if you don't want to take the time to make your own (which is always better) to season this mayonnaise. The same brand comes in a tube, but it is not as spicy or flavorful. Adding roasted red pepper (canned or jarred is fine) gives the sauce a nice red hue.

⟩ MAKES 1¹/₂ CUPS ⟨

2 tablespoons Homemade Harissa (page 255) or purchased harissa

1 large egg

1 tablespoon freshly squeezed lemon juice

2 tablespoons chopped roasted red pepper

¹/₄ teaspoon chopped garlic

¹/₂ teaspoon kosher salt

¹/₂ cup canola oil

¹/₂ cup extra-virgin olive oil

Place the harissa, egg, lemon juice, red pepper, garlic, and salt in the bowl of a food processor, and process until smooth. With the machine running, add the oils in a thin stream through the small tube in the bowl's lid until the mixture becomes a thick mayonnaise. Store refrigerated in an airtight container for up to 3 days.

Aioli

The word aioli comes from ail, the French word for garlic. So please don't ever call it "garlic aioli," at least not in front of me. Because this French version of Alioli contains acid, the emulsion is much more stable and can therefore be made in a food processor.

{ MAKES 1 1/2 CUPS }

1 large egg

1 large egg yolk

2 small cloves garlic, crushed

1 1/2 teaspoons freshly squeezed lemon juice

1 1/2 teaspoons kosher salt

1 cup canola oil

1/2 cup extra-virgin olive oil

Place the egg, egg yolk, garlic, lemon juice, and salt in the bowl of a food processor, and process until smooth. With the machine running, add the oils in a thin stream through the small tube in the bowl's lid until the mixture becomes a thick mayonnaise. Store refrigerated in an airtight container for up to 3 days.

Alioli

This is the Spanish preparation of aioli, made with egg yolks and olive oil. The French version uses whole eggs and lighter oil and is therefore not as intensely flavored.

Because the alioli has no acid in it to denature the egg's protein, you need to whip air into it in order for the oil molecules to bond with the protein molecules. For this reason, it is best to use a stand mixer.

{ MAKES 2 1/2 CUPS }

2 large egg yolks

2 cloves garlic, crushed

2 teaspoons kosher salt

1/4 cup water, at room temperature

2 cups extra-virgin olive oil

Place the egg yolks, garlic, salt, and 2 tablespoons of the water in the bowl of a stand mixer fitted with the whisk attachment; beat on high speed for 10 minutes, until the yolks have doubled in volume and are pale white. Add half of the oil in a thin stream, then add the remaining 2 tablespoons of water. Stream in the rest of the oil; the allioli will be yellow and very thick. Season with more salt if you wish. Store refrigerated in an airtight container for up to 3 days.

Hollandaise Sauce

Hollandaise sauce is relatively easy to make as long as you follow the rules. Keep the cooking temperature steady and make sure the eggs are cooked properly—this gives you a stable sauce. The sauce should taste of butter, not egg. If it tastes of egg, you need to add more butter. The clarified butter should be slightly warm when you add it, the same temperature as the yolks. It's all about keeping everything at about the same temperature, so you don't want to add the lemon juice cold.

Note: Making the sauce requires beating egg yolks into foam over direct heat and then off the heat, and ladling melted clarified butter into them while whisking at the same time. This means you don't have a hand free to hold the bowl. To keep it from moving during this step, roll a large, damp kitchen towel from one corner to the other to create a long, 2-inch-diameter cylinder. Form the cylinder into a ring wide enough to create a nest for your bowl and have it ready on your work surface.

Hollandaise sauce cannot be made ahead of time, but you can shorten the preparation time by clarifying the butter as much as several days in advance, refrigerating it, and then melting it just before making the sauce.

⁕⦃ MAKES 2 CUPS ⦄⁕

6 large egg yolks
3 tablespoons water

1¹/₂ cups warm clarified butter (see How to Clarify Butter, opposite)
Juice of 1 lemon, at room temperature

A few dashes of Tabasco sauce
Kosher salt

Beat the egg yolks: Using a large whisk, beat the yolks and water in a large stainless steel bowl until well combined. Then place the bowl directly over low heat and whisk vigorously until the yolks become frothy and very pale, resembling beaten egg whites, about 5 to 7 minutes. Continue to cook and whisk until the yolks are completely cooked and thickened and the whisk makes visible furrows in the foam.

Add the butter: Remove the bowl from the heat and anchor it on a rolled towel on your work surface (see recipe note). With one hand, continue to whisk the yolks while with the other hand you slowly ladle the warm clarified butter into them. Add the butter in a continuous stream, incorporating it completely into the yolks with your whisk as you go along. After you add about half of the butter, add half of the lemon juice. Continue adding butter until the sauce is the texture of mayonnaise and tastes buttery, not eggy. (You may not need all of the butter. Freeze whatever remains for future use.) Add a few dashes of Tabasco, some salt, and the rest of the lemon juice if the sauce needs it. Strain the sauce through a fine-mesh sieve into a bowl that has been warmed with hot tap water and towel dried. Serve immediately.

To make clarified butter, melt 2 pounds of unsalted butter in a large saucepan over medium-low heat. As the protein coagulates and rises to the surface, skim it off and discard it. Stir occasionally to keep the solids from resting in the bottom of the pan and burning. The idea is to cook the butter, get rid of its solids, and create a clear, golden liquid, not a nutlike one. The process will take about 20 minutes. Remove the butter from the heat and let it rest, discarding any more solids that rise to the surface. After a few minutes, pass the butterfat through a coffee filter or cheesecloth into a large measuring cup, stopping when you get to the water that has settled to the bottom of the pot. The yield is about 1 1/2 cups.

Parsley Sauce

This is a parsley-seasoned white sauce we serve warm with Boiling Bacon (page 122), a specialty of the Halloween table. You could also use it for fish, such as baked or poached cod or salmon.

⁕❴ MAKES 2 CUPS ❵⁕

2 tablespoons unsalted butter

2 1/2 tablespoons all-purpose flour

1 1/2 cups whole milk, warmed

1/2 teaspoon kosher salt

1/4 teaspoon freshly ground black pepper

Pinch of freshly ground nutmeg

1/2 cup chopped parsley

In a saucepan over medium heat, heat the butter until it bubbles. Whisk in the flour and cook for 2 to 3 minutes, whisking constantly, until the mixture is blond in color. Whisking continually, slowly add the milk. Bring the sauce to a boil and cook until it thickens, about 3 minutes, whisking continually to keep lumps from forming. Add the salt, pepper, nutmeg, and parsley, whisking to incorporate. Season with more salt and pepper if you wish. It can be stored in the refrigerator for up to 2 days. (To reheat, heat 1/2 cup milk in a saucepan over medium heat and stir in the sauce in batches, warming each one through before adding the next.)

Horseradish Cream

To me, there's no point in eating horseradish unless you use it fresh. I never even saw prepared horseradish before I came to America. The stuff in a jar has absolutely no flavor at all.

❋❴ MAKES 1¹/₄ CUPS ❵❋

¹/₄ cup grated fresh horseradish
1 cup crème fraîche or sour cream
1 tablespoon freshly squeezed lemon juice
1 tablespoon chopped chives
Kosher salt

In a small bowl, whisk together the horseradish, crème fraîche, lemon juice, and chives until combined. Season with salt to taste. If not using immediately, store refrigerated in an airtight container for up to 3 days.

Homemade Harissa

Use harissa as you would any chile sauce, such as Sriracha or Tabasco. It has a distinctly North African profile and adds extra dimension to any recipe or when served as a condiment, especially for roasted meats.

2 1/2 pounds red Fresno chiles, stems removed, halved lengthwise

4 1/2 teaspoons coriander seeds

4 1/2 teaspoons caraway seeds

1 1/2 teaspoons cumin seeds

1 teaspoon smoked Spanish paprika (pimentón)

1 tablespoon chopped garlic

1/4 teaspoon kosher salt

4 1/2 teaspoons extra-virgin olive oil

1 tablespoon freshly squeezed lemon juice

2 tablespoons chopped fresh mint leaves

Roast the chiles: Preheat the oven to 350°F. Place the chiles skin-side down on rimmed baking sheets. Bake until the skins begin to pull away from the flesh, 5 to 7 minutes. Transfer the chiles to a large bowl and cover with plastic wrap. When the chiles are cool, peel them, discarding the skins and as many of the seeds as you can. Transfer the chiles to the bowl of a food processor. (There should be about 3 cups of peeled chiles.)

Make the harissa: In a spice grinder, grind the coriander, caraway, and cumin seeds and add them to the chiles in the food processor, along with the paprika, garlic, salt, and olive oil. Purée until smooth. Turn the purée into a bowl and stir in the lemon juice and mint leaves. The harissa can be refrigerated in an airtight container for up to 2 weeks.

Tomato Marmalade

This is a very versatile condiment. We use it at Restaurant Eve on the Irish BLT (page 138), but it would be great to use on any sandwich that would routinely have tomatoes on it.

} MAKES 1 CUP {

12 Roma tomatoes, cored and cut crosswise into 1/2-inch slices

1 clove garlic, chopped

18 medium fresh basil leaves

1 sprig fresh rosemary, leaves only

1/4 cup extra-virgin olive oil

Kosher salt and freshly ground black pepper

Roast the tomatoes: Preheat the oven to 275°F. Line a rimmed baking sheet with aluminum foil or parchment paper and arrange the tomato slices in a single layer. In a blender or small food processor, process the garlic, basil, rosemary, and oil for about 20 seconds, or until they form a coarse pesto. Spread some pesto on each tomato slice. Bake the tomatoes for 2 hours, until they are completely softened. Cool completely on the baking sheet.

Finish the marmalade: Remove and discard the tomato skins. Transfer the flesh to a cutting board and chop it with a chef's knife. Scoop the marmalade into a container and season it with salt and pepper to taste. Store the marmalade in an airtight container in the refrigerator for up to 3 days.

Caramelized Onions

Sautéeing onions in a very hot pan and stirring intermittently allows them to retain some texture but still caramelize nicely. If you have caramelized onions on hand, they won't go to waste; they work well as a sandwich or pizza topping, an omelet or tart filling, a soup or gravy base, or an accompaniment for roast beef or lamb or grilled chicken breasts.

❋⟨ MAKES ABOUT 1/2 CUP ⟩❋

1 teaspoon canola oil
1 yellow onion, halved lengthwise and sliced into 1/4-inch half moons
1/2 teaspoon kosher salt

Heat a slope-sided sauté pan over high heat for several minutes to get it very hot. Add the oil and spread the onions in an even layer on the bottom of the pan. Leave undisturbed for 1 minute, then stir and leave them for another minute. Repeat this process several times, until the onions are golden brown, about 5 minutes. Transfer them to a baking sheet and spread them in a flat layer to cool. (This way they won't be soggy.) Season with salt. The onions can be refrigerated for up to 3 days.

Piccalilli

This vegetable relish, a derivative of Indian pickle, is served cold, as a traditional accompaniment to rich stews. For this version, which features cipollini onions, do NOT use red beets, as they will stain the onions. The idea is to cut the vegetables so that they are all about the same size, giving the relish a nice finished look. The recipe calls for about 4 pounds of vegetables; feel free to mix and match them according to your taste or use others, such as carrots, broccoli, white turnips, or zucchini.

The piccalilli can be stored in the refrigerator for up to 2 weeks. Or if you like, it can be preserved, which requires a precise method that calls for special equipment; see Canning Instructions, page 25.

✻⟩ MAKES 5 PINTS ⟨✻

2 pounds large (3-inch-diameter) white or golden beets, unpeeled but trimmed of greens and tips

6 tablespoons kosher salt

2 quarts water

2 cups cauliflower florets (cut into 1-inch pieces, about 10 ounces)

5 cups whole peeled and trimmed cipollini onions (about 24 ounces)

2 cups halved radishes (stem and root ends removed, about 12 ounces)

³/₄ cup ground turmeric

³/₄ cup all-purpose flour

1 cup sugar

¹/₂ cup Dijon mustard

4 cups Champagne vinegar

Cook the beets: Cover the beets with cold water in a heavy saucepan and boil until fork tender, about 1¹/₂ hours. Drain them in a colander and let them cool just until you can handle them. Peel them warm (the skin slides right off if they're warm), then cut them into ³/₄-inch cubes. You should have about 3 cups.

Brine the vegetables: Place the salt and 1 quart of the water in a 2-gallon zip-top bag. Seal the bag and massage it a few times to help dissolve the salt. Add the beets, cauliflower, onions, and radishes to the bag along with the remaining 1 quart of water. Seal the bag again, pressing out any air, so that the vegetables are completely submerged. Place the bag in a large bowl (to stabilize it) and let the vegetables sit on the counter for several hours, or refrigerate overnight. When ready to use, drain the vegetables in a colander, rinse them in cold water, and drain again.

Make the sauce: In large flameproof casserole, whisk together the turmeric, flour, sugar, mustard, and 1 cup of the vinegar to make a paste. Add the remaining 3 cups of vinegar and whisk until smooth. Over medium heat, bring the sauce to a boil and cook until it thickens, about 3 minutes, whisking continually to keep lumps from forming. Add the vegetables, stirring to coat them, and cook for 5 minutes. Remove from the heat and allow the mixture to cool to room temperature.

Store the piccalilli: Refrigerate the piccalilli or preserve and store it per the instructions on page 25.

GLOSSARY

Berkshire pork: A breed of heritage pork originally from Berkshire, England, known for its flavor and high fat content.

Beurre monté: An emulsion of butter and water.

Blanch: To cook food briefly in boiling water, then plunge it into ice water to stop the cooking process. The method is often used to par-cook green vegetables to set their color, or to help remove skins from some nuts (almonds, pistachios) and fruits (tomatoes, peaches).

Bomba: a very absorbent, short-grained, almost round Spanish rice often used for paella.

Calasparra: a very absorbent, short-grained, almost round Spanish rice often used for paella.

Chine bone: Part of the backbone sometimes still attached to the loin, making it difficult to slice.

Chinois: A conical fine-mesh strainer, also called a China cap.

Cippolini onions: Bulblike vegetables similar to onions, but not from the Allium genus; they are actually the bulbs of grape hyacinths.

Collagen casings: Sausage casings manufactured from edible animal collagen, which some people prefer using instead of natural casings made from intestines.

Court bouillon: A poaching liquid, often used for fish, made from water simmered with aromatic vegetables and acid, such as vinegar, wine, or citrus.

Crème fraîche: A rich, soured cream high in butterfat.

Daube: A stew, usually made with red meat, red wine, and vegetables.

Deckle: The fatty flap of meat attached to the flat cut of a beef brisket.

Demi-glace: A rich, syrupy reduction of beef or veal stock or a brown sauce base made from beef or veal stock.

Dublin spice: A spice blend of ground juniper berries, black pepper, allspice, and cloves.

Foie gras: The liver of a duck or goose that has been fattened through the force-feeding of corn.

Forcemeat: A mixture of ground meat and fat, usually used as a stuffing.

Frenching: To remove all fat and sinew from the bones of lamb, veal, or beef racks and scrape them clean.

Frisée: A variety of endive with dark green outer leaves, yellowish-green inner leaves, and a slightly bitter flavor.

Gastrique: A sauce made from a base of caramelized sugar and vinegar.

Glace: A highly concentrated reduction of demi-glace.

H-bone (aitch bone): The hip bone of a four-legged animal.

Harissa: A spicy North African red pepper paste.

Herbes de Provence: An herb blend popular in the Provence region of France, usually containing savory, fennel, lavender, thyme, and basil.

Hotel pan: A rectangular stainless steel pan with a lip that allows it to rest in a steam table. A full-size pan is a 12 by 20-inch rectangle, with depths 2, 4, or 6 inches. They also come in other sizes: half pans, two-thirds, third, fourth, sixth, and ninth pans.

Insta Cure #1: A commercially sold cure containing salt and sodium nitrite, effective in keeping meat, especially in pâtés and sausages, from oxidizing and turning brown.

Jus: Pan juices or a sauce made from them.

Kurobuta pork: The Japanese name for Berkshire pork.

Lardons: Small strips or cubes of fatback, pork belly, or bacon that have been blanched, sautéed, or both.

Meat glace: Meat stock that has been reduced to a very syrupy, dark-brown consistency, often the base of red meat sauces.

Micro greens: The small, flavorful leaves of various plants, lettuces, and herbs (such as arugula, mizuna, basil) used as a garnish.

Mirepoix: A combination of coarsely chopped aromatic vegetables, usually celery, carrots, and onions, used to flavor stocks and braising liquids.

Panko: Japanese bread crumbs, larger and more textured than the American version.

Pavlova: A dessert made from meringue baked to be crispy on the outside and chewy on the inside, usually topped with whipped cream and fresh fruit.

Piccalilli: A bright yellow (from turmeric), vinegar-based vegetable relish, usually containing cauliflower florets. A derivation of Indian mustard pickle.

Quatre épices: A blend of spices, often ground cloves, ground ginger, ground nutmeg, and ground white pepper, used to flavor pâtés in French cooking.

Rasher: A slice of bacon.

Ricing: Removing lumps from cooked potato pieces by putting them through a tool (ricer) that pushes them through a die with small holes drilled into it.

Roux: A mixture of flour cooked in butter or oil, used as a thickening agent.

Sel rose: A pink preserving salt containing nitrates and pinkish-red food dye, useful for retaining color and flavor in pâtés, sausages, and cured meats.

Shocking: Plunging foods, usually vegetables, in ice water to stop the cooking process and to cool them quickly.

Silverskin: A thin layer of chewy connective tissue attached to various meat muscles.

Simmering: Cooking in liquid maintained just below the boiling point. The method usually involves bringing liquid to a boil over medium high to high heat, then lowering the heat to medium or medium low so to maintain a slight bubbling at the surface.

Sous-vide: "Under vacuum" in French; a method of cooking in which food vacuum sealed in plastic bags is cooked for extended periods of time in a heated water bath.

Sweating: Cooking vegetables, usually diced aromatics such as onions, shallots, garlic, celery, or carrots, over heat in a small amount of fat so that water releases from them, allowing the vegetables to cook slowly in their own natural moisture.

Tamis: A sieve that resembles a large springform pan, except with fine mesh screening stretched across the bottom. Using a scraper, puréed food is pressed through the mesh to make it lump-free.

Turbinado sugar: A coarse, crystalline, light-brown sugar, also known as raw sugar.

Wondra flour: A very fine, freeze-dried flour used to impart a light, crisp coating when used to dredge items (such as fish fillets or chicken cutlets) before sautéing them. Available in most grocery stores.

RESOURCES

Some of the resources listed here sell their products regionally. I've included purveyors I've come to know and trust over the years. I recommend that you source fresh produce, meats, fish, seafood, dairy products, and poultry locally and support farmers and farmers' markets.

For all sausage-making equipment, such as Insta Cure #1, sel rose, sausage casing, meat grinders, sausage stuffers, and sausage prickers:
The Sausage Maker, Inc. | www.sausagemaker.com

For cooking equipment such as paella pans, various sizes of hotel pans, baking pans, Christmas pudding bowls, potato ricers, tamis, thermometers, coarse- and fine-mesh sieves, and chinois:
La Cuisine | www.lacuisineus.com

For sous-vide cooking equipment, such as a vacuum sealer, vacuum seal bags, circulators, and water bath receptacles: **PolyScience | www.cuisinetechnology.com**

Micro greens, such as micro arugula, micro cilantro, micro beet greens, micro tatsoi, micro mizuna, and micro celery: **Planet Earth Diversified**
www.shop.planetearthdiversified.com

Dairy products: **Trickling Springs Creamery**
www.tricklingspringscreamery.com

Grade-A foie gras, rendered duck fat: **Society Fair**
www.hudsonvalleyfoiegras.com

Chickens: For a list of retailers who carry Polyface Farms chickens (they do not ship):
www.polyfacefarms.com

Fresh Maryland blue jumbo lump crabmeat:
Linton's Seafood | www.lintonseafood.com

Bomba and Calasparra rice:
La Tienda | www.tienda.com

Cashel Blue and other Irish farmhouse cheeses:
Murray's Cheese | www.murrayscheese.com

Irish foods, such as digestive biscuits, black and white pudding, Irish sausage, Irish bacon, Irish-style wholemeal flour, and Kerrygold butter:
Food Ireland | www.foodireland.com

Irish-style wholemeal flour:
King Arthur Flour | www.kingarthurflour.com

Venison: **Shaffer Venison Farms, Inc.**
www.shafferfarms.com

Lamb: **Shenandoah Valley Lamb | www.svlamb.com**

INDEX

CONVERSION CHARTS

Volume

U.S.	IMPERIAL	METRIC
1 tablespoon	$\frac{1}{2}$ fl oz	15 ml
2 tablespoons	1 fl oz	30 ml
$\frac{1}{4}$ cup	2 fl oz	60 ml
$\frac{1}{3}$ cup	3 fl oz	90 ml
$\frac{1}{2}$ cup	4 fl oz	120 ml
$\frac{2}{3}$ cup	5 fl oz ($\frac{1}{4}$ pint)	150 ml
$\frac{3}{4}$ cup	6 fl oz	180 ml
1 cup	8 fl oz ($\frac{1}{3}$ pint)	240 ml
$1\frac{1}{4}$ cups	10 fl oz ($\frac{1}{2}$ pint)	300 ml
2 cups (1 pint)	16 fl oz ($\frac{2}{3}$ pint)	480 ml
$2\frac{1}{2}$ cups	20 fl oz (1 pint)	600 ml
1 quart	32 fl oz ($1\frac{2}{3}$ pints)	1 l

Temperature

FAHRENHEIT	CELSIUS/GAS MARK
250°F	120°C/gas mark $\frac{1}{2}$
275°F	135°C/gas mark 1
300°F	150°C/gas mark 2
325°F	160°C/gas mark 3
350°F	180 or 175°C/gas mark 4
375°F	190°C/gas mark 5
400°F	200°C/gas mark 6
425°F	220°C/gas mark 7
450°F	230°C/gas mark 8
475°F	245°C/gas mark 9
500°F	260°C

Length

INCH	METRIC
$\frac{1}{4}$ inch	6 mm
$\frac{1}{2}$ inch	1.25 cm
$\frac{3}{4}$ inch	2 cm
1 inch	2.5 cm
6 inches ($\frac{1}{2}$ foot)	15 cm
12 inches (1 foot)	30 cm

Weight

U.S./IMPERIAL	METRIC
$\frac{1}{2}$ oz	15 g
1 oz	30 g
2 oz	60 g
$\frac{1}{4}$ lb	115 g
$\frac{1}{3}$ lb	150 g
$\frac{1}{2}$ lb	225 g
$\frac{3}{4}$ lb	350 g
1 lb	450 g

Published in the United States by Ten Speed Press,
an imprint of the Crown Publishing Group,
a division of Random House LLC, New York,
a Penguin Random House Company.
www.crownpublishing.com
www.tenspeed.com

Ten Speed Press and the Ten Speed Press colophon
are registered trademarks of Random House LLC.

Food and prop styling for photographs on pages iii,
    18, 24, 26, 33, 43, 52, 58, 89, 90, 95, 96, 104, 106, 116,
    123, 125, 128, 139, 150, 153, 157, 161, 164, 173, 213, 237,
    249, 258 by Lisa Cherkasky
Food styling for front cover photograph by
    George Dolese
Prop styling for front cover photograph by
    Glenn Jenkins

Library of Congress Cataloging-in-Publication Data
Armstrong, Cathal.
My Irish table : recipes from the homeland and
Restaurant Eve / Cathal Armstrong, David Hagedorn.
— First edition.
        pages cm
Includes index.
1. Cooking, Irish. 2. Cooking, American. I. Hagedorn,
David, 1959- II. Restaurant Eve. III. Title.
TX717.5.A762 2014
641.59417--dc23
                                        2013039099

Hardcover ISBN: 978-1-60774-430-6
eBook ISBN: 978-1-60774-431-3

Printed in China

10 9 8 7 6 5 4 3 2 1

First Edition